高等院校双语教材
A College Bilingual Textbook
汽车工程师英语向导
An English Guide for Automotive Engineers

中国汽车工程学会推荐图书

主　编　李卓森
副主编　何莉萍　李理光
主　审　林　逸　喻　凡
顾　问　[美]马芳武　[美]门永新

AUTOMOTIVE FUNDAMENTALS

汽车概论

人民交通出版社

内 容 提 要

本书是我国高等院校汽车专业自编的第一部双语教材，内容包括：汽车分类、社会纵览、发展历史、结构知识、行驶原理、驾驶维修、道路交通、设计试验、制造技术、展览营销、汽车竞赛、发展趋势等，并附有多媒体教学音像光盘一张。

本书专供理工科院校汽车专业开展双语教学使用，并可作为我国汽车工程技术人员提高专业英语交流能力的拓展教材。

图书在版编目（CIP）数据

Automotive Fundamentals 汽车概论：汉、英/李卓森主编．—北京：人民交通出版社，2009.6
ISBN 978-7-114-07747-0

Ⅰ.A... Ⅱ.李... Ⅲ.汽车-双语教学-高等学校-教材
Ⅳ.U46

中国版本图书馆 CIP 数据核字（2009）第 071887 号

AUTOMOTIVE FUNDAMENTALS

书　　名：汽车概论
著 作 者：李卓森
责任编辑：张　淼
出版发行：人民交通出版社
地　　址：(100011)北京市朝阳区安定门外外馆斜街 3 号
网　　址：http://www.ccpress.com.cn
销售电话：(010)85285656，59757969，59757973
总 经 销：北京中交盛世书刊有限公司
经　　销：各地新华书店
印　　刷：北京鑫正大印刷有限公司
开　　本：880×1230　1/32
印　　张：10.375
字　　数：273 千
版　　次：2009 年 7 月第 1 版
印　　次：2009 年 7 月第 1 次印刷
书　　号：ISBN 978-7-114-07747-0
印　　数：0001－3500 册
定　　价：39.00 元

编 者 名 单

主　　编　李卓森（吉林大学）
副 主 编　何莉萍（湖南大学）　李理光（同济大学）
顾　　问　马芳武（美国）
　　　　　门永新（美国）
主　　审　林　逸（北京汽车研究总院）
　　　　　喻　凡（上海交通大学）
统　　筹　付于武（中国汽车工程学会）
参加编写　徐　冰（燕山大学）　丁舟波（湖南大学）
　　　　　李　克（湖南大学）　张维刚（湖南大学）
　　　　　廖晓军（湖南大学）　徐雯霞（同济大学）
　　　　　阮届望（同济大学）　朱宇方（同济大学）
　　　　　周红丽（湖南大学）

光 盘 制 作

编　　绘　李卓森（吉林大学）
界　　面　闫文亮（天津一汽产品开发中心）
配　　音　Sherry Liu（美国）
录　　音　Sherry Liu（美国）
合　　成　闫文亮（天津一汽产品开发中心）
词　　汇　程　嘉（燕山大学）　姚俊贤（北京阿尔特）
　　　　　何宁宁（北汽福田汽车公司）

a) Smart Fortwo

b) Volkswagen Polo

c) Toyota Corolla

d) Ford Mondeo

e) Audi A4

f) Chrysler 300

g) Volvo S80

h) Mecerdes-Benz S600

Fig.1-1　Passenger Cars

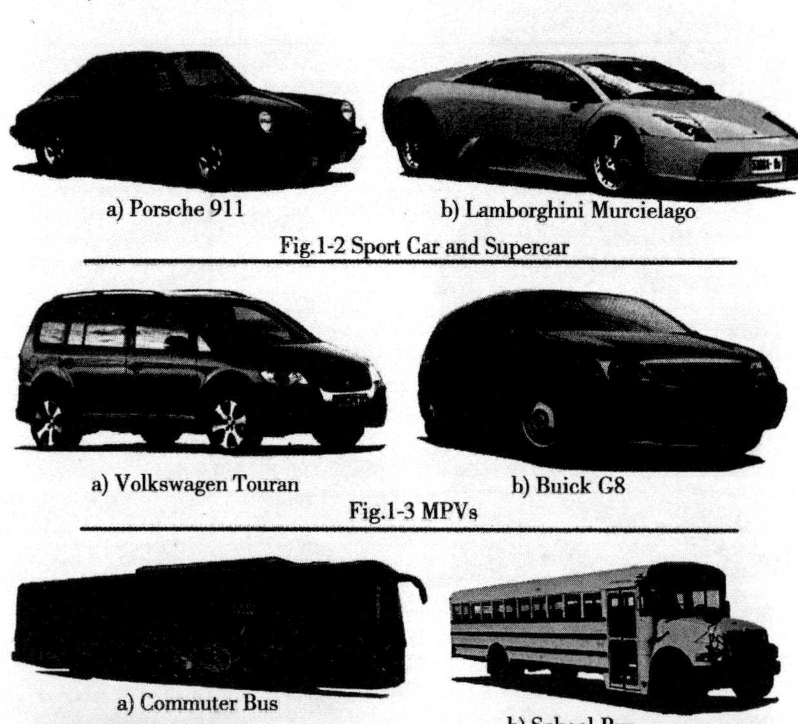

a) Porsche 911　　b) Lamborghini Murcielago

Fig.1-2 Sport Car and Supercar

a) Volkswagen Touran　　b) Buick G8

Fig.1-3 MPVs

a) Commuter Bus　　b) School Bus

c) Double-Decker Bus 　　d) Motorcoach

Fig.1-4　Buses

1 GENERAL MOTORS

BUICK CADILLAC CHEVROLET PONTIAC OLDSMOBILE SATURN SAAB

OPEL VAUXHALL SUZUKI ISUZU DAEWOO HOLDEN HUMMER

2 FORD

 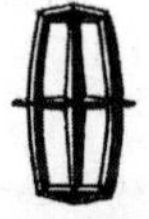    

FORD LINCOLN MERCURY MAZDA VOLVO JAGUAR

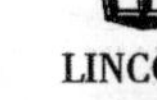  

ASTON MARTIN LANDROVER

3 DAIMLER-CHRYSLER

MERCEDES-BENZ MAYBACH CHRYSLER DODGE PLYMOUTH JEEP SMART

4 TOYOTA

TOYOTA LEXUS DAIHATSU SUBARU SCION

Fig.6-1A Brand Marks of Famous Automotive Companies

(Information before 2008)

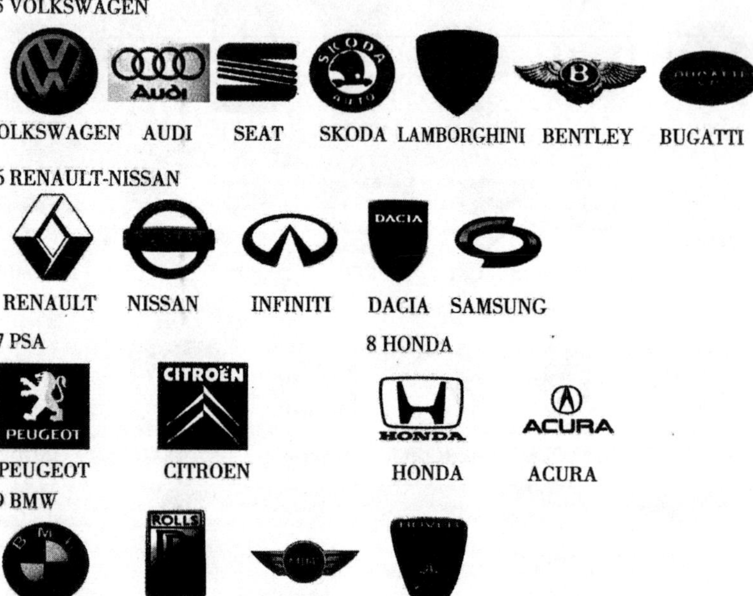

BMW ROLLS-ROYCE MINI ROVER

10 FIAT

FIAT LANCIA FERRARI ALFA-ROMEO MASERATI

11 THE OTHERS

PORSCHE MITSUBISI HYUNDAI KIA LOTUS MG

Fig.6-1B Brand Marks of Famous Automotive Companies

(Information before 2008)

序

近年来，国内许多高校开始推广专业基础课双语教学。汽车专业的双语教学实践也已开展多年。但是，国内汽车专业双语教材十分缺乏，而国外汽车专业教材价位高、内容深，且专业口径定位较宽，一般侧重为大机械专业，与国内目前汽车专业课程内容有较大差别。为满足对汽车专业双语教学的需要，吉林大学、湖南大学，同济大学多位留学回国教师共同合编了双语教材《Automotive Fundamentals》。这是我国汽车行业首次自行编写的汽车专业双语教材，该教材以“汽车概论”为切入点，具有如下特点：

(1)专业定位清晰、体系完整，贯穿整个汽车产业前、后市场；

(2)内容丰富，基本覆盖了汽车领域最常见的专业语汇；

(3)双语同译(文词、语音)准确、易于交流，附有多媒体教学光盘(含课文选读、写作模拟、结构图精注)。

另获悉，本书已获中国汽车工程学会行业推荐，相信本书出版后定能推动汽车专业双语教学的开展，同时也为汽车工程技术人员普及汽车专业英语知识，提高英语综合交流能力提供专业的指导与帮助。

很高兴能为此书做序。

湖南大学校长、中国工程院院士：钟志华

二〇〇九年六月

编 者 寄 语

高等院校双语教学，是近年来教育部大力倡导的教学模式，目前已在国内许多院校推广、试行。随着高校教改步伐的加快，理工科院校专业课程开展双语教学已成大势所趋。

双语教学应是汽车专业的实训课程，其有别于现行的汽车专业英语课程，就在于注重专业英语的综合技能运用，而后者仅侧重阅读理解。

本书是我国汽车行业第一本自编的双语教材，全部课文用英文撰写，附有少量中文注释，专门为我国高等院校普及汽车知识的校级公共课程“汽车概论”而编写。

●本书适用：

1. 高等院校双语教学；

2. 作为我国汽车工程技术人员提高专业英语交流能力的拓展教材。

●本书内容：

本书内容包括：汽车分类、社会纵览、发展历史、结构知识、行驶原理、驾驶维修、道路交通、设计试验、制造技术、展览营销、汽车竞赛、发展趋势等，覆盖了这些方面的最基本英语词汇及词组1700余条。

●本书特点：

本书所编入的术语和定义规范准确，数据和资料详实可靠。另附光盘，内有400余幅彩色幻灯片（结构图采用双语注释），以便于多媒体课堂教学和课余学习。每幅幻灯片有标准美语配音，有助于提高听力和口语学习。光盘内还有汽车工程基础词汇表，利于查阅。

本书获得中国汽车工程学会推荐用书，中国工程院院士、湖南大学钟志华校长为本书作序，参编人员多为国内知名汽车院校海归教师。全书由吉林大学李卓森教授担任主编，湖南大学何莉萍教授、同济大学李理光教授担任副主编，北京汽车研究总院林逸教授和上海交通大学喻凡教授担任主审。本书特邀国外资深汽车专家马芳武博士和门永新博士为顾问，二人及其美国同事提供了大量写作资料和修改建议。

本书的出版旨在推动我国高等院校汽车专业双语教学，无论对普及汽车知识或是提高大学生和汽车工程技术人员的英语水平，均有较大的现实意义。

目前，国内汽车行业双语教学尚缺乏成熟的经验，本书编写中的不足和欠妥之处在所难免，殷切期望使用本书的师生和读者们提出宝贵意见。

编者

2009 年 5 月

AUTHOR'S PREFACE

Bilingual teaching in higher educational institutes has been actively advocated by the Ministry of Education in recent years and it has been tested and promoted currently in many institutes in China. With the teaching reform drive in colleges and universities pacing up, it has been a trend for the institutes of science and technology to carry out bilingual teaching of their specialty courses.

For the automotive major, bilingual teaching should be a practical training course. It differs with the existing automobile English course in that it emphasizes more on learners' overall and practical skills while the latter only caters to reading comprehension.

This book is the first bilingual textbook of its kind designed by ourselves for China's automobile industry. All the texts are written in English except very few Chinese notes. It is designed specially for "General Introduction to Automobile", the public course aiming to promote students' knowledge of automobiles.

●Target readership of this book:

1 Teachers and students in colleges and universities for bilingual teaching;

2 The technical personnel in automobile engineering to improve their communicative abilities.

●Contents of this book:

Automobile classification, society overview, development history, automobile structure, operation principles, motoring, maintenance and repair, road and transportation, designing and testing, manufacturing technology, exhibition and promotion, automobile racing and development trends and over 1700 English words and phrases frequently used in these aspects.

●Features of this book:

This book contains standard and accurate terminology and definitions with detailed and reliable data and resources. A compact disc is also provided containing over 400 colored slides (structure diagram with bilingual notes) to facilitate multimedia teaching and self-learning after class. Each slide is dubbed with standard American English helpful in listening and speaking improvement. The disc also includes a basic glossary of automotive engineering for convenient search.

This book is recommended by the Society of Automotive Engineers of China and President of Hunan University Zhong Zhihua, Academician of Chinese Academy of Engineering, Wrote the preface for this book. The authors are mainly teachers with oversea education background and currently working in the prestige automotive colleges and universities. Prof. Li Zhuosen from Jilin University is chief-editor with Prof. He Liping from Hunan University and Prof. Li Liguang from Tongji University as deputy editors. The examiners-in-chief are Prof. Lin Yi from Beijing Automotive Technology Center and Prof. Yu Fan from Shanghai Jiaotong University. We have also invited senior foreign automotive experts Dr. Ma Fangwu and Dr. Men Yongxin as our consultants. They and their American workmates have provided us a great deal of resources and amendment suggestions.

The publication of this book aims to promote the bilingual teaching of Automotive Engineering in colleges and universities in China. It has great significance in popularizing automotive knowledge and improving the English ability of college students and automotive engineering and technical personnel.

Since successful experience is still lacking in the current bilingual teaching of automotive major, demerits are unavoidable in this book, therefore, valuable opinions and suggestions from teachers, students and other readers will be highly appreciated.

The authors

May 2009

对使用本书的建议

1. 课程定位和教学建议

本书是专为我国高等院校的校级公共课程“汽车概论”编写的双语教材。授课时，教师可用英语或双语讲解。建议起初采用双语教学，在逐步取得教学经验后，向全部英语授课过渡。

本教材与现行的《汽车专业英语》教材的主要区别是：其重点培养学生专业英语听、说、读、写的综合交流能力，而后者仅偏重于阅读理解。本课程是专业英语的拓展实训课程，在教学中，教师应把握住上述重点，采用教与学互动的方法。

为配合课堂教学，本教材制作了400余幅汽车多媒体幻灯片。幻灯片采用双语注释，附有标准美语配音。教师在课堂上可酌情播放配音。

由于本书内容较全面，可供教师授课选择。对于理工类学生，可着重汽车结构知识和行驶原理，而对文科学生则可偏重讲授汽车文化方面的内容。

2. 学习建议

为提高听力，建议学生课前不预习，听力较差的学生例外。上课时，注意聆听教师的讲解而尽量不看课文。

阅读课本时，不要急于查阅段落下方的注释，最好采用快速阅读的方法先掌握全段的大意，然后再重复精读。不要死记硬背词汇表中的单词，而要结合课文对词汇作更深入的理解，达到活学活用。

学生要努力争取课堂发言，应尽量用英语准备，可以参考课文中的词语和句法，模仿光盘中的发音进行准备。如学生一人单独准备有困难,可以几个学生一起准备,然后由一个学生做中心发言,其他学生补充发言。在课外,学生可以请助课教师辅导。

3. 工程技术人员学习建议

本书收录了汽车专业最常用的英语词汇及词组1700余条,基本涵盖了该专业日常书面或口语涉外交流的多数用语,为使双方的交流更加顺畅(即正确理解和准确表达),每个工程技术人员都应下决心掌握好课文中最基本的专业词汇和术语用法。

本书还为读者提供了检索功能,如要查找词汇,可到书中的相关章节内容中查找,也可以在光盘的词汇表中检索,如要查找某个结构名称,可直接从光盘的双语结构图中查寻,还可从彩图中查找国外企业名称以及从本书后部索引中查找车坛名人。

尽量争取机会与国外同行进行交流,在实践中不断锻炼和提高能力。

HOW TO USE THIS BOOK

1 Course positioning and suggestions for teaching

This book is a bilingual textbook designed for the public course "General Introduction to Automobile" in China's higher educational institutions. Teachers could teach this book in English or bilingually. It is recommended that teachers could begin the course bilingually. With their experience growing, they can come to teaching completely in English in the end.

This textbook differs from another book entitled "Automobile English" mainly in that the former aims to foster the students' overall communicative ability including listening, speaking, reading and writing while the latter only caters to reading comprehension. In whole, it expands the "Automobile English" and offers practical training to learners. Teachers should realize this focus and adopt the interactive teaching methods.

For a better teaching effect, over 400 slides are made with bilingual notes and standard American English dubbing. Teachers can use them when they feel it needed.

The coverage of this book is fairly comprehensive so it offers teachers substantial flexibility in course design. For science students, teachers can emphasize on the sections about automobile structures and operation principles, while for art students, more automobile culture could be introduced.

2 Suggestions for learning

In order to improve listening, it is not advisable for students to preview except those with poor listening. While attending classes, students should try not to read their textbooks but to be attentive to the teacher's lecturing.

While reading this book, do not rush to the notes following each section. It is highly recommended that students should read through the whole paragraph quickly and then reread it intensively. Do not try to remember the vocabulary list by rote but to gain a deeper understanding of the words by the context and to be able to make use of the words skillfully.

Students should seize every opportunity to speak English in class. They can prepare their speech with the words and sentence patterns in the textbook and imitating the pronunciation in the compact disc. If students find it difficult to prepare individually, they can do it together with several classmates. One student is chosen to make a speech and other teammates can contribute their own thoughts to the speech. After class, students can ask their assistant teacher to tutor them.

3 Suggestions to technical personnel

This book covers over 1700 frequently used English words and phrases which could meet the basic needs of those in automotive industry in terms of written or oral communication. In order to smooth their communication with their foreign counterparts, i. e. proper understanding and accurate expression, the engineering and technical personnel should be determined to grasp the basic technical terms and their usage.

This book offers an indexing system which makes it easy for readers to look for words in the concerned chapters of this book. Readers can also search for the words in the glossary contained in the compact disc. If they want to look for the name of a certain structure, they could search for it directly in the bilingual structure diagram in the disc. Readers could also search for the names of foreign companies in the colored pages and celebrites in automobile circle in the index attached.

The engineering and technical personnel should take every opportunity to communicate with their foreign partners and improve their language proficiency gradually.

CONTENTS

CHAPTER ONE INTRODUCTION OF MOTOR VEHICLE … 1
1.1 MOTOR VEHICLE CLASSIFICATION …… 1
1.2 MOTOR VEHICLE AND SOCIETY …… 15
CHAPTER TWO HISTORY OF MOTOR VEHICLE …… 26
2.1 THE BIRTH OF MOTOR VEHICLE …… 26
2.2 THE EARLY DAYS …… 34
2.3 THRIVING ERA …… 53
CHAPTER THREE STRUCTURE OF MOTOR VEHICLE … 85
3.1 VEHICLE STRUCTURE …… 85
3.2 ENGINE …… 88
3.3 CHASSIS …… 110
3.4 BODY …… 138
CHAPTER FOUR OPERATION OF MOTOR VEHICLE …… 149
4.1 BASIC OPERATION PRINCIPLE …… 149
4.2 VEHICLE PERFORMANCES …… 151
4.3 MOTORING …… 159
4.4 MAINTENANCE AND REPAIR …… 169
4.5 TRANSPORTATION AND ROAD …… 177
CHAPTER FIVE DESIGN AND MANUFACTURE …… 187
5.1 DESIGN STUDIO …… 187
5.2 AUTOMOTIVE PROVING GROUND …… 213
5.3 WORKSHOP …… 227

CHAPTER SIX THE FUTURE ······································· 247
6.1 AUTO SHOWS ······································· 247
6.2 MOTOR RACING ······································· 261
6.3 FUTURE OF AUTOMOTIVE TECHNOLOGY ··················· 283
INDEX CELEBRITIES IN AUTOMOBILE CIRCLE ··········· 310

CHAPTER ONE
INTRODUCTION OF MOTOR VEHICLE

1.1 MOTOR VEHICLE CLASSIFICATION

1.1.1 *PASSENGER CAR*

Passenger cars are motor vehicles that carry people. The classification may differ from country to country. Even the same kind of vehicle can be named differently by region. The classifications in Table 1-1 are commonly used. The relevant classifications of EuroNCAP (European New Car Assessment Program[1]) and China's standard are also shown.

1.1.1.1 MICROCAR

Microcars[2] are a type of motor vehicles straddling the range between cars and motorbikes. Although a small amount of microcars are three wheelers, they are not classified into the category of motorbike. The reason is that a microcar has seats and is operated by a steering wheel but a motorbike has a saddle[3] and a handle bar to steer. Microcars were popular in post-war Europe where their appearance earned them to be called the name Bubble cars[4]. Examples of microcars are Subaru 360 (Fig. 2-49) and Smart Fortwo (Fig. 1-1a).

两节注释：[1]欧洲新车评估体系；[2]相当于我国的“超微型汽车”；[3]鞍座；[4]带圆形透明顶(像泡泡)的微型轿车。

Car Classifications Table 1-1

<table>
<tr><th>America</th><th>Britain</th><th>EuroNCAP</th><th>China</th></tr>
<tr><td>Microcar</td><td>Micro car or Bubble car</td><td>—</td><td rowspan="2">Mini class car</td></tr>
<tr><td>—</td><td>City car</td><td rowspan="2">Super mini</td></tr>
<tr><td>Subcompact car</td><td>Super mini</td><td rowspan="2">Popular class car</td></tr>
<tr><td>Compact car</td><td>Small family car</td><td>Small family car</td></tr>
<tr><td>Mid-size car</td><td>Large family car</td><td rowspan="2">Large family car</td><td rowspan="2">Medium class car</td></tr>
<tr><td>Entry-level luxury car</td><td>Compact executive car</td></tr>
<tr><td>Full-size car</td><td rowspan="2">Executive car</td><td rowspan="2">Executive car</td><td rowspan="2">Mid-high class car</td></tr>
<tr><td>Mid-size luxury car</td></tr>
<tr><td>Full-size luxury car</td><td>Luxury car</td><td>—</td><td>High class car</td></tr>
<tr><td>Sport car</td><td>Sport car</td><td>—</td><td rowspan="5">Roadster</td></tr>
<tr><td>Grand tourer</td><td>Grand tourer</td><td>—</td></tr>
<tr><td>Super car</td><td>Super car</td><td>—</td></tr>
<tr><td>Convertible</td><td>Convertible</td><td>—</td></tr>
<tr><td>Roadster</td><td>Roadster</td><td>Roadster</td></tr>
<tr><td>—</td><td>Leisure activity vehicle</td><td rowspan="3">Small MPV</td><td rowspan="4">MPV</td></tr>
<tr><td>—</td><td>Mini MPV</td></tr>
<tr><td>Compact minivan</td><td>Compact MPV</td></tr>
<tr><td>Minivan</td><td>Large MPV</td><td>MPV</td></tr>
<tr><td>Mini SUV</td><td>Mini 4×4</td><td rowspan="2">Small off-roader</td><td rowspan="5">SUV</td></tr>
<tr><td>Compact SUV</td><td>Compact 4×4</td></tr>
<tr><td>Mid-size crossover SUV</td><td>Large 4×4</td><td rowspan="3">Large off-roader</td></tr>
<tr><td>Mid-size SUV</td><td rowspan="2">Off-roader</td></tr>
<tr><td>Full-size SUV</td></tr>
</table>

1.1.1.2 HATCHBACKS,SEDANS AND STATION WAGONS

A hatchback car[1], refers to a small size car with an upper hinged back door[2]. The term sedan[3] is used to describe a four-door car with a trunk[4]. A station wagon[5] is a car with a roof extending to the rear. The rear body is roomy to carry more luggage than a sedan and suitable for the service at railway station and airport. A station wagon can be equipped with an upper hinged back door, but is not called hatchback car.

CITY CAR

Unlike microcars, a city car with greater speed and safer occupant protection is more adaptable to mixed traffic environments and weather conditions. In Japan, city car is called "kei car[6]". Kei car has to meet strict size and engine requirements: engine has a maximum displacement of 660 mL and the car's length must be under 3400 mm. Examples of city cars are Peugeot 107, Fiat Cinquecento and Suziki Alto.

SUBCOMPACT CAR

Subcompact car[7] is known as supermini in Europe and light car in Austria. Superminis have three, four or five doors and are designed to seat four passengers comfortably. Current supermini hatchbacks are approximately 3900 mm long, while sedans and station wagons are around 4200 mm long. Today, subcompact cars are of the best selling vehicles in most of the developing countries. Examples of subcompact cars are Ford Fiesta, Suzuki Swift and Volkswagen Polo (Fig. 1-1b).

COMPACT CAR

Compact cars[8] refer to the longest hatchbacks and sedans and station wagons with similar size. They are approximately 4250 mm long in case of hatchbacks and 4500 mm in the case of sedans and station wagons. Compact cars have room for five adults and usually have engines between 1.6 and 2.2 liters. These are the most popular vehicles in most developed countries. Examples of compact cars are Ford Focus, Toyota Corolla (Fig. 1-1 c) and Volkswagen Golf.

MID-SIZE CAR

Mid-size cars[9] have room for five adults and a large trunk. Engines are more powerful than compact cars, six-cylinder engines are more common used than in smaller cars. In Europe, large family cars are rarely over 4700 mm long, while in North America and Australasia they may be well over 4800 mm. Examples of Mid-size cars are Ford Mondeo (Fig. 1-1 d), Toyota Camry, Honda Accord and Volkswagen Passat.

ENTRY-LEVEL LUXURY CAR

Entry-level luxury car[10] is luxurious equivalent to large family car and compact car. Powerful six- and eight-cylinder engines are common, but rear seat room and trunk space are more reduced than in "non-luxury" models since the extra room is needed to accommodate the larger engine. Examples of entry-level luxury cars are Audi A4 (Fig. 1-1e) and BMW 3 Series.

FULL-SIZE CAR

The term full-size car[11] is used most in North America and Australia where it refers to the largest sedans on the market. Full-size cars may be well over 5000 mm long and are the roomiest vehicles. Examples of full-size cars are Buick Park Avenue, Chrysler 300 (Fig. 1-1f), Hyundai Grandeur/Azera and Toyota Avalon.

MID-LUXURY CAR

A mid-luxury car[12] is larger than an entry-level luxury car. They are usually very roomy, powerful and luxurious, making them more expensive than "standard" sedans. Examples of mid-luxury cars are BMW 5 Series and Volvo S80 (Fig. 1-1g).

The full-size car and mid-luxury car are equivalent to the EuroNCAP class "Executive Car[13]".

FULL-SIZE LUXURY CAR

A full-size luxury car[14] is typically a four-door sedan. These are the most powerful sedans, with eight and twelve-cylinder engines and have more equipment than smaller models. Examples of full-size luxury cars are Audi A8, Mercedes-Benz S-Class (Fig. 1-2 d) and Rolls-Royce Phantom.

本节注释：[1]掀背式轿车；[2]顶部装铰链的背门；[3]轿车、四门轿车；[4]行李箱；[5]旅行车(直译:接站车)；[6]轻四轮车；[7]准紧凑型轿车；[8]紧凑型轿车；[9]中型轿车；[10]准豪华型轿车；[11]大型轿车；[12]中型豪华轿车；[13]行政轿车；[14]大型豪华轿车。

1.1.1.3 SPORT CARS AND GRAND TORUERS

SPORT CAR

Sport car[1] is a small lightweight class combining power and handling performance. Often inspired by racing vehicles, this class ranges from sporty vehicles such as the Mazda Miata/MX-5 to derivatives of true racing thoroughbreds[2] such as the Lotus Elise. Examples of sports cars are Austin-Healey 3000, Honda NSX and Porsche 911 (Fig. 1-2 a).

GRAND TOURER

Grand tourer[3] is larger, more powerful and heavier than sports cars, these vehicles typically have a FR layout and seating for four passengers (2 +2). These are more expensive than sports cars but not expensive as supercars. Some grand tourers are hand-built. Examples of grand tourers are Aston Martin DB9, Ferrari 612 Scaglietti, Jaguar XK8, Maserati Coupe and Mitsubishi GTO.

SUPERCAR

Supercars[4] are ultra-high performance cars, typically very expensive, luxurious and exceptionally fast. Supercars typically contain cutting-edge technology[5] and are usually assembled by hand. Examples of supercars are Bugatti Veyron, Lamborghini Murcielago (Fig. 1-2b), McLaren F1 and Porsche Carrera GT.

CONVERTIBLE

Convertible[6] is also called an open saloon, roadster[7] or drop-head coupe. This type of car has a roof (fabric, vinyl, metal or glass) which can be folded away. Convertibles were very popular in hotter places before the advent of automotive air-conditioning. 2-seat convertible sports cars are commonly named roadster or spyder. Examples of convertibles are Fiat Barchetta, Volkswagen Eos, Mercedes-Benz SLK and Porsche Boxster.

本节注释：[1]运动汽车；[2]纯血统；[3]跑车、轿跑车；[4]超级跑车；[5]尖端技术；[6]敞篷轿车；[7]活顶跑车。

1.1.1.4 OFF-ROADERS[1]

SUV

SUVs (Sport Utility Vehicles) are off-road vehicles with a body-on-frame chassis[2], four-wheel drive and true off-road capability. They can be troublesome in accidents. A high center of gravity in SUVs means that they rollover more easily than passenger cars. Examples of off-roaders / SUVs are Mitsubishi Pajero, Land Rover, Range Rover and Suzuki Samurai. This category is equivalent to the EuroNCAP class "Large Off-Roaders".

CROSSOVER SUV

Crossover SUVs[3] have a monocoque construction[4] and lower ground clearance[5] than SUVs. Some of them have traction control[6] and adjustable suspension[7] to improve off-road capabilities. Examples of crossover SUVs are Acura MDX, Toyota RAV4 and Volvo XC90. This category is equivalent to the EuroNCAP class "Small Off-Roaders".

本节注释：[1]越野汽车；[2]非承载式车身、车身与车架分开的结构；[3]轿车式SUV；[4]承载式车身、无车架的整体车身结构；[5]离地间隙；[6]驱动力控制装置；[7]可调节车身离地高度的悬架。

1.1.1.5 MINIVANS[1]/MPVS (Multi-Purpose Vehicles[2])

Also known as people carriers, this class of cars resemble tall station wagons[3]. Larger minivans may have seating for up to eighth passengers. Being taller than a family car improves visibility for the driver (while reducing visibility for other road users) and may help access for the elderly or disabled[4]. They also offer more seats and increased load capacity than hatchbacks or station wagons. Examples of mini MPVs are Fiat Idea, Hyundai Matrix, Renault Modus and Suzuki Wagon R. Examples of compact MPVs are Chevrolet HHR, Volkswagen Touran (Fig. 1-3 a) and Mazda 5. Both categories are equivalent to the EuroNCAP class "Small MPVs". Examples of large MPVs / minivans are Buick G8 (Fig. 1-3 b), Dodge Caravan, Peugeot 807 and Toyota Previa. This category is equivalent to the EuroNCAP class "MPVs"

In some countries, the term "van" can refer to a small panel van[5] based on a passenger car design (often the station wagon / estate model); it also refers to light trucks, which themselves are sometimes based on SUVs or MPVs. (But note that those retaining seats and windows, while being larger and more utilitarian than MPVs, may be called "minibuses".) The term is also used in the term "camper van[6]", equivalent to a North American recreational vehicle[7]. In the United States, the term "van" refers to vehicles that, like European minibuses, are even larger than large MPVs and are rarely seen being driven for domestic purposes, except for "conversion vans[8]". These possess extremely large interior space and are often more intended for hauling cargo than people. Most vans use body-on-frame construction and are thus suitable for extensive modification and coachwork, known as conversion. Conversion vans are often quite luxurious, boasting comfortable seats, soft rides, built-in support for electronics such as television sets, and other amenities. The more elaborate conversion vans straddle the line between cars and recreational vehicles. Examples of North American "vans" are Dodge Ram Van, Ford E-Series and GMC Savana. Examples of European "vans" are Ford Transit, Mercedes-Benz Sprinter and Renault Trafic.

本节注释：[1]小厢式车；[2]多用车；[3]加高旅行车；[4]功能障碍者、残疾人；[5]小型厢式货车（两侧的后窗用钢板封闭）；[6]野营厢式车；[7]娱乐车；[8]经装修的厢式车。

1.1.2 BUS

A bus is a large road vehicle designed to carry numerous passengers in addition to the driver and sometimes a conductor[1]. The name is a neologic version of the Latin "omnibus", which means "for everyone."

Types of Buses Table 1-2

America	China	
	Name	Bus length (m)
Commuter bus	Urban bus, City bus	Medium ($7<L\leqslant10$) or Large ($10<L\leqslant12^*$)
Motorcoach	Intercity bus	
Double-decker bus	Double-decker bus	$10<L\leqslant12^*$
Articulated bus	Articulated bus	$L\leqslant18$
—	Microbus	$L\leqslant3.5$
Minibus	Light bus	$3.5<L\leqslant7$
Midibus	Medium bus	$7<L\leqslant10$
Trolley bus	Trolley bus	
* Length of a triple-axle single unit bus can be up to 13.7 m.		

1.1.2.1 BUS FOR LOCAL TRANSPORTATION

COMMUTER BUS

Commuter bus[2] (Local transit bus or City bus) (Fig. 1-4 a) usually has two axles (duallies[3] on the drive axle), and two doors (one front, one mid-rear), allowing efficient internal traffic flow. Their seats are usually fixed and limited, leaving room for standing passengers. Having no need for a luggage compartment, many have low floor design, further easing entry and exit. Double-decker buses[4] (Fig. 1-4c), articulated buses[5] or extra-long triple-axled buses are often used on urban routes with heavy passenger loads. An articulated bus is sometimes called a bendy bus.

SCHOOL BUS

School buses[6] (Fig. 1-4b) are lighter, they have only one passenger door, seats more closely spaced, and no standing room. North American versions are based on truck chassis, and must meet special USDOT(US Department of Transportation)[7] standards including distinct color, design or markings to make the bus recognizable as a school bus, and warning lights and signs to warn traffic when children are getting in and out.

TROLLEY BUS

Trolley buses[8] are similar in appearance and function to commuter buses, but powered by an electric motor supplied by overhead power cables[9] rather than by an onboard internal combustion engine.

两节注释：[1]乘务员、售票员；[2]城市客车(注意:不要误译为我国的“班车”)；[3]指双胎；[4]双层客车；[5]铰接式客车；[6]校车；[7]美国交通局；[8]无轨电车；[9]电力架线。

1.1.2.2 MOTORCOACH

Motorcoaches[1] (Fig. 1-4d), also known as intercity coaches, are heavier, with usually three axles, one passenger door and no standing room. Seats are usually soft and able to recline. The floor is high, allowing large under-floor luggage compartments. There is usually a small carry-on luggage rack within the passenger cabin. Besides their use for intercity transportation, motorcoaches are used for long-distance airport shuttle service[2], local touring and charters[3], for large groups, and so on. They have seats for 47 to 62 passengers. Tour coaches[4], especially cross-country touring coaches, are often equipped with a lavatory, video system, PA system[5], and other amenities appropriate for hours of comfortable travel.

Short-distance tour buses are simpler, having a PA system and sometimes a video system. Some retired double-deckers and specialty vehicles are used in the local tour bus business.

本节注释: [1]长途客车; [2]穿梭于两地的营运; [3]包车; [4]旅游客车、游览客车; [5]有线广播系统。

1.1.2.3 OTHER TYPES OF BUSES

MINIBUS

Minibuses[1] are one size up from large passenger vans, and seat up to 25 passengers. Some may include a small space for luggage. Usually derived from heavy-duty small truck platforms such as cutaway van chassis, minibuses are often used for short-distance shuttles, city tours, and local charters. Many are wheelchair-lift[2] equipped and used in paratransit[3] capacities.

MIDIBUS

Midibuses[4], or mid-sized buses, are larger than minibuses, but smaller than motorcoaches, thus seating between 26 and 47. They can be front- or rear-engined, and have a variety of designs depending on specific needs. For example, they may be used to transport airport passengers between the terminal and distant parking lots; such vehicles may sacrifice seats for interior luggage space. The truck-based ones[5] can pack in enough seats to rival a motorcoach, but lack the luggage space and other amenities. However, they are also much cheaper.

SHUTTLE BUS

Shuttle bus[6] provides transit service between two destinations, such as an airport and city center. Shuttle bus services are often provided by colleges, airports, shopping areas, companies, and amusement destinations.

TOUR BUS

Tour bus service shows tourists notable sights by bus. City tour buses often simply pass by the sites while a tour guide[7] describes them. Longer distance tour coaches generally allow passengers to disembark at specific points of interest.

PARKING LOT TRAMS

Parking lot trams are a specialized form of bus, found in the parking lots of amusement parks such as Disneyland[8] and Walt Disney World. Those vehicles consist of an engine-car or motor-car (which may or may not be passenger-carrying) chained up to a passenger-carrying trailer or number of trailers, thus making a kind of road train.

本节注释：[1]相当于我国的轻型客车，或“中巴”（注意：不要误译为微型客车）；[2]轮椅提升器；[3]运送残疾人；[4]中型客车；[5]在货车的基础上改装的客车；[6]穿梭客车；[7]导游员；[8]迪斯尼乐园。

1.1.3 *TRUCK*

1.1.3.1 AMERICAN DEFINITIONS

The following definitions are given by the United States Federal Highway Administration (FHWA).

Trucks are motor vehicles to carry goods. They are further subdivided by number of axles and number of units, including both power and trailer units[1]. Note that the addition of a light trailer to a vehicle does not change the classification of the vehicle.

In reporting information on trucks the following criteria should be used:

(1) Truck tractor units[2] traveling without a trailer will be considered single-unit trucks.

(2) A truck tractor unit pulling other such units in a "saddle[3] mount" configuration will be considered one single-unit truck and will be defined only by the axles on the pulling unit.

(3) Vehicles are defined by the number of axles in contact with the road. Therefore, "floating" axles[4] are counted only when in the down position.

(4) The term "trailer" includes both semi- and full trailers[5].

Types of Trucks Given by FHWA Table 1-3

Type	Number of axles	Number of units	Number of trailers
1	2		
2	3	1	0
3	4 or more		
4	4 or fewer		
5	5	2	1
6	6 or more		
7	5 or fewer		
8	6	3 or more	2 or more
9	7 or more		

(1) Two-Axle, Six-Tire, Single-Unit Trucks— All vehicles on a single frame[6] including trucks, camping and recreational vehicles, mobile homes, etc. , with two axles and dual rear wheels[7].

(2) Three-Axle Single-Unit Trucks — All vehicles on a single frame including trucks, camping and recreational vehicles, mobile homes, etc. , with three axles.

(3) Four or More Axle Single-Unit Trucks — All trucks on a single frame with four or more axles.

(4) Four or Fewer Axle Single-Trailer Trucks — All vehicles with four or fewer axles consisting of two units, one of which is a tractor or straight truck power unit[8].

(5) Five-Axle Single-Trailer Trucks — All five-axle vehicles consisting of two units, one of which is a tractor or straight truck power unit.

(6) Six or More Axle Single-Trailer Trucks — All vehicles with six or more axles consisting of two units, one of which is a tractor or straight truck power unit.

(7) Five or fewer Axle Multi-Trailer Trucks — All vehicles with five or fewer axles consisting of three or more units, one of which is a tractor or straight truck power unit.

(8) Six-Axle Multi-Trailer Trucks — All six-axle vehicles consisting of three or more units, one of which is a tractor or straight truck power unit.

(9) Seven or More Axle Multi-Trailer Trucks — All vehicles with seven

or more axles consisting of three or more units, one of which is a tractor or straight truck power unit.

本节注释: [1]包括有动力的主车和无动力的挂车两种单元; [2]货车拖车单元; [3]牵引半挂车的鞍座; [4]可抬起的车轴(适用于摆臂式平衡悬架); [5]半挂和全挂车; [6]在单一的车架上; [7]后轮双胎; [8]拖车(无货箱)或纯属货车(有货箱)的动力单元。

1.1.3.2 CHINESE DEFINITIONS

In China, trucks are classified by their gross mass (Table 1-4). Only a single truck unit is considered. The information of trailers is given by another standard. Types of off-road trucks (all wheel drive) are not included in Table 1-4.

Types of Trucks Given by the Chinese National Standard

Table 1-4

Type	Gross mass (t)
Mini truck	$M \leqslant 1.8$
Light truck	$1.8 < M \leqslant 6$
Medium truck	$6 < M \leqslant 14$
Heavy truck	$M > 14$

Mini truck[1] and light truck[2] are used to deliver small commodities for little stores and families. Medium truck[3] and heavy truck[4] are used to meet batch orders[5]. Heavy truck is always used for long distance delivery.

本节注释: [1]微型货车; [2]轻型货车; [3]中型货车; [4]重型货车; [5]成批地订货。

1.1.3.3 EXTERIOR FEATURES

According to its exterior feature, the cab of the truck can be classified into two types:

NORMAL CONTROLLED TYPE

The normal controlled type[1] has a "long nose" and provides some front panels[2] (hood[3], fenders[4], etc.) to cover the engine and front wheels. The driver's seat and the control devices are behind the engine. This type is also called CBE (cab behind engine) type.

FORWARD CONTROLLED TYPE

The forward controlled type[5] puts the driver's seat and the control devices over the engine, thus the front panels are not required (flat nose). This type is also called COE (cab over engine) type. In the old forward controlled cab, the engine projects over the floor and is called CAE (cab alongside engine) type.

本节注释: [1]长头式; [2]车前板制件; [3]发动机罩; [4]翼板、翼子板; [5]平头式。

1.1.4 *OTHER TYPES OF MOTOR VEHICLES*

1.1.4.1 MODIFICATIONS

Modifications[1] are rebuilt on the chassis of mass production motor vehicles to meet particular requirements. Many modifications are provided with special equipments to carry out special tasks. In China, they are called special purpose vehicles[2].

Special purpose vehicles are classified into two types - vehicles for special transportation[3] and vehicles for special work[4].

VEHICLES FOR SPECIAL TRANSPORTATION

Vehicles for special transportation are used to carry special goods. Examples are: vehicle with a closed body for easy-contaminated goods[5], vehicle with a refrigerator body for perishable foodstuff[6], dump truck[7] for sand, soil or stones, flat-bed semi-trailer[8] for large-size cargo and tanker for liquid, powder or grain[9] (Fig. 1-5-a and b).

VEHICLES FOR SPECIAL WORK

Vehicles for special work have special equipments to meet the requirements of special work. Examples are: mobile-shop[10], ambulance[11], fire engine[12] and vehicles for urban sanitation and road cleaning[13] (Fig 1-5-c and d).

本节注释: [1]改装车; [2]专用汽车; [3]运输型专用汽车; [4]作业型专用汽车; [5]装运易污货物的闭式车身的汽车; [6]装运易腐食品的冷藏车身的汽车; [7]

自卸汽车；[8]平板半挂车；[9]运液体、粉状或粒状货物的罐车；[10]流动商店(售货车)；[11]医疗救护车；[12]消防车；[13]城市卫生和道路清扫车辆；[14]90 m 高的云梯；[15]垃圾处理车。

a)　　b)　　c)　　d)

Fig. 1-5　Special Purpose Vehicles

(by courtesy of SCANIA Beijing Representative Office)

a) cement mixer truck with a transfer pump (8×4); b) dumper (10×4); c) SKYLIFT truck with a scaling ladder of 90 m height [14] (10×4); d) garbage disposal truck [15] (6×4)

1.1.4.2　RACING CAR

Racing car[1] is constructed for particular race criteria. There are quite many worldwide famous motor races such as Formula one[2], Rally[3], Le Mans 24 hour[4] and Indianapolis 500[5]. Because the components of the racing cars might be examined under critical conditions during the competitions, smart constructions should be made using cutting-edge technologies. Detailed description of motor races is given in Section 6.2 of Chapter 6.

本节注释：[1]竞赛汽车；[2]一级方程式汽车竞赛；[3]汽车拉力赛；[4]勒芒24小时汽车竞赛；[5]印第安纳波里斯500汽车竞赛。

1.2 MOTOR VEHICLE AND SOCIETY

If we review the history of human society, it is easy to find that the greatest contribution to the human civilization in the 20th century is the motor vehicle. Motor vehicles have changed the living style of our society, brought us a modern industry production mode, and pushed forward the transportation revolution, city planning and social progress.

1.2.1 *THE MOST IMPORTANT TRANSPORTATION TOOL*

Motor vehicle is the most important transportation tool. In modern society, there is no transportation tool which can compare favorably[1] with the motor vehicle. Although a railway train or a water ship may carry more passengers and goods than a motor vehicle, it is clear that they can only operate along particular routes (railways or water routes) and pick up or drop off passengers and goods at particular points (railway stations or wharfs). Although airplane is suitable for distant and fast transportation, it needs airports too. Evidently, railway train, water ship and airplane are those kinds of transportation tools can only function along "lines and points"[2] whereas motor vehicle is not. It is a kind of transportation tool functioning on "surface"[3], that is, motor vehicles can go to almost everywhere in cities or country-sides. Moreover, they also have the advantage of "door to door" convenience[4], that is, to carry passengers and goods conveniently from one door to another door. Therefore, for the past several decades motor vehicle has become the most important and the most favorable[5] transportation tool in the society.

Nowadays, motor vehicles have become necessities not only in public transportation, but also in people's daily life. Compared with the other transportation tools, the transportation quantity of motor vehicles is the most and compared with the other machine products, the number of motor vehicles is the most too. There are more than 900 million motor vehicles throughout the world. Among them 80% are passenger cars. Average rate of ownership[6], i.e. the population divided by the total number of motor vehicles, is about 7 persons per motor vehicle in the world. This rate is 1.2 in U.S.A, about 2 in many developed countries such as Japan, west and north European countries and Australia, and 5 to 10 in South Korea, Russia and east European countries. (Table 1-5). The reason why motor vehicles are so popular is that they can keep pace with people's daily activities[7]. That is to say, motor vehicles can speed up work efficiency and living tempo[8]. Once you own a car, you can go somewhere in your own way[9] without constraint by the schedule and the route of public transportation tools. The motor vehicle has become such a satisfactory tool in everyone's mind, efficient, convenient and comfortable.

AVERAGE RATE OF MOTOR VEHICLE OWNERSHIP IN SOME COUNTRIES IN 2006 Table 1-5

Country	Rate of ownership (persons/vehicle)	Country	Rate of ownership (persons/vehicle)
U.S.A.	1.2	Mexico	5.0
Japan	1.7	Brazil	8.1
Germany	1.7	China	35
South Korea	3.5	India	59

本节注释：[1]媲美；[2]在点和线上起作用的交通工具；[3]在面上起作用的交通工具；[4]"门对门"的便利；[5]最受青睐的；[6]平均拥有率；[7]与人们的日常活动合拍；[8]提高工作效率和加快生活节拍；[9]随自己的意愿到某个地方。

1.2.2 *PILLAR INDUSTRY OF NATIONAL ECONOMY*[1]

Motor vehicle became a product in large quantities at the beginning of 20th century. Since then, human civilization developed with the motor vehicle industry progress. So far, motor vehicle has been a pillar industry of our society. The first "assembly line" appeared in Model T mass production by Henry Ford in 1913, who was the founder of Ford Motor

Company. The new production method made the massive production of cars possible and high productivity resulted in low price and popularity. This new production technology was introduced to all the other industry processes and it led to a revolution of production method and a new era for the modern industry. But in the same time increasing requirements and the automotive union make the automotive industry in the western shrink and face big challenge in surviving.

The annual production of motor vehicles in the world is nearly 70 million units (Table 1-6). A modern vehicle consists of more than 10 thousand parts which are made of various materials such as steel, alloys, plastics, rubber, glass, textures, wood and coatings[2], and by various manufacturing technologies such as smelting, casting, forging, cutting, welding, assembling and painting[3]. Many kinds of industries are involved such as metallurgy[4], machine-building, chemical industry,

Top 15 Motor Vehicle Producing Countries in 2006

Table 1-6

Rank	Country	Production (1 000 units)
1	United States	10 802
2	Japan	10 774
3	China	7 280
4	Germany	5 601
5	South Korea	3 828
6	France	3 100
7	Spain	2 698
8	Canada	2 497
9	Brazil	2 471
10	Mexico	1 956
11	India	1 684
12	United Kingdom	1 629
13	Russia	1 392
14	Thailand	1 281
15	Italy	1 165
	Total Global Production	67 265

electronic industry, electric power industry, petroleum industry and light industry[5]. Many kinds of business are also involved such as banking[6], commerce[7], transportation, tourist trades[8] and service trades[9] (Fig. 1-6). It is for sure that none of the aspects of industry and businesses in the national economy does not concern automotive industry.

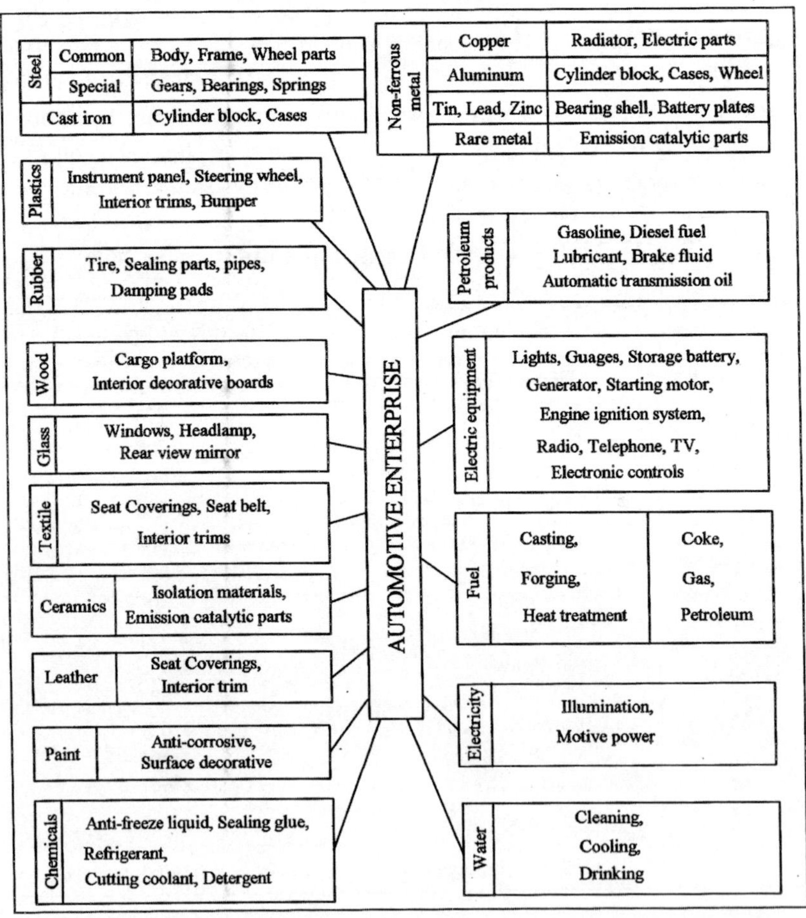

Fig. 1-6 Wide Involvement of Automotive Industry in National Economy

Another contribution of motor vehicle is its huge demand for labor force, from production line, marketing, after-sale service and car maintenance, to public transportation, highway construction, 1/9 of the total laborers work in the automotive sectors in Japan now, and this ratio is even higher in the U. S. and Germany, which is 1/6. There are more than 3 million technical, management personnel and blue-collor workers in the manufacturing plants of motor vehicle in China now. Automotive sectors in China have created more than 30 million job positions which make up 1/7 of salary laborers in this country (Table 1-7). Undoubtedly, motor vehicles have brought a huge labor group and high rate of employment to the society.

Comparison of Laborers in Three Countries (1 000 people)

Table 1-7

Item	U. S.	Japan	China
Number of laborers in automotive sectors	21 000	7 270	30 000
Total number of laborers in the country	129 520	64 360	202 000*
Comparison of the upper two items	1/6	1/9	1/7
* Laborers in cities and towns, total laborers in China are about 800 million.			

The automotive industry is also highly profitable. In the developed countries, lots of automotive firms such as GM, Daimler-Chrysler, Toyota, Ford and Volkswagen are powerful giants and rank top places among the list of "global top 500 companies" (Table 1-8). In these countries, the total production value of the automotive industry is 7% to 8% of GDP (Gross Domestic Product)[10] and 30% of the production value of the machine-building industry. Therefore, all the developed countries in the world regard the automotive industry as "the pillar industry of national economy" without exception.

本节注释：[1]国民经济的支柱产业；[2]涂料；[3]冶炼、铸造、锻造、切削加工、焊接、装配和油漆；[4]冶金；[5]轻工业；[6]银行业(金融业)；[7]商业；[8]旅游业；[9]各种服务业；[10]国内生产总值；[11]总收入。

Rank of Powerful Automotive Firms among Global Top 500 Companies in 2006 Table 1-8

Global top 500 rank	Automotive firm	Revenues[11] ($ millions)
5	GM	192 604
7	Daimler-Chrysler	186 106
8	Toyota Motor	185 805
9	Ford Motor	177 210
17	Volkswagen	118 377
31	Honda Motor	85 511
41	Nissan Motor	83 274
60	Peugeot	69 915
78	BMW	57 973
79	Fiat	57 834
80	Hyundai Motor	57 435
100	Renault	51 365
178	Volvo	32 184
235	Mazda Motor	25 789
249	Suzuki Motor	24 258
345	Mitsibishi Motors	18 725
470	China FAW	14 511
475	Shanghai Automotive	14 057
491	Isuzu Motors	13 971

1.2.3 *INDICATOR OF LATEST SCIENCE AND TECHNOLOGY*

The modern automobile uses a lot of state-of-the-art science and technology[1], such as leading-edge materials and new structures in various components, including improved electronics in its gauges and panel controls. These improvements have come as a result of many skilled and talented people performing constant research and development. This R & D (Research and Development)[2] process is carried out through many means, for example, through thousands of scientific studies utilizing the latest theories, advanced methods of measuring, the latest in computer programming, computer design, and in precision-controlled test environments. From there, the automotive industry has also seen improvements being made through advances in manufacturing processes, increases in the use of automation, and even through the introduction of newer management styles. Without doubt, the motor vehicle has become a product that displays the best that science and technology can offer. It is also an indicator and measure of greater capability for a nation that is on the rise. Ongoing development within the automotive industry will also result in helping to promote advances being made in the general science and technology fields.

本节注释：[1]现代化科学技术；[2]研究与开发。

1.2.4 *CHANGING OF LIVING STYLE*

Today, motor vehicles can be seen everywhere in our daily life. A new living style can be created as people can move from one place to another more easily and quickly. With the help of a car a person can live in suburb and work in downtown. People also can travel wherever they want to go by their car easily. There are so many examples for the benefit of motor vehicles. It is unbelievable for us to live without the motor vehicle now.

Motor vehicle has brought to our society lots of changes in the living style. For example, Americans have been described as having a love affair with their motor vehicles. The U. S. has become "A nation on wheels"[1] as affordable cars have revolutionized their way of life and changed living patterns. Many middle class families[2] are no longer willing to live in the apartments[3] of the crowded tower buildings[4] but buy their comfortable houses in the suburb which are provided with garages, even swimming pools and tennis courts. Then, the family should drive to the supermarket for shopping enough food for several days or a week. Most is not raw but frozen or packed food[5] which is kept in refrigerators, easy to cook or even ready to eat. It is evident that the way of living and eating has been different from the old days. The motor vehicle has led to a number of motels[6], shopping centers, highways, drive-in restaurants and drive-through banks[7] everywhere in this country. During the whole life of an American, from the day of birth in the hospital going home by vehicle to the day of death sent to the cemetery[8] by vehicle, it is almost impossible to live without motor vehicle. This seems to be a joke, but it is true!

As more and more people in China have purchased their family cars, the living style of the car owners have changed a lot. Because the highways have been greatly improved (it is possible driving 1 000 km within one day), more and more people can enjoy their long travels by cars. For example they can travel to their hometown during Spring Festival.

We can see roads divided by lanes, controlled traffic lights and signs, connected fly-over junctions, parking lots, city ring roads and highway networks between cities[9]. Have you ever thought that all these facilities are built to meet the requirements of motor vehicles? Indeed, the motor vehicle has changed the city planning and our environment tremendously. Moreover, the effect of the motor vehicle on our society is not only substantial, but also spiritual[10]. Motor vehicle brings us lots of cultural products and activities. Everyday you can find the news related the motor vehicle from media such as TV programs, radios and newspapers. Not only lots of specialists work hard on their design, research, sales, service and advertisements, but also citizens take the motor vehicle as an interesting topic in their ordinary conversations. There are so many movies and magazines for enjoyment where the motor vehicles play important roles under the camera shots[11]. Auto museums, auto shows and motor races have become the interesting activities around the world. They are usually most crowded places and attract so many auto fans, collectors and even fanatics[12] in the society.

One of the famous books was titled as "The Machine That Changed The World". After long term investigation, James P. Womack, a professor of MIT (Massachusetts Institute of Technology[13]) and his fellow researchers wrote this book. Here the machine means the motor vehicle. It might be proper to take the title of the book as conclusion of this section.

本节注释：[1]在车轮上的国家；[2]中产阶级家庭；[3]公寓；[4]高层建筑；[5]不是生的产品，而是冷冻和包装食品；[6]汽车旅馆；[7]汽车驶入的即取餐馆和在汽车上办理业务的银行；[8]坟墓；[9]划分车道的道路、交通红绿灯和交通标志、高架立交桥、停车场、城市环路和城间公路网络；[10]不仅是物质的，而且是精神的；[11]最上镜的重要角色；[12]车迷、收藏家、甚至狂热者；[13]美国麻省理工学院。

1.2.5 *PROBLEMS CREATED BY MOTOR VEHICLES*

As each coin has two sides, motor vehicles bring us many advantages and at the same time some problems which cannot be solved easily.

As thousands of motor vehicles running fast along crowded roads, it is difficult to avoid collisions. According to the world statistic figures, every year traffic accidents cause about 700 thousand deaths, 12 million injuries and losses of more than 50 billion US dollars. The number of motor vehicles in use in China is only 5% of the total in the world, but the number of annual traffic deaths is about 1/9 of the total in the world. As we know, heart desease and cancer are top sicknesses of death rate[1]. Unfortunately, losses of lives and properties in motor vehicle accidents are by no means less than[2] heart desease or cancer.

How much fuel do motor vehicles consume globally every year? It is more than one billion tons, one third of the world's annual petroleum production. That is, the prospected petroleum reserves in the world[3] would be used up within the next 40 years.

As we know, fuel burning of motor vehicle engines would exhaust harmful gas which consist of carbon monoxide, hydrocarbons, nitro-oxides, sulphur dioxide and lead particles[4]. when gas exposed to the sunshine it changes into chemical smoke which may be the cause of poisoning, stifling[5] and cancer, as well as acid rain[6]. Normally, the harmful gas equal to 5% of the weight of the fuel consumed.

Suppose population of a city in the U. S. is 2 million, it would have 1.5 million motor vehicles by the rate of ownership 1.2 mentioned above.

Every year, motor vehicles in this city would consume 3 million tons of fuel, thus produce 150 thousand ton harmful gas, Its volume is about 100 million cubic meters and average volume every day is about 200 thousand cubic meters. If the gas continues to accumulate for several days over the city out of low atmospheric pressure and bad ventilation[7], what a terrible disaster it would be! Here is a miserable example of the emission event caused by motor vehicles in Los Angeles (population 2.8 million) in 1943[8]. Thousands of casualties[9] were poisoned within one day. This paragraph describes 1.5 million motor vehicles only. You could imagine that how serious the pollution of 900 million motor vehicles would be!

The rapid growth of the number of motor vehicles also leads to problems such as traffic jam and shortage of parking lots. Today, traffic safety, energy economy and environmental protection have become the three main issues created by automotive technology which wait for us to solve (see Section 6.3 Chapter 6).

How can we free ourselves from this albatross[10], and create for ourselves and for future generations a transportation system which provides commuters[11] with economical, environmental and sustainable[12] solutions?

No challenge means no success. Mankind developed with both achievements and failures in her evolution history. For the motor vehicle, how to take its advantages and keep away from its blemishes[13] will be our challenges for today and future.

本节注释：[1]心脏病和癌症是死亡率最高的疾病；[2]绝不少于；[3]全世界探明的石油储量；[4]一氧化碳、碳氢化合物、氮氧化合物、二氧化硫和铅微粒；[5]中毒、窒息；[6]酸雨；[7]大气压低，通风不利；[8]1943年洛杉矶汽车废气事件；[9]受害者；[10]沉重的负担；[11]上班族，泛指乘客；[12]可持续发展的；[13]污点，瑕疵。

本章参考文献

1.1 陈家瑞. 汽车构造 上、下册 第五版. 北京：人民交通出版社，2006
1.2 陈礼璠，顾剑青. 现代轿车知识手册. 上海：上海科学技术文献出

版社, 2002
1.3 [美]Robert Lacey 著. 刘先涛,董培继 译. 福特家族. 北京:中国经济出版社,1991
1.4 林平. 汽车夜话-汽车社会大观. 北京:电子工业出版社,2005
1.5 孙益年. 世界汽车浪潮. 北京:经济管理出版社,1991
1.6 日本汽车研究所. 刘秀娟 译. 二十一世纪汽车社会. 长春:吉林科学技术出版社,1991
1.7 Car Classification. Wikipedia, the free encyclopedia. May 2007
1.8 Global Top 500-auto rank. Motor Vehicles & Parts. July 24, 2007

CHAPTER TWO
HISTORY OF MOTOR VEHICLE

2.1 THE BIRTH OF MOTOR VEHICLE

It is difficult to say who invented the motor vehicle. As a complicated machine made up by many components, the structure of the motor vehicle might not be developed by one or two persons. It has taken quite a long time to make improvement step by step, accumulated by thousands of people's creative ideas. In other words, the birth of the motor vehicle could be the certain outcome of the progress of human society, which was closely related to the industrial revolution and scientific and technological development.

British were the early designers of the steam engine. In 1712, Thomas Newcomen built his first steam engine which was used to draw the pit water[1]. It was a giant and was strictly stationary. In 1765 James Watt developed the first pressurized steam engine which was proved to be much more efficient and compact than the Newcomen's engine. Watt's engine was said to be an important step of industrial revolution.

The earliest vehicle to move under its own power was designed by a French artillery[2] engineer Nicholas Joseph Cugnot in 1769 (Fig 2-1). It was a tricycle and had a steam boiler with a diameter of 1.3 m at the front. Steam was sent to two 50 liter cylinders behind the boiler to drive the front wheel. The vehicle was 7.3 m long, the same size as a modern medium truck. Cugnot planned to let his vehicle pull cannon[3]. But it was rather clumsy and difficult to steer due to the heavy load on the front wheel. On its first test it knocked down a wall, which was considered "the first motor vehicle accident in the world" several decades later.

Although Cugnot's vehicle was not practical, it was generally recognized as the first self-propelled road vehicle in the world and also the first self-propelled transportation tool in the world (Table 2-1). Therefore, it marked the division between ancient transportation (horse and wind powered) and modern transportation (machine powered).

Fig. 2-1 Nicholas Cugnot's Steam Powered Vehicle

The early steam powered vehicles were big and heavy. They were suitable to move on rails and use to pull a train of many cars carrying cargoes and passengers. As the picture shown in Figure 2-2, many attempts had been made to develop a practical vehicle that didn't need rails. Several commercial vehicles were built but they were more like trains without rails, big and heavy.

Invention of Steam Transportation Tools Table 2-1

Transportation tools	Year of invention	Inventor
Steam tricycle	1769	Nicholas Cugnot (F)
Steam ship (driven by oars)	1786	John Fitch (A)
Steam railway locomotive	1808	Richard Trevithick (B)
Steam airship	1852	Henri Giffard (F)
Steam motor-cycle	1867	L. G. Perraux (F)
(A)-USA; (B)-GB; (F)-France		

Some of the businessmen thought that steam vehicle would be profitable to carry more passengers and goods than horse carriages. The first coach company in the world, the Scotland Coach Transportation Company was founded in 1834. But the problem was that it was difficult to control the large size vehicles. Accidents could be heard quite often. The first steam coach disaster happened when the boiler of John Scott Russell's coach exploded after a wheel collapsed near Paisley, Scotland in July 1834, and five passengers were killed. Russell's disaster was a rare chance of propaganda for the opponents who were against steam road vehicles.

Fig. 2-2 A Picture Described the Steam Vehicle in Early Nineteenth Century

In 1865 the English Parliament[4] passed an Act, the so-called "Red Flag Act[5]" known as the earliest motor vehicle safety regulation in the world, to claim the speed limit of 4 miles per hour (6.4 km/h) and the need of a man with a red flag or a red lantern in his hand, walking in front of the steam vehicle to warn pedestrians. Because of road tolls[6] and restrictive legislations[7], development of steam road vehicles was held up and horse carriages were still active everywhere.

In 1860, a Frenchman named Etienne Lenoir patented[8] the first practical gas engine in Paris. The first gas engine used coal gas, which was generated by heating coal in a pressure vessel or boiler. His 0.37 kW (1/2 hp) engine had a bore[9] of 127 mm (5 in.) and stroke of 610 mm (24 in.). It was big and heavy, turned 100 rpm and consumed 2 800 liters of gas per horsepower (3 800 L/kW). Nobody was willing to put Lenoir's engine into production. He spent his later years in poverty.

Alphonse Beau de Rochas realized that the fault in Lenoir's engine was that the gas was not compressed before burning. In 1862, He figured out how to compress the gas in the same cylinder in which it was to burn.

Siegfried Marcus, of Mecklenburg, built his first car in 1868. The car had no clutch and should be started by jacking the wheels up, spinning them and dropping them back to the ground. His second car called the Strassenwagen had about 3/4 horse power (0.55 kW) at 500 rpm. It ran on crude wooden wheels with iron rims and stopped by pressing wooden blocks against the iron rims[10], but it had a clutch, a differential and a magneto[11] ignition. Marcus is believed to have built 4 cars, although his position in automotive history is disputed[12] by some people.

In 1876, Nikolas Otto (Fig. 2-3), an engineer of a company making gas engines at Dutz in Germany, patented an engine of almost the same working process as that found by Rochas. This process of bringing the gas into the cylinder, compressing it, combusting the compressed mixture[13],

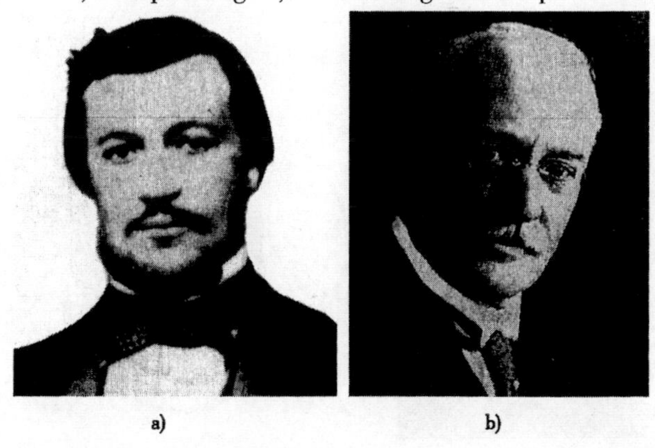

a) b)

Fig. 2-3 Famous Inventors of Internal Combustion Engines
a) Nikolas Otto (1831-1891); b) Rudolph Diesel (1858-1913)

then exhausting it is known as the Otto cycle or four stroke cycle which takes the name of the principle founder. Although the working process had already been discovered by Rochas, he had not been specific enough in his description.

The internal combustion engine was a kind of light weight power source and had profound effect on the structural revolution of motor vehicles in late nineteenth century. It was different from the steam engine. Fuel burning inside the cylinder was much more efficient than coal burning in the boiler outside the cylinder of the steam engine which was considered to be an external combustion engine[14].

In 1885, at Mannheim in Germany, an engineer Karl Benz made a single cylinder, water cooled, 0.55 kW (3/4 hp) engine and installed it beneath the seat of a tricycle (Fig. 2-4). At the rear of his car, a horizontal flywheel was used to start the engine. The car was patented as a complete unit on January 29, 1886. Germen claimed that the approved date of Benz's patent was significant and called him "the father of motor car". But Frenchmen argued that Edouard Delamarre Debottaville had driven a tricycle with a gas engine in 1884, two years earlier than Benz's patent.

Fig. 2-4 Karl Benz (1844-1929) and His First Tricycle

Any new matter has a hard time at its beginning. The performance of

Benz's first tricycle was not good enough compared with the horse carriage. As the gear was shifted, sudden pull could make the passenger uncomfortable. Some people joked: "The car jumped just like a billy-goat[15]". One summer morning in 1888, Mrs. Bertha Benz rolled the car from the workshop while her husband was still asleep. Together with two sons Bertha started off on a secret excursion. Because the car had no fuel tank, one of the boys had to run behind with a bottle of fuel in his hand. The engine was too weak to clime every slope and the boys had to push the car. Troubles such as blockage of carburetor, short of electric circuit and poor brake happened. Mrs. Benz was very keen on her husband's cause and she was capable of dealing with every trouble just like a qualified mechanic[16]. It was well past dark when they arrived in Pforzheim, 140 km far from Mannheim. What a daring adventure it was! It might be the first long distance drive in the world. Bertha Benz is recognized as the first woman driver of motor vehicle in the world.

Gottlieb Daimler (Fig. 2-5), a German engineer in Cannstatt near Stuttgart, was experienced in making engines. He had experience of making a visit to Lenoir and collaborating with Otto. His first motor vehicle was a wooden motorcycle. In 1886, he made a single cylinder, air cooled engine of 0.462L, 0.81 kW (1.1 hp) and successfully installed it onto a second-hand horse carriage (Fig. 2-6). Daimler and his friend Wilhelm Maybach were the makers. They worked such secretly in their workshop that the neighbors became suspicious[17]. Metal banging noise could be heard till late into the night. The policemen were informed and broke into the workshop to find any evidence of crime[18]. All they found were tools and car parts.

Fig. 2-5 Gottlieb Daimler (1834-1900)

Cannstatt was just 100 km from Mannheim. Daimler and Benz did not know each other but they did almost the same kind of work.

Fig. 2-6 Gottlieb (on the rear seat) and his son Paul (the driver) were testing the horseless carriage.

Rudolph Diesel (Fig. 2-3) was a German refrigeration engineer but was obsessed[19] with making a new kind of engine. In 1892 he registered his first patent for an internal combustion engine of compressed ignition. That is, only air was drawn to the cylinder and then greatly compressed to a temperature high enough to ignite the fuel sprayed into the cylinder by a nozzle. In 1897 his engine passed the performance test successfully and had an efficiency of 38%, much higher than any other kind of engines before. At the 1897 Munich Exhibition, Aldof Bush, a German-American bought the patent and put the engine into small scale production. Owing to many quality problems the products were not sold well. Diesel was very depressed at the failure. One night in 1913 while traveling on a ship to England he disappeared forever in the waters of the North Sea. It was a pity that Diesel did not live to see the great achievement of his engine many years later. The engine was named "Diesel engine[20]" in memory of his contribution.

At the same time, both Benz and Daimler founded their companies and ran them successfully. Their engines were sold well and their cars were demonstrated at many Motor Shows. The first gasoline omnibus was made by Benz's company in 1895. Its appearance was just like a big horse carriage with eight seats (Fig. 2-7). The omnibus served in Siegtal successfully. The first gasoline truck was developed by Daimler's

Fig. 2-7 The First Gasoline Bus Developed by Benz in 1895

company in 1896 (Fig. 2-8). Its cargo platform covered almost the whole

Fig. 2-8 The First Gasoline Truck Develop by Daimler in 1896

length of the truck and the driver's seat was at the front. A big steering wheel mounted on the truck was more convenient for the driver to operate than a long steering handle.

The achievement of Daimler and Benz might be that they put the motor vehicle into practical use and industrial production.

本节注释:[1]矿井积水;[2]炮兵;[3]牵引大炮;[4]英国议会;[5]红旗法案;[6]交费;[7]立法;[8]取得专利;[9]气缸直径;[10]指用木块与车轮的轮缘摩擦的方式进行制动;[11]磁电机;[12]质疑;[13]可燃混合气;[14]外燃机;[15]公羊;[16]合格的技师;[17]怀疑;[18]罪证;[19]着迷;[20]狄赛尔发动机(柴油机)。

2.2 THE EARLY DAYS

2.2.1 *FRENCH PIONEERS*

The pioneers[1] of putting cars into small scale production[2] in France were Louis Rene Panhard together with Emile Lavassor in 1889, and Armand Peugeot in 1891. They began with installing engines from Daimler. Panhard-Lavassor was the earliest company of introducing gearbox to car. The company was too small to produce all the parts and had to rely on the cooperation of Peugeot's company.

Business of Peugeot's family began in 15th century including flour mill, dyeing factory, leather factory and textile factory[3]. In the early 19th century the Peugeots founded a steel corporation to make pipes, wires, springs and panels.

Armand Peugeot began to make bicycle in 1880 and production was up to 20 thousand units in 1900. He failed to install a steam engine onto a tricycle. But in 1891 he was successful to make a four-wheel motor vehicle (Fig. 2-9) with an engine bought from Daimler. Because of Peugeot's solid background of industrial manufacturing, his production grew fast. 500 cars were sold in 1899. Attracted by Armand's profitable business, three nephews joined their uncle and expanded the enterprise. A trade mark of lion was registered since then[4].

Fig. 2-9 A Peugeot Car Made in 1892 (notice the bicycle wheels)

Albert Marquis De Dion together with his engineering partner Georges Bouton, began producing self-propelled steam vehicles in 1882. Their company patented a light rear axle, which was named after De Dion, to improve the ride of the vehicles. A patent for a high-speed single-cylinder gasoline engine was filed in 1890, production started five years later. By 1900, De Dion-Bouton was the world's largest car maker with an annual production of 400 cars and 3 200 engines. De Dion founded the first automobile club in 1895 and organized the world's first auto show in Paris in 1898.

In addition, he looked for ways to transfer automotive applications to commercial vehicles and public transportation. Not satisfied, De Dion also produced road maps, developed military equipment and was an aviation pioneer.

De Dion lost his motivation as an innovator and pioneer after World War I. In 1932 he withdrew from his company, which had stopped making cars.

The world's first motor race was held in 1895, from Paris to

Bordaeux[5] and return, a distance of 1 178 km. 22 cars competed, including 15 gasoline cars, 6 steamers and 1 electric car. The winner was Emile Lavassor together with his partner Louis Panhard (Fig 2-10). They used 48 hours to finish their driving, 6 hours ahead of their nearest rival. Their average speed of 24.5 km/h was not fast but they were very exhausted by the continuous driving of two days. Night driving depended on kerosene lanterns and therefore was difficult to see. On the road returned it was Panhard's turn to drive but he fell in sleep. So, Lavassor kept on driving all the way back. Although the motor race was far from perfect, it was said to be a good way for the makers to promote their products.

Fig. 2-10 Lavassor and Panhard drove their car to the race

The first world land speed record was established by a Frenchman Gaston de Chasselop-Laubat in 1898. He drove a "Jeantaud" electric car at 63.15 km/h over a measured distance near Paris and proclaimed himself the fastest man in the world. Camille Jenatzy, a Belgian nicknamed[6] the "Red Devil" because of his red hair and beard, accepted the challenge and took an electric car of his own design, "La Jamais Contente (Never Satisfied)" to the same road and reached 68.27 km/h. Alternative competitions between the two men were followed and the record was rewritten four times within five months. The last winner was the Red Devil at a speed of 105.88 km/h. As shown in Figure 2-11, the shape of Janatzy's electric car was just like a shell[7], because he thought the shape might be low air resistant.

本节注释:[1]先驱者; [2]小批量生产; [3]面粉厂、印染厂、皮革厂、纺织厂; [4]从此以后; [5]波尔多(法国西海岸城市); [6]绰号;[7]炮弹。

Fig. 2-11 Janatzy drove his electric car and made a world record in 1898.

2.2.2 *GASOLINE ENGINE BECAME DOMINANT*

2.2.2.1 FLOURISHING AGE OF STEAM VEHICLES

There were up to 200 brands of motor vehicles in the world in 1902 and 700 in 1905. Their power sources were three kinds mainly, i. e. gasoline engine, electric motor and steam engine.

In late 19th century steam vehicles had made some progress and became smaller and lighter. In 1875 Leon Serpollet, a French pioneer of steam vehicles, invented a more efficient steam boiler of flame-pipe type. In 1900 he built a steamer and began to use paraffin[1] in the boiler which was beneath the rear seats and close to the under-floor engine with four cylinders and a total volume of 0.965 L.

At that time, steamers became very popular in the United States. For example, in 1901 there were 8 000 powered vehicles in use in the U. S.

Half of them were steamers, 3 000 were electric cars and only a few were gasoline cars.

Stanley twins[2] began to build their steam cars in 1897 and their cars continued to be made until 1927. The cars not only took part in some races, but also were sold to the American police and fire department.

The world's largest enterprise to produce steam vehicles was the Locomobile Company in Connecticut[3] where 4 000 steamers were made from 1899 to 1901. This kind of steamer (Fig. 2-12) had a boiler of 35.6 cm (14 in.) under the driver's seat to supply a twin cylinder engine. Its main problem was "thirsty", needed to be refilled with water every 30 km or so.

Fig. 2-12 Steamer Made by Locomobile Company in 1901

Another large company was the White Steamer by Rollin White in Cleveland, Ohio[4], an original sewing machine manufacturer. Its annual production was up to 1 000 units. White's cars took part in some races and performed quite well. Therefore President Theodore Roosevelt had a White at the White House, which helped to make the company the most famous.

In 1902 Serpollet in a steamer took the world land speed record to

120.79 km/h at Nice in France, writing a glorious chapter of steamer in the history.

After that, no technical break-through could be seen in the steam engine. A big disadvantage of the steam engine was difficult to start. It took almost half an hour for the boiler to preheat and produce enough steam, especially in winter. In 1903, Locomobile abandoned steam and shifted to gasoline engine. The production change of the largest steamer enterprise ended the flourishing age of this kind of vehicles. The research of steam engine faded when Serpollet died in 1907.

本节注释:[1]煤油;[2]孪生兄弟;[3]康奈狄格州;[4]俄亥俄州。

2.2.2.2 ELECTRIC VEHICLES IN LATE 19TH CENTURY

In the late 19th century, electricity greatly changed the society and the style of people's daily life. The following were some great inventions. In 1800, an Italian physician Alesandro Volta invented the storage battery which provided the human society with continuous and stable electric current and made the invention and application of telegraph[1] (1835) and telephone (1876) possible. The invention of electric motor in 1821 by an English physician Michael Faraday provided the human society with a new kind of motive force and his inventions of generator and transformer[2] in 1831 led to the birth of electric power plant[3]. After that, various kinds of electric transportation tools were invented and used (Table 2-2).

Compared with the gasoline car, the electric car was easier to

Invention of Electric Transportation Tools Table 2-2

Transportation tool	Year of invention	Inventor
Electric ship (driven by oars)	1839	(Russia)
Experimental electric car	1847	Moses Farmer (A)
Elevator[4]	1854	Eli Otis (A)
The first electric railway	1879	Werner Siemens (G)
Electric airship	1889	Charles Renard (F)
Electric underground railway	1890	(London)
(A)-USA; (G)-Germany; (F)-France		

operate and had less trouble. Its main problems of small electric capacity and heavy weight led to low speed, short operation mileage and long rechargeable[5] time. If the car was used in a limited area, such as the urban area, it might be practical and beneficial. In fact, electric taxis were very active in London, Paris and other cities at that time (Fig. 2-13). But the charging cost within one year was very expensive, worth the price of a new electric car. In the city, tramcars might be the most effective transportation tool with the largest volume to beat the others in the early 20th century. The overhead cables provided them with everlasting and more reliable power compared with storage batteries on electric cars. As there was not any technical break through, the electric cars faded.

Fig. 2-13 An Electric Taxi in New York in 1898 (front wheel drive)

本节注释:[1]电报机; [2]发电机和变压器; [3]发电厂; [4]电梯(升降机); [5]重新充电。

2.2.2.3 PROGRESS OF GASOLINE ENGINE

Before long, the gasoline engine had improved greatly to become lighter and more powerful than the steam engine and the battery-motor. Its quality and structure were changing with every passing day[1]. A comprehensive target to show its progress was specific power or liter power[2], i. e. how many kilowatts of power output developed by one liter of its working volume. (Table 2-3). The progress of this target meant that many structural innovations were carried out by hundreds of skillful inventors year by year. That was why the gasoline car could beat the steam car and electric car. In the late 1920s, no horse carriages, steamers and electric cars could be seen on the roads except those vehicles equipped with internal combustion engines.

Liter Power Progress of Some early Gasoline Engines

Table 2-3

Engine of car	Year	Power output (kW)	Working volume (L)	Liter power (kW/L)
Daimler's horseless carriage	1886	0.81	0.462	1.75
Mercedes car	1902	20.59	5.3	3.88
Renault racing car	1906	66.18	13.0	5.09
Austin racing car	1908	73.53	9.6	7.66
Audi racing car	1912	29.41	3.6	8.17
Campbell's Bluebird	1923	257.35	13.8	18.65
Segrave's Sunbeam Tiger	1926	220.60	4.0	55.15

本节注释:[1]日新月异;[2]比功率或升功率。

2.2.3 *MERCEDES*

Gottlieb Daimler's company received strong support from an Austrian Emil Jelinek who was a sales agent in Nice, a city by the Mediterranean Sea[1] in south France. Jelinek was an enthusiast of motor race. In 1897 he had Daimler build a car on his own specifications. He drove this Daimler-Phoenix car to win Nice Motor Race at 84.8 km/h in 1899. He gave the car another name "Mercedes". It was his eleven year old daughter's name (Fig. 2-14). After Daimler's death in 1900, Jelinek became an important member of the board of directors[2] and made great contribution to the Daimler Company. Since 1902, all the cars produced by the company took the name "Mercedes".

Figure 2-15 shows a 1902 Mercedes car, equipped with a 4 cylinder, 5.3 L and 20.59 kW (28 hp) engine. A passenger car or a racing car could be built on the same chassis. Structures of the car were more progressive than those of the Oldsmobile "Curved Dash[3]" car (Fig. 2-16) made by Ransome Eli Olds with a single cylinder, 1.5 L and 3.7 kW engine beneath the driver's seat. "Curved Dash" was cheap and sold well, but its structures were traditional. However, some assemblies of the Mercedes car were similar to those of a modern car. In order to provide enough room for a larger and more powerful engine, its position was moved from the seat bottom to the front. The car was equipped with a gearbox, a rear drive axle, pneumatic tires and an offset steering wheel[4].

Fig. 2-14 Eleven Year Old Mercedes Jelinek

Fig. 2-15 The 1902 Mercedes Car

Economic situation in Germany became worse after it was defeated in World War I. In 1923, among the 15 million registered car, over 80% of them were registered in the US and over 1/2 were Fords. Benz built 1 382 cars in 1923 while Daimler only built 1 020. German auto makers were at a low point although racing success for the companies continued.

In 1924, from sheer economic necessity[5], Benz and Daimler signed

Fig. 2-16 The Oldsmobile "Curved Dash" car was sold well from 1901 to 1905 in the U. S.

an "Agreement of Mutual Interest." Although both companies retained their identities, the agreement was valid until the year 2000. The two companies merged[6] with relative ease on June 28, 1926.

A symbol Mercedes-Benz was chosen for the combined products of Daimler and Benz. The new insignia[7] was a three-pointed star wreathed with laurel[8]. The word "Mercedes" was at the top and the word "Benz" was at the bottom.

Then the merger did the new company some good. Production of Mercedes-Benz rose to 7 918 Mercedes-Benz motor vehicles in 1927. The Mercedes-Benz diesel truck was also put into production in 1927.

本节注释:[1]地中海; [2]董事会; [3]驾驶员脚前面的挡板(前围板); [4]偏置一侧的转向盘; [5]纯属经济上的需求; [6]合并; [7]徽章、标志; [8]月桂环绕的三尖星。

2.2.4 *RENAULT BEGAN TO CROP OUT*[1]

The Renault Automobile Company was founded at Billancourt in France by Renault brothers, Fernand, Marcel and Louis in 1898. The first product was a Type A car (Fig. 2-17) with a single cylinder, 0.273 L and 1.29 kW engine and a three-speed gear box. Renault products initiated[2] the remarkable features of direct gear in the gearbox and propeller shaft[3] which made the cars very special in the early years.

Fig. 2-17 Renault "Type A" Car (with Louis at the wheel)

In 1902, the most ambitious intercity race, the Paris-Vienna Race was held. It was hailed as "the Race of Races". The race spanned 990 km including the Arlberg Pass which was said to be the most difficult. The cars were required to clime 1 500 m in 16 km, with the unfenced road ending on one side in a precipitous cliffs[4]. Cars were divided into big car class and light car class. Only 80 out of 130 cars completed the course. It was surprised that the overall winner was not the big and powerful car, but a Renault car of mere 3.8 liters driven by Marcel Renault (Fig. 2-18), 35 minutes ahead of the next arrival. Under such a complicated road condition, big engine size might not be of first importance.

Unfortunately, in the next year the skillful motorist Marcel Renault

Fig. 2-18 The 1902 Renault Car (with a propeller shaft)

died in the Paris-Madrid Race which was a big disaster and ended on the midway because of so many accidents and fatalities. It also ended the dangerous intercity races.

In 1909 the eldest brother Fernand died too and the youngest Louis became the only leader of the company.

After the 1902 victory, Renault's products became famous and the company ran well. In 1914 the World War I broke out and the famous "Taxis de la Marne" made a historic contribution to victory over the German troops at the battle of the Marne, by helping transport 6 500 soldiers to the front. Renault also produced tanks, ambulances and aircraft engines for the Allied Army. After the War, Louis got another Chevalier medallion[5] for his contribution to the war.

After the World War II, Louis Renault was arrested for collaboration with the German army. His firm was taken over and run by the government (state owned[6]) and he died in the jail in 1944.

本节注释：[1]初露锋芒(崭露头角)；[2]首创；[3]变速器中的直接档和传动轴；[4]没有围栏的道路一边有陡峭的悬崖；[5]骑士大奖章；[6]国营。

2.2.5 *RUBBER PNEUMATIC TIRE*

Wooden road wheels were the main components of the ancient vehicles. Then an iron hoop[1] was added to the circumference of the wheel. The horse carriages and the early motor vehicles used iron hooped wheels. But this kind of wheels was not suitable for fast driving because of serious vibration, making the passengers uncomfortable. Application of the rubber pneumatic tires[2] to motor vehicles was a great achievement to solve the problem of low comfort at high speed.

An American, Charles Goodyear (Fig. 2-19) made outstanding contribution to the rubber industry and was called "the father of rubber industry". His invention of vulcanized technology[3] in 1844 was very important to improve the property of rubber, putting rubber into practical use. In 1898 Goodyear Tire and Rubber Company was formed in America by Frank Seiberling. Then Firestone Tire & Rubber Company was started by Harvey Firestone in 1900. Other tire makers followed.

Fig. 2-19 Charles Goodyear (1800-1860)

In the late 19th century the tire makers always used a rubber tire casing stuffed by sawdust, cloth pieces or other elastic materials to damp the road shock. This kind of tires was called the solid tire. The popularity of bicycles in the late 1800s revived the idea of the pneumatic tire, and in 1888 a Belfast veterinary surgeon[4] named John Boyd Dunlop obtained a patent for a pneumatic bicycle tire.

The first use of pneumatic tires for motor cars was pioneered by the Michelin brothers, Andre and Edouard. They equipped a car with pneumatic tires and drove it to 1895 Paris-Bordeaux road race. The winner of the race, Lavassor did not use the pneumatic tire but the solid rubber tire because the pneumatic tires were not reliable at that time. He affirmed that the pneumatic tire would not be successful. But the rapid development of rubber pneumatic tires in the coming years proved that Lavassor was totally wrong.

In 1908 Seiberling invented the technology of making deep pattern[5] on tire tread[6] to increase tire and road adhesion. Before his invention, the tire tread was smooth and easy to slip. Ropes should be used to bind the tire to prevent from slippery on wet roads. Until this time, problems of both ride comfort and road adhesion could be solved and the increase of speed was made possible. After that, structure and manufacturing technology had made great progress and tire had become an important component of motor vehicle.

本节注释：[1]铁箍；[2]橡胶充气轮胎；[3]硫化工艺；[4]兽医；[5]轮胎花纹；[6]胎面。

2.2.6 *BRITISH PIONEERS*

The first British gasoline car was made in Surrey in 1895 by John Henry Knight, who had previously built steam cars. It was a tricycle with a single cylinder, water-cooled engine and was capable of about 14.5 km/h. He might be short-sighted[1] to make only one car.

Wolseley's car production began in Birmingham in 1899 with Herbert Austin as manager. It was Britain's leading car company. 500 cars had been sold by 1902. In this year it introduced two models, a four cylinder 5.2 liter car and a twin cylinder 2.6 liter car. It also made racing cars which took part in the 1902 Paris-Vienna and the 1903 Paris-Madrid competitions.

In 1908 Austin quit the Wolseley Company and started his own firm in Longbridge, Birmingham. In the 1920s his product model "Austin 7" was sold well and became famous. In the 1980s Austin-Rover became the largest enterprise in Britain with a production volume of 500 thousand units per year.

Another famous brand is the MG which stands for "Morris Garages". The enterprise was founded by William Richard Morris, later Lord[2] Nuffield. He designed his first car, the Bull Nosed Morris in 1912 and began large-scale production at the former site of a military training college in the Cowley area of Oxford. Morris opened car manufacturing plants at Abingdon, Birmingham, and Swindon between 1919 and 1925, and introduced Henry Ford's mass production technique to the United

Kingdom. He is remembered not only as an industrialist, but also as a philanthropist[3] who gave away approximately £ 30 million over of his lifetime. (That is the equivalent of more than £ 600 million, or approximately $ 1 billion in today's money.)

Two British pioneers Charles Rolls and Henry Royce, their names are forever linked by a hyphen[4]. Royce was an engineer who made electric cranes and dynamos in Manchester. One day, a friend brought him a car to repair. He was not satisfied with the structure of the car and said: "I can do better than this". He built his first car with a two cylinder engine and a three speed gearbox in 1903. There was nothing new in the car but it ran well and was exceptionally quiet and smooth. A racing motorist and car salesman Charles Rolls enthused over Royce's products and decided to cooperate with him. The company Rolls-Royce began in 1906. Rolls drove one of their first models, a six cylinder 14.7 kW (20 hp) car and won the 1906 Isle of Man TT Race[5]. This success brought them more orders than they could meet. They bought land at Derby to expand their enterprise. Their product Silver Ghost was comfortable and elegant and earned the company an unofficial title of "the best car in the world" (Fig. 2-20).

Fig. 2-20 Rolls-Royce Silver Ghost of 1906 was in production until 1925.

They had separate roles. Royce was the practical, hard-working man who designed every element of Rolls-Royce engines and chassis. Rolls provided much of the finance and the social connections that generated sales. It was a great partnership, but lasted only six years. In 1910, Rolls, an aviation pioneer, became the first Briton to die in an air crash[6] when he piloted a plane to create a record. Royce continued to make all the company's engineering decisions, but was aided on the commercial side by Claude Johnson, a man many years later called the hyphen in Rolls-Royce.

During World War I, Rolls-Royce began designing and manufacturing airplane engines, a business that was to become the dominant company activity. In 1931, Rolls-Royce bought the assets of the bankrupt Bentley Motors.

本节注释: [1]目光短浅; [2]勋爵; [3]慈善家; [4]连字符号(短划); [5]马恩岛 TT 汽车赛; [6]死于空难的第一个英国人。

2.2.7 *FIAT*

FIAT is the initials of Fabbrica Italiana Automobili Torino (Italian Car Factory of Turin). The name began to use since 1906.

The company was founded in 1899 by a group of joint stock[1] Italians including Giovanni Agnelli, a former cavalry officer turned amateur engineer[2]. Since 1902 the company has always been guided by a member of Agnelli's family. Giovanni Agnelli led the company until his death in 1945.

In 1902 Vincenzo Lancia who was the company's chief tester drove Fiat's first real competition car with a 6.4 liter 17.6 kW (24 hp) engine to won the Sassi-Superga uphill race. In the same year he also won Portugal's first race. In 1903, Fiat produced its first truck. In 1908, the first Fiat was exported to the US. That same year, the first Fiat aircraft engine was produced. Also around the same time, Fiat taxis became popular in Europe. By 1910, Fiat was the largest automotive company in Italy, a position it has retained ever since.

本节注释: [1]股票; [2]转为业余工程师的前骑兵军官。

2.2.8 *THE FIRST GRAND PRIX*

In 1906, three years after the Paris-Madrid disaster, a new kind of race was introduced. The race lasted two days in Le Mans near Paris. Cars should run six laps on a closed public road circuit of 103.18 km every day. Total mileage was 1 238 km. It was the first Gran Prix[1].

The race was organized by ACF (Automobile Club de France). 32 cars of 11 types from Germany, Italy and France took part in the race. The cars were big and heavy and their brakes were not good. Some roads were tarred to stop dust from blinding the drivers. But the weather was so hot that the tar melted and splashed on their faces. Renault entered three cars with four cylinder 13 liter and 66 kW (90 hp) engines. Only one of the Renaults finished and won the race by one minute less than a Fiat. The winner Ferenc Szisz, a Hungarian, covered all the roads nearly 12 hours at an average speed of 101.195 km/h. His car had two seats because a riding mechanic was needed. The car utilized detachable rims[2] created by Michelin which enabled him to save time when changing tires in 2 to 3 minutes instead of the normal 15 minutes.

The first Grand Prix was very successful. It was safer than the 1903 Paris-Madrid Race and easier for the organizer to manage the racing cars. Wooden fences were built to control the crowds and thus selling tickets to earn money became possible. Advertisements were also active in the race. Since then, Grand Prix was considered to be a good kind of race and Le Mans became famous.

本节注释：[1]汽车大奖赛(注意读音)；[2]可拆卸的轮辋。

2.2.9 *AUDI*

August Horch (Fig. 2-21) was a former engineer and motorist of Benz's company. He founded a factory named "Horch" in 1899 and began to produce cars in 1901. His business ran well and became a large enterprise within 8 years. After disagreements with his partners, he left the enterprise and began another in 1909. His new enterprise was impossible to use the name "Horch" which was already registered. When he had no idea to find another good name, his son said: Why don't you use "Audi"? The word "Audi" in Latin means "hearing", just the same meaning of the word "Horch" in German. So the father was very happy to accept his boy's suggestion.

Fig. 2-21 August Horch (1868-1951)

From 1912 to 1914, August Horch drove his Audi sport cars and won Austrian Alpine Trials three times. Since then, Audi products became famous.

In 1932, four companies, Audi, Horch, Wanderer and DKW merged together to form a new firm named "Auto Union". After that, a four-link symbol was used as the trade mark of this firm. In 1964, Audi was taken over by Volkswagen.

2.2.10 *THE FIRST AUTO-MARATHON FROM BEIJING TO PARIS*

The first auto-marathon[1] was held in 1907. It was more than 16 thousand kilometers from Beijing to Paris. Five cars took part in the race and they were shipped to Beijing in advance. Cars drove on a long journey across deserts, swamps[2], rivers and the wastelands of Siberia[3] in Russia. For much of the way there were no roads and cars drove along the Trans-Siberian railway tracks (Fig. 2-22). Every car was packed with food, tools, spare parts and medicine. In fact, it was an adventure.

The winner was Prince Scipio Borghese in an "Itala" of 7.4 liters built by an Italian company founded in 1904. Accompanied by Luigi Barzini, he covered the race in 60 days, three weeks ahead of the other finishers, two French De Dions and one Dutch Spyker.

Fig. 2-22 The car Itala drove along the Trans-Siberian railway tracks.

本节注释：[1]汽车马拉松；[2]沼泽；[3]西伯利亚。

2.2.11 *GUN-POWDER ROCKET CAR*

A car propelled by gun-powder[1] might be very dangerous, but it was true. In 1928, Fritz Opel tested this car named "Rak 2" on Avus track in Germany. It had a round head and short wings (Fig. 2-23), fitted with 24 gun-powder rockets. Fritz fired the rockets in stages and lived to tell the tale. In fact, the car worked and achieved the speed of

Fig. 2-23 Fritz Opel drove his gun-powder rocket car along the track.

201.16 km/h.

The significance of the test was not Fritz's confidence and courage but the jet propulsion[2], though the structure was impossible to be introduced to the market.

本节注释：[1]火药；[2]喷气驱动。

2.3 THRIVING ERA

2.3.1 *EARLY DAYS OF AUTOMOTIVE INDUSTRY IN THE UNITED STATES*

Automotive industry in the United States developed rapidly. At the beginning of the twentieth century it overtook all the European countries, although motor vehicles were born in Europe. In 1895, there were only 4 motor vehicles in use in the US, whereas there were 450 in France and 100 in Germany. Before the World War I in 1914, there were nearly two million motor vehicles in use throughout the world, 65 percent of them were American motor vehicles. From 1914 to 1918, European economy was seriously destroyed by the World War I. But in the same period, Americans carried out a lot of technical reforms and left Europeans far behind.

A variety of pioneers were working hard at building the groundwork for a future American automotive industry. Oliver Evans, a pioneer of the steam engine, had driven a combination wagon[1] and flatboat[2] over land and water as early as 1805 in Philadelphia. Many followed Evans in constructing steam vehicles or electric cars, but gasoline vehicles were still in the experimental stage prior to 1893. Charles Duryea built a three-wheeled, gasoline powered vehicle in 1893, and his company built 13 cars of the same design in 1896. Gasoline automobiles were produced by Elwood Haynes in 1894, by Ransom Olds in 1895, and Charles King and Henry Ford in 1896. Motor races stirred the public interest and bicycle and buggy[3] manufacturers began to convert on making motor vehicles.

One of the major factors which led to the dominance of the American automotive industry was the discovery in 1901 of vast oil fields near Beaumont, Texas. These rich deposits of petroleum made gasoline become an abundant supply of the economical fuel.

本节注释：[1]指主车与挂车的组合；[2]平底船；[3]轻便马车。

2.3.2 *DETROIT*

Detroit is the heart of the American Automotive industry. It is in Michigan, near the Great Lakes[1]. Many famous automotive companies and their manufacturing plants were set in Detroit.

In late seventeenth century, Detroit was just an uncultivated land. Regarding its important strategic position and excellent natural conditions, Antoine Cadillac, a French officer served in the colonial army in Canada, reported to the King Louis XIV[2] that the French army should control this area. In 1701, Cadillac together with 50 soldiers and some businessmen settled there and began to exchange goods with the native Indians. He named the area "Detroit" which meant "strait" in French to describe the narrow water passages at the Great Lakes.

Fertile soil and good climate made crops and fruits grow well. For the next 50 years, Detroit thrived and became a densely residential area. After the independence of the United States in 1786, Detroit was within her boundary. Industry began with the excavation for iron and cooper mines and more people went there to earn their living.

An important step in the history of Detroit was the Canal Erie's opening to navigation in 1825. Goods could be shipped to Detroit from the Atlantic Ocean through the canal. Freight volume[3] handled by Detroit was not inferior to those harbors by the Atlantic Ocean such as Boston and Baltimore. In 1870 population in Detroit was only 80 thousands, but in 1899 it became the top tenth city in the US. Another important step was the development of automotive industry which made it rank into the top five cities of American economy in the mid-twentieth century.

本节注释：[1]美国北部五大湖；[2]法国国王路易十四；[3]吞吐量。

2.3.3 *FORD*

The achievement of the American automotive industry in the early days was much concerned with Henry Ford's success.

Henry Ford (Fig. 2-24) built his first crude but successful "quadricycle" in 1896. Three years later he became the manager of the Detroit Automobile Company. He soon left the company and turned to racing. He built racing cars and won the Manufacturer's Challenge Cup. Based on that success Ford Motor Company was founded in 1903.

Fig. 2-24 Henry Ford (1863-1947)

When founded, Ford Motor Company was just one of 15 car manufacturers in Michigan and 88 in the US. The first Ford, the Model A, was being sold in Detroit a few months later. But as it began to turn a profit within its first few months, it became clear that Henry Ford's vision for the automotive industry was going to work, and work in a big way. Henry Ford's insistence that the company's future lay in the production of affordable cars for a mass market caused increasing friction between him and the other investors. As some left, Ford acquired enough stock to increase his own holdings to 58.5 percent. Henry Ford became president in 1906.

The best selling car Model T (Fig. 2-25) was introduced in 1908. It had four seats, a four cylinder engine of 2.88 L and 20 hp (14.7 kW) with hand controlled throttle and a two-speed gear box. Model T was economical and reliable. In 1909 one Model T won the New York-Seattle Race in 22 days.

In 1913, a moving assembly line began to produce Model Ts at Highland Park in Detroit (Fig. 2-26). The new technique was the

Fig. 2-25 Ford Model T

Fig. 2-26 Ford's Assembly Line in Highland Park

so-called flow process[1]. It was quite different from the on-site assembling technique which required versatile workers to do all kinds of work. The new technique allowed individual workers to stay at one place and perform the same task repeatedly, which resulted in high productivity and low cost. After that, the production volume of Model Ts increased tremendously, 300 thousand units in 1914 and 730 thousand units in 1917. At the same time, Ford built his Model T assembly plants in Germany, France, Mexico and Denmark. 1923 was the year of top production and 1.8 million Model Ts were produced totally in the world. From 1908 to 1927, more than 15 million Model Ts were sold. The price of a single car was greatly cut down from $ 850 to $ 265. In 1920s, more than 50 percent of the cars in the world were Model Ts.

The years between the world wars were a period of hectic expansion. In 1917, Ford Motor Company began producing trucks and tractors. In 1919 Henry Ford and his shareholders[2] disputed the investment of several millions to build the giant Rouge manufacturing complex[3] in Dearborn. Henry Ford desired to buy all the shares and this led to the company becoming wholly owned by him and his son, Edsel, who then succeeded his father as president.

In 1914, Dodge brothers, John and Horace moved to Detroit where they opened their machine shop and became the sub-contractors to the Olds Motor Works. Later Henry Ford offered them shares in his company and they built engines for him. With Ford's success their business became prosperous. The brothers strongly disagreed to Henry Ford's huge investment to build the Rouge Manufacturing Complex and led a band of rebel shareholders[4]. Ford wanted them out of his company and the price he paid was sufficient to found the Dodge Motor Company.

Henry Ford was not only a man who brought car to the masses, but also a man of great vision. He established the eight-hour working day, guaranteed a minimum wage, and gave help and encouragement to scholars.

本节注释：[1]流水作业；[2]股票持有者、股东；[3]综合设施；[4]一群叛逆的股东。

2.3.4 *GENERAL MOTORS*

The General Motors Corporation became the world's largest motor vehicle manufacturer in 1931 and maintained that status into the 21st century. It operates manufacturing and assembly plants and distribution centers throughout the United States, Canada, and many other countries. Its major products include cars and trucks, automotive components, and engines. Its subsidiary General Motors Acceptance Corporation (GMAC), founded in 1919 to finance and insure the installment sales of GM products, entered the mortgage business in 1985 and expanded into commercial finance in 1999. GM's headquarters are in Detroit, Michigan.

William Crapo Durant (Figure 2-27 a), a former horse carriage builder founded the General Motors Company in 1908 to merge several motor car companies including Buick, Oldsmobile, Cadillac, Oakland (later Pontiac), Ewing, Marquette, and other autos, as well as Reliance and Rapid trucks.

a) b)

Fig. 2-27 Famous Leaders of General Motors Corporation
a) William Crapo Durant (1861-1947); b) Alfred Pritchard Sloan Jr. (1875-1966)

David Dunbar Buick, a former bathroom designer founded his motor car company in 1903. But the company's financial control was taken over by his co-investor Durant soon. Buick found his share becoming less and he was only a nominal member of the board[1]. He left the company in 1908 and never returned. But he left behind him a memorial, a car name which remained in the forefront of American automotive industry through the succeeding decades and became famous all over the world.

Ransome Eli Olds began to make Oldsmobile cars in 1896. His "Curved Dash" cars (Fig 2-16) dominated the car market from 1901 to 1905. The car was very famous and suitable for rough dirt roads which abounded in the US at that time. By the end of 1905, the Olds Motor Works had produced 18 500 cars. Olds found he could keep costs down and sell the car for $ 650 by concentrating on a single model, using efficient production methods, and producing cars in large quantities. His success in placing inexpensive cars in the hands of average people helped popularize the automobile and remove the label of "rich man's toy". He also helped to establish Detroit as the Motor City since many of his suppliers went on to become auto manufacturers.

Henry Martin Leland was regarded as the giant of the developing motor industry. He was the leader of Cadillac Motor Car Company from 1902 to 1917. The company was named after the founder of the city Detroit. Many Leland's ideas subsequently appeared both in General Motors and Ford cars. At that time, a big problem was that one part did not fit different cars. With a background in the precision tool industry, Leland began applying the interchangeable principle[2] in the manufacturing of cars. In 1907, a demonstration was held to prove that Cadillac parts were completely interchangeable. The individual components of three cars piled indiscriminately about an open shed. In a short time Leland's mechanics had built three complete cars from the assortment of parts. The cars easily completed a 800 km test run and Cadillac was awarded the Sir Thomas Dewar Trophy for the most meritorious automotive performance of the year. Parts became interchangeable, something that was to have a tremendous impact both in the production of cars and the services. In 1912, Cadillac introduced the Kettering electric self-starter commercially in its car and was again awarded the Dewar Trophy. Without hand cranking[3], cars were easier to start and it was now practical for women to drive. Besides, having a solid foundation of precise manufacturing, Cadillac was the first company to use synchronizer[4] onto the gearbox in 1928.

Durant lost control of GM in 1910. A banker's trust[5] took over management of the firm. In 1916 Durant returned to GM with his Chevrolet Motor Car Company. Durant's partner, Louis Chevrolet had worked for Mors and De Dion Bouton in France. He went to work for the New York branch of De Dion and from there he began his racing life. Louis became one of the most famous American racing drivers in Buick racing team and soon the first Chevrolet car was on the market. But Chevrolet had a row[6] with Durant and in 1912 left the company which bore his name.

Durant was forced out of the company in 1920 and was succeeded by Alfred P. Sloan Jr. (Fig 2-27 b), who served as president (1923-1937) and then as chairman of the board of directors (1937-1956). Sloan reorganized GM from a sprawling, uncoordinated collection of business units into a single enterprise consisting of five main automotive divisions — Cadillac, Buick, Pontiac, Oldsmobile (discontinued in 2004), and Chevrolet—the activities of which were coordinated by a central corporate office equipped with large advisory and financial staffs. The various operating divisions retained a substantial degree of autonomy within a framework of overall policy; this decentralized concept of management became a model for large-scaled industrial enterprises in the United States. Sloan also greatly strengthened GM's sales organization, pioneered annual style changes in car models, and introduced innovations in consumer financing.

General Motors added overseas operations, including Vauxhall of England in 1925, Adam Opel of Germany in 1929, and Holden of Australia in 1931. The Yellow Truck & Coach Manufacturing Co. (now GMC Truck & Coach Division), organized in 1925, was among the new American divisions and subsidiaries established.

本节注释：[1]董事会；[2]互换原理；[3]手摇起动汽车；[4]同步器；[5]

托拉斯、联合企业；[6]争吵。

2.3.5 *CHRYSLER*

Walter Percy Chrysler (Fig. 2-28), a former locomotive mechanic was offered the position of works manager at the Buick plant in 1912. With Chrysler's developments and improvements installed, the production at the plant was increased to 550 cars per day. The innovation of painting parts before they were assembled reduced bottlenecks in the assembly line. A new painting method of pressurized air spray was also developed to apply the finish to the car bodies. The method was soon used throughout the industry. Because he had saved Buick millions of dollars and increased production, in 1916 he took the presidency of Buick at an annual salary of one half million dollars. Later, he was also the executive vice-president of GM. Furious at the interference from Durant, he resigned on March 20, 1920. The argument was recalled by Sloan: "I remember the day. He banged the door on the way out, and out of that bang came eventually the Chrysler Corporation."

Fig. 2-28 Walter Percy Chrysler (1875-1940)

The origins of Chrysler Motor Corporation lie in Maxwell Motor Company, Inc. (first formed in 1913). The first Maxwell car was made in 1904 by Jonathan Maxwell and Benjamin Briscoe, who in 1909 joined the short-lived United States Motor Company. With the collapse of this combine in 1913, Maxwell continued on alone until the postwar recession[1], when Walter P. Chrysler was brought in to revitalize the company in 1920.

In early 1924, Chrysler produced the first car to bear his name, the Chrysler Six (Fig. 2-29). It was featured as medium-priced with a high compression ratio[2] and high speed engine and four wheel hydraulic brakes[3], i. e. more standard features than many higher priced cars. At the 1924 automobile show, Chrysler Six drew huge crowds and was widely acclaimed in the trade publications[4]. Bankers were deeply impressed with the car and the public reactions to it, which allow Chrysler a negotiation on a loan of five million dollars during the show successfully. Within 12 months 32 000 Chrysler Sixes were sold.

Fig. 2-29 Chrysler Six, The Company's First Production Model

On June 6, 1925 the old Maxwell Motor Company was changed its name into the Chrysler Motor Corporation, with Chrysler as president. The corporation was greatly enlarged by the purchase of Dodge Motor Company in 1928 and the establishment of two new plants Plymouth and Desoto in 1929. The Chrysler Corporation became a major presence in the American automotive industry.

From the beginning of the twentieth century to early 1930s, almost all the mass production cars were built with square body corners, separate fenders and running boards[5] which could be called the "square box" type. Air resistance of this type of body was too large to meet the requirement for high speed. In 1934 Chrysler caught the industry and the public with "Airflow" cars (Fig 2-30). The Airflows created a new concept of weight distribution and featured round body corners, smooth curved surfaces and built-in headlamps. Soon the new style was called "streamlined style[6]" and it had great influence on the car design several years later.

Fig. 2-30 The 1934 Chrysler Airflow

本节注释：[1]战后的经济衰退；[2]压缩比；[3]4 轮液压制动器；[4]商业报刊；[5]与车身两侧分开的翼子板和踏脚板；[6]流线型。

2.3.6 *CITROEN -PIONEER OF FLOW PRODUCTION IN EUROPE*

In 1906 Andre Citroen was appointed managing director of Automobiles Mors, a company that made its name by beating a number of speed records at the turn of the century. Andre Citroen reorganized the workshops and involved in the design of the new models. In ten years, he doubled Mors's annual production. Later, he went to the US to learn advanced production technique.

Before World War I, Citroen owned a company to produce gears. He was special at making herring-bone gears[1]. Citroen established his own trademark which was somewhat like two herring-bone gear teeth. During the World War I the company turned to make ammunitions[2].

In 1919 Citroen reconverted his company to produce motor cars. He played the pioneer role, first in introducing American mass production methods in Europe. But his company was not as powerful as Peugeot and Renault in France and had many financial difficulties. He had to rely on advertisements. During the period of the Paris International Exhibition he spent a lot of money to hang an extra large poster of 100 m high on the

Eiffel Tower[3]. 250 thousand bulbs were used to shine on the poster. It was approved as a Guiness World Record[4] later.

Citroen was creative in new structures. In 1934, he launched the car 7CV (Fig. 2-31) which was a front wheel driven car with monocoque body[5], torsion bar suspension[6] and a gearbox attached to the front of the engine. The tooling and development costs of the car brought bankruptcy to his company which was sold to the Michelin Tire Company. Andre Citroen was forced to resign and the company continued to bear his name. But after the teething troubles[7] were solved, the 7CV became tremendously successful and remained production for 22 years until it was replaced by the DS-19 (Fig. 2-46) in 1956. Citroen could not live to see the achievement. He died in 1935.

Fig. 2-31 Citroen 7CV

本节注释：[1]人字齿轮；[2]弹药；[3]埃菲尔铁塔；[4]吉尼斯世界记录；[5]承载式车身；[6]扭杆悬架；[7]开始时期的困难。

2.3.7 *MYTH OF THE BEETLE CAR*

The Beetle Car designed by Dr. Ferdinand Porsche (Fig. 2-32) in Germany in 1930s became a living myth not only in Europe but all over the world. Having a very unique shape and design, the Beetle has indeed traveled a long journey from West to East. No other car has had such a moving life so far. No other car has such a long and successful history. No other car represents both the German and the world culture at the same time better. And as Arthur Railton has said, "No other automobile has had such a social effect".

Fig. 2-32 Dr. Ferdinand Porsche (1875-1951)

At that time, Hitler was exasperated by German Industry's failure to produce a cheap "people's car" (Volkswagen in German). What Hitler wanted was an affordable car selling for 900 marks with an annual volume of 350 thousand units. He commissioned Porsche to design one with state backing[1]. The German auto makers did not want to accept the idea because the cheapest DKW cost 1 680 marks and the small Opel cost 1 450 marks. In 1936, three prototypes[2] (Fig. 2-33) had passed 30 000 mile (48 800 km) endurance test. The beetle car had a rear flat engine[3] of four cylinders, a monocoque body and four wheel independent suspensions[4]. In May 1938 the construction of a new Volkswagen factory started in Wolfsburg, a city 170 km west from Berlin.

By early 1939 the Wolfsburg factory was the largest motor factory in Europe, capable of producing 150 000 cars per year, with plans to increase the production rate potential to 1.5 million cars by 1942. Then World War II broke out and the factory was handed over to the German Air Force. During the war the factory turned to make airplanes and military vehicles. One famous type of military vehicles was the VW 82 (Fig. 2-34) with almost the same structure and components as the beetle car. By the end of the war both the Volkswagen factory and the city of Wolfsburg were in ruins. After the war Allied Countries[5] attempted to revive the West German auto industry centered on the Volkswagen. The

Fig. 2-33 Volkswagen 30 Prototype

Fig. 2-34 VW 82

British Army ordered 10 000 Volkswagens for use and this kept the factory busy. In little more than a decade the company was producing half of West Germany's motor vehicles.

In 1946 a total of 7 677 Volkswagens had been built and in 1947 this figure rose to 8 987. In 1973 the total production of Beetles passed 16.5 Million and broke Henry Ford's Model T record as the most popular car in the world.

Because the Volkswagen Beetle had hardly changed from its original design, in 1974, with increasing competition from other compact foreign cars, Volkswagen was forced to reevaluate their concentration on a one-model policy. This spurred the company to develop newer, sportier car models, among them the Rabbit and its successor, the Golf. Production of the Beetle in Wolfsburg stopped in 1974, Beetle manufacturing continued in Emden until noon on January 19, 1978. And in the late 1979 production of the convertible[6] was also stopped. Most think that this marked the end of the beetle.

The Beetle is arguably the best car ever made, and looking at the sales perspective, it is the most popular car in the world's history.

本节注释：[1]国家支持；[2]样车；[3]卧式发动机；[4]独立悬架；[5]同盟国；[6]敞篷车。

2.3.8 *MATURE AGE OF AUTOMOTIVE TECHNICAL PROGRESS*

The late 1930s was the mature age of automotive technical progress. At that time, the motor vehicle had become an important transportation tool in the society. Not only cars, but also buses and trucks were playing main roles in land transportation. With the increase of vehicle speed, road construction was greatly improved. Social requirements for motor vehicles led to rapid development of automotive structure as well as manufacturing methods.

However, in the early days, the motor car was far from perfect. At that time, to drive a car was not a matter of happiness and comfort, but a kind of physical labor. To start the car, the driver had to crank the engine. Owing to a lot of troubles, the car might break down on the midway and had to be cranked again and again, which required effort and thus kept women from driving. Poor steering system led to directional deviation and even dangerous situation. The braking system was not good and only two rear wheels were equipped with brakes. And poor adhesion of tires made the matter even worse, it was difficult to stop the car immediately at emergency. Rough road and tough operation made the driver nervous and exhausted. The early day cars were not equipped with windshields and roofs to prevent the occupants from bad weather. Drivers had to wear leather caps and goggles[1]. Under complicated traffic conditions the driver had to ring the bell to warn the pedestrians. Night driving was also difficult because the kerosene lantern was very dim.

It is not easy to count how many innovations to make the car become mature.

The six-cylinder engine had largely replaced the four by 1916, and the "straight eight[2]" was adopted by most manufacturers by 1930. An important exception was Ford's famous V-8 of 1932, remarkable in its single casting and excellent performance.

Good quality gasoline of high anti-knock property[3] resulted in a high compression ratio to increase engine efficiency.

Battery ignition system not only improved the engine performance, but also made the use of electric equipments such as head lamps[4], indicators[5], horn and gauges possible, and especially the use of self-starter.

In addition to transmissions with synchronized gears, final drive with hypoid gears[6] in 1928 and four-wheel brakes, almost exclusively hydraulic by 1936, independent suspensions in 1938 this made driving and riding more comfortably.

All steel body supported by new technologies of stamping and welding replaced the heavy wooden structure. Laminated safe glasses[7], windshield wipers[8], rear view mirrors[9], heaters and radios became popular accessories.

An outstanding step to show the technical progress was the automatic transmissions[10] launched by GM in its Cadillac, Buick and Oldsmobile cars in 1938. Not only design skill, but also manufacturing potential had reached a considerably high level.

The motor car was no more a troublesome machine or a clumsy carriage. It became the symbol of wealth and status. It was fast, convenient, safe and comfortable. It was a favor to catch everybody's eye with elegant streamlined style[11], colorful painting surfaces and glittering decorations.

本节注释：[1]皮帽和风镜；[2]直列8气缸；[3]抗爆性能；[4]前照灯；[5]指示灯；[6]双曲线齿轮的主减速器；[7]夹层安全玻璃；[8]风窗刮水器；[9]后视镜；[10]自动变速器；[11]优雅的流线型。

2.3.9 *AUTOMOTIVE INDUSTRY IN WORLD WAR II*

During the World War II, motor vehicles were used extensively for land transportation tasks and greatly increased the mobility of the military troops and their rear-service[1] capability. In addition, automotive plants could readily be converted into facilities for manufacturing military equipment, including tanks and aircrafts.

Early in 1934, in order to build a highly motorized army for blitzkrieg[2], the Nazis worked out a program to produce military vehicles and took over a great number of civilian vehicles for military use.

In September 1939, when Hitler made a swift attack on Poland, Britain and France declared war on Germany. In April 1940, the German army occupied Denmark and Norway and on May 10 turned back to sweep across Netherlands and Belgium. Not more than 10 days, 400 thousand soldiers of the British-French allied army were squeezed to a small area in Dunkirk[3]. This time, Hitler put 143 infantry divisions[4] into action with 10 armored divisions in advance[5]. All the troops were transported by motor vehicles, mobile and agile. Dominated by the swift concentration of troops, arms and ammunitions in one place, Hitler was capable of giving his enemy a death blow.

Differing from the Germen, the Frenchmen did not pay attention to motor vehicles. They spent six billion francs building the 390 km long Maginot Line[6] extending along the north boundary of France and divided most of their forces on the Line for defense. As the German enemies broke through the Line and deployed at the rear of the French troops, the Line was no more functional. French soldiers could not find enough motor vehicles to retreat and a large number of them were captured. On June 25, the French government surrendered to the German invader.

Englishmen were successful to prevent the German troops from crossing the Dover Strait. The British government built "shadow factories" adjacent to their automotive plants, equipped them for military production (principally aircraft) when war came, with managerial and technical personnel drawn from the automotive industry.

In the United States the preparation for industrial mobilization was negligible until 1940; in fact, there was no serious effort even to restrict civilian automobile production until after the attack on Pearl Harbor in December 1941. Still, the American automotive industry represented such a concentration of productive capacity and skill that, once its resources had been harnessed to war production, its contribution was tremendous. Between 1940 and 1945 automotive firms made almost \$ 29 billion worth of military materials, one fifth of the country's entire output. The list included 2.6 million military trucks and 660 thousand jeeps, but production extended well beyond motor vehicles. Automotive firms provided 455 thousand aircraft engines, 22 thousand complete airplanes, one-half of the machine guns and carbines, 60 percent of the tanks, all the armored cars and 85 percent of the military helmets and aerial bombs.

Fig. 2-35 shows some military truck models produced by the American automotive industry in the War. At that time, the most famous military vehicle was Jeep (Fig. 2-36). It had a four cylinder and 2.2 liter engine, four wheel drive and tires with off-road pattern. It had a 2032 mm wheelbase, was 3359 mm long and 1575 mm wide. Its convertible and low body was convenient for soldiers to jump over. The Jeep could pull through deep mud, snow, sand and loose coral, carrying three times of its rated payload. It could be fitted with machine gun or communication apparatus, transported by train, ship or aircraft, and even used to pull B-17 bomber. For its wide use, it was designated as "General Purpose" vehicle or GP (Jeep). After the War many Jeeps were abandoned or sold to the local people. In the United States the surplus Jeeps were converted to snowplows and utility vehicles. Since they could be acquired by colleges, local governments and local schools at essentially no cost, so Jeeps were often seen on college campuses and in

Fig. 2-35　Some American Military Truck Models in Wartime
a) Dodge T-234 4 ×2 truck; b) GMC 6 ×6 truck; c) Chevrolet C-60 4 ×4 light truck; d) Dodge T- 214 4 ×4 light truck

Fig. 2-36　The World War II Jeep

government fleets. An investigation from the United States Department of Agriculture (USDA) reported that the Jeep was suitable for light plowing[7]. The military continued to use evolutionary models of Jeeps well into the 1980s. They are now being replaced by Hummer[8], a much more sophisticated and expensive off-road vehicle.

本节注释：[1]后勤；[2]闪电战；[3]敦刻尔克；[4]步兵师；[5]先锋、先头部队；[6]马奇诺防线；[7]犁地；[8]悍马。

2.3.10 *AUTOMOTIVE INDUSTRY AFTER WORLD WAR II*

When the war was over, many countries faced difficulties such as damage of enterprise, shortage of investment, loss of engineers and lack of raw materials. Their production volumes of motor vehicles were much less than the pre-war levels. The cars to go on sale were based on pre-war designs and completely new models were not seen for two or three years. The only exception was the United States. Without destruction from gunfire, the American automotive enterprises soon returned to normal and dominated over the world market. For example, in 1950 the US production volume of motor vehicles was 8 millions, more than four times compared with the sum of the volumes of 1.96 millions in five European countries and Japan (Table 2-4).

Post-war Annual Productions of Motor Vehicles in Some Countries (in unit) Table 2-4

Year	US	UK	Soviet Union	France	West Germany	Italy	Japan
1950	8 005 859	783 677	362 895	357 552	306 064	127 847	31 597
1946	3 100 820	359 634	102 171	96 092	30 671	28 983	14 921

Based on different social economic backgrounds, European car design and American car design went different ways. Living a frugal life, the European people wanted small and economical cars whereas the American people were in easy life and wanted big and comfortable cars.

In 1950s, small cars dominated the European market. Some famous models were: the French Citroen 2CV, the German BMW 600, The Italian Fiat 500, the British Austin Mini and the Soviet Moskvich[1] 407. For example, the curb weight of the BMW 600 (Fig. 2-37) was 561 kg, only one third of the curb weight of an American big car, its engine volume of 0.585 liter was only one eighth of an American big car and its fuel economy of 54 MPG (4.4 L/100km) was four times better than an American big car.

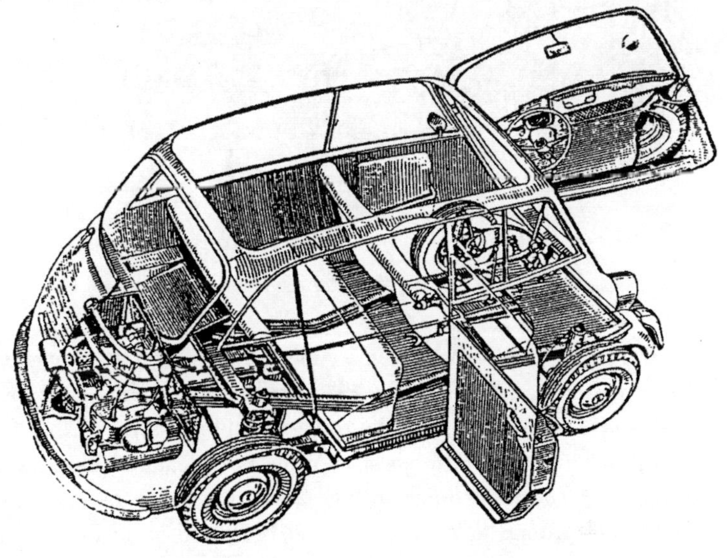

Fig. 2-37 The 1958 BMW 600

Another example was the Austin Mini (Fig. 2-38) created by Alec Issigonis. It pioneered in a lateral four cylinder engine and front wheel drive. A tight package at the front end made its passenger compartment comfortable for four people though its overall length of 3050 mm was quite short. Its suspension developed by Alex Moulton was very special which had rubber cone springs, later surprised by hydrolastic system[2] of interconnecting pipes containing a mixture of alcohol and water. More than five million Mini cars had been sold by the year of 2000.

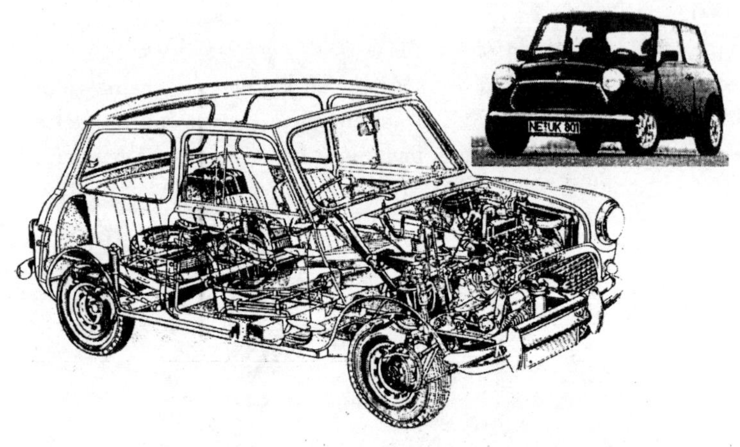

Fig. 2-38　The 1959 Austin Mini

Several attempts were made by the American designers to change the style of the post-war car models. The 1946 Ford shown in Fig. 2-39 was a typical post-war car model, almost the same streamlined style as the 1934 Chrysler Airflow (Fig. 2-30). Both sides of its body featured "four bulges over the wheels". The 1948 Buick in Fig. 2-40 tried to let the curved surface of the front fender extepd to the rear and the 1948 Hudson in Fig. 41 had elegant and flat body sides to wipe out the bulges.

Fig. 2-39　The 1946 Ford, Typical Style of Post-war Models

Fig. 2-40 The 1948 Buick

Fig. 2-41 The 1948 Hudson

In 1949, a famous industrial designer[3], Raymond Loewy successfully attracted the public with his Studebaker Commander Coupe[4] (Fig. 2-42). The passenger compartment of the car was moved forward to form a big trunk at the rear. It was the first car of the so-called "three box form" [5], apparently divided into three segments — the front end (the engine compartment), the passenger compartment and the trunk. This style was also called "pontoon" form[6] which was soon followed by most of the stylists.

At that time, petroleum was cheap enough, not more than $ 2 per barrel (1 barrel = 158 L). That was why Americans liked roomy and imposing cars. In 1950s, most of the American big cars had V8 engines with a volume about five liters and they were more than five meters long (Fig. 2-43). Harley Jefferson Earl, the chief stylist of GM offered a strong impact to the American car style in late 1950s. Three Firebird "dream cars"

Fig. 2-42 The 1949 Studebaker Commander Coupe, Pioneer of "Three Box Form"

developed by Earl impressed the public with long thin bodies, tail fins[7], gas turbine engines, independent suspensions and four wheel disc brakes[8]. Soon, hydraulic automatic transmissions, dual headlamps, wrap-round windshields, tail fins and more chrome trims became popular in the late 1950s for the big American cars (Fig. 2-44).

Fig. 2-43 The 1956 Chevrolet Bel Air, A Typical American Car in 1950s

Fig. 2-44 The 1959 Cadillac Fleetwood

Three Middle East Wars in 1948, 1967 and 1973 between Arabic countries and Israel made petroleum price rise up quickly, from $ 2.48 per barrel in 1971 to $ 11.65 per barrel in 1974 (4.7 times). Petroleum crisis hurt the world automotive industries tremendously. American cars of large fuel consumption soon became bad-selling goods and American automotive enterprises were at great losses. In 1975 the production of motor vehicles in the US was cut down 29 percent compared with the production in 1973 (Table 2-5). The automotive enterprises in other countries were also at losses, but not as heavy as the American enterprises. Some of them went bankrupt and some were reorganized.

Annual Productions of Motor Vehicles in Some Countries (in unit) Table 2-5

Year	US	Japan	West Germany	France	UK	Italy
1973	12 674 613	7 082 757	3 949 065	3 569 179	2 163 941	1 957 994
1975	8 991 091	6 941 591	3 186 208	2 861 305	1 648 399	1 458 629
Cut down	29.1%	2%	19.3%	19.8%	23.8%	25.5%

Increasing competition from small European cars in the US market reduced the share of the big cars. The style of European cars was not as luxury and over-decorated as the American cars, but emphasized on elegant appearance and delicate curves. The examples were the Italian Fiat 1800 (Fig. 2-45) and the French Citroen DS-19 (Fig. 2-46) which expressed the plain and modest ideas of their designers. Italy, a country rich in artistry since the Renaissance[9], had many auto designers of high attainments[10] such as Pininfarina, Nuccio Bertone, and Vittorio Jano. They had design many outstanding cars and became famous in 1950s. Production volume of Italian cars was not as large as some other countries, but Italian designers were able to demonstrate their eye-catching new models in the world motor shows. This time, the American firms had to reconsider their design ideas. Their engines were changed from the majority of V8 to the majority of V6 and the volumes were cut down from 5 liters to 3 liters. In late 1970s dimensions and weights of most American cars were reduced (Fig. 2-47) , and front wheel drive initiated by European cars some years earlier became popular (Fig. 2-48).

Fig. 2-45 Elegant Style of The 1958 Fiat 1800

Fig. 2-46 The 1956 Citroen DS-19 was special in style and structure.

Fig. 2-47 The 1978 Chevrolet Chevette, the GM's Smallest Car

Fig. 2-48 The 1978 Cadillac Eldorado, A Big Front Wheel Driven Car

After the World War II, the American automotive firms took measures of "annual model change" [11] and "dynamic obsolescence" [12] to promote the sale of their products. Dynamic obsolescence means that a car during its whole operation life from birth to discard is not held by one owner but can be passed several times to different owners. Automotive firms build up such social pressure to the customers that they should buy new cars every two or three years to show their wealth and status. The fact that many customers sold their old cars to the second-hand car agents[13] and frequently returned to new car market increased the sales volume of the new cars greatly. If the automotive firms did not change their car models annually, 20 million new car buyers would not return to the car market every 3 years but every 6 years and the sales volume of new cars would reduce one half. Evidently, the measures of "annual model change" and "dynamic obsolescence" had great effect on the social economy. For example, in 1960, GM invested $ 600 million to renew its manufacturing equipments and had a total sales volume of $ 9 billion. Comparison of the expenditure with the income indicated that it was a worth while investment. However, the situations of the small automotive companies were totally different from that of GM, because the tooling investment of small scale production could not be taken back within one or two years. If the small companies did not want to change their models, there would be a risk of bad selling, but if they spend a lot of money to renew the manufacturing equipments annually, it was unable to make their ends meet. The competition of annual model change resulted in a domino effect[14] of small companies such as Nash, Studebaker, Hudson,

Packard and Kaiser to collapse. By the end of 1980s the automotive industry in the United States was concentrated in the Big Three, GM, Ford and Chrysler.

The same story also happened in other countries. The French automotive industry was concentrated in two big companies, Peugeot and Renault and the Italian in only one, Fiat. The German Volkswagen shared half the production. Then, the Japanese Big Three, Toyota, Nissan and Honda as well as the Korean Big Three, Hyundai, Daewoo and Kia were well-known.

本节注释：[1]莫斯科人；[2]液压平衡系统；[3]工业设计师；[4]双门轿车；[5]三箱式；[6]浮桥式；[7]尾翅；[8]盘式制动器；[9]文艺复兴；[10]造诣很高；[11]年度车型更新；[12]动态报废；[13]二手车经销商；[14]多米诺骨牌效应。

2.3.11 *DEVELOPMENT OF JAPANESE AUTOMOTIVE INDUSTRY*

The most spectacular increases in automotive production after World War II occurred in Japan. From a negligible position in 1950, Japan in 30 years moved past the western countries one by one to becoming the world's leading automotive producer.

After the World War II, Japanese people had a very hard time. GDP[1] in 1946 was only $ 1.4 billion, i.e. not more than $ 15 per capita[2]. In 1950, the production of motor vehicles was 30 thousand units, far less than the production of 50 thousand units in the pre-war 1941.

In 1950 the Korean War broke out. The US Army took Japan as a rear service base and many order sheets[3] were given to the Japanese enterprises. Thus the Japanese economy stood firm and began to recover. Through ten year (1946-1955) regulation and twenty year (1956-1975) development, Japan made a big leap to become a country of powerful economy. Such an economic miracle was created by the introduction of the advanced technique and the effective management.

In the early stage, the strategy of the Japanese automotive industry was to avoid competing with the American and the European powerful enterprises. That is, the Japanese manufacturers did not make the same kinds of motor vehicles dominated by the foreign firms but popular products of two-wheelers, three-wheelers and small four-wheelers (Fig. 2-49) to meet the domestic requirements. By this way, they accumulated funds and experiences for further development. Then, they began to import advanced technologies and stepped into a flourishing period. Japan produced 480 thousand motor vehicles in 1960. It overtook Italy in 1961, France in 1964, Great Britain in 1966, West Germany in 1967 and US in 1980 (Table 2-6). From 1980 to 1993 Japanese annual production volume of motor vehicles ranked the first position in the world.

Fig. 2-49 The 1958 Subaru 360

Japanese Productions of Motor Vehicles Compared with Some Countries (in unit) Table 2-6

Year	Japan	US	West Germany	France	UK	Italy
1961	813 879	6 650 282	2 147 825	1 244 223	1 464 134	759 140
1964	1 702 475	9 304 403	2 909 657	1 615 896	2 332 376	1 090 078
1966	2 286 399	10 363 418	3 050 708	2 024 552	2 042 354	1 365 898
1967	3 146 468	8 996 490	2 484 319	2 009 672	1 937 199	1 542 669
1980	11 042 884	8 010 374	3 878 553	3 378 443	1 312 904	1 611 856

Japanese were good at learning the advanced experiences. During the period of petroleum crisis in 1970s their cars characterized by low price and low fuel consumption were highly competitive. Japanese were also good at enterprise management, manufacturing arrangement and laborer motivation. The Toyota Motor Company was considered an epitome[4] of the Japanese automotive industry.

本节注释：[1]国内生产总值；[2]人均；[3]订单；[4]缩影。

2.3.12 *TOYOTA*

The origin of Toyota Motor Company was the Automotive Department of Toyota Automatic Textile Machine Works founded by Sakichi Toyota[1], the son of a carpenter. He was an industrious man and invented an automatic textile machine. In 1906, he collected one million yens[2] to found the company and put the machine into production. In 1934, the Automotive Department in Toyota's company was established and headed by his son Kiichirou[3]. In 1935 the department began to produce its earliest car, the Model A-1 (Fig. 2-50). In 1937 the department was reorganized to becoming Toyota Motor Company.

Fig. 2-50 The 1935 Toyota A-1

After the World War II, Toyota Motor Company was in financial crisis. In 1950 the company received some order sheets from the US Army and began to recover. In 1952 Eiji Toyota[4] (Fig. 2-51) replaced his cousin Kiichirou to be the chairman of the board[5] and was the man leading the company to great achievements. Nowadays, Toyota has become a group of enterprises including the industries of motor vehicle, steel, machine tool, electric and electronic equipments, textile machine, chemistry and architecture.

The success of Toyota Motor Company was based on effective production management, the so-called "Toyota Pattern" [6] which was highly evaluated as a good example of lean production[7]. The basic idea of Toyota Pattern is "to stop an end to all wastes and to look for rational production methods". The concept of waste is critical. Not only waste of products and loss of work time, but also over-production, overstock, backward operation, bad cooperation and unreasonable design are all regarded as waste. Toyota's idea of flow production is distinctive and is called "reverse flow line" [8]. That is, design of the line begins with the last operation process reversely or the former operation process should meet the requirement of the latter process. Two main supports of Toyota Pattern are "just in time (JIT)" [9] and "automation" [10]. JIT means that the supply just meets the required quantity and timing. More or less and earlier or later would be regarded as waste. Automation concerns not only machines, but also enthusiasm of laborers. Differing from the western TQC (Total Quality Control [11]), Toyota Pattern not only attaches importance to production organization, but also pays attention to the motivation of the laborers. Not only the headquarters, but also everybody should be responsible for the quality control.

Fig. 2-51 Eiji Toyota

Several decades have passed from the start of Toyota Pattern in 1950. Outstanding achievements have proven the active function of this kind of management.

本节注释: [1]丰田佐吉; [2]日元; [3]喜一郎;[3] [4]丰田英二; [5]董事长; [6]丰田方式; [7]精益生产; [8]倒流水线; [9]准时制; [10]自働化; [11]全面质量管理。

本章参考文献

2.1 陈礼璠,顾剑青. 现代轿车知识手册. 上海:上海科学技术文献出版社,2002

2.2 林平. 汽车史话(汽车发展史). 北京:电子工业出版社, 2005

2.3 罗伯特·莱西 著. 俞再林 等译. 汽车大王—福特. 北京:中国展望出版社,1989

2.4 小野吉郎 著. 胡天放 译. 世界汽车今昔. 北京:机械工业出版社,1985

2.5 白泽照雄 著. 季云飞 译. 日本汽车工业. 上海:上海译文出版社,1983

2.6 Kevin Cunningham. The History of the Automobile. Child's World, 2004

2.7 Alfred D. Chandler Jr. Giant Enterprise: Ford, General Motors, and the Automobile Industry. New York, 1964.

2.8 Flower, Raymond and Michael Wynn Jones. One Hundred Years on the Road: A Social History of the Automobile. New York: McGraw-Hill, 1981.

2.9 Sears, Stephen W. The American Heritage History of the Automobile in America. New York: American Heritage Publishing Co. , 1977.

2.10 Martin Derrick. Detroit Cars: 50 Years of the Motor City. PRC Publishing, 2001

2.11 Beverly R. Kimes. Pioneers, Engineers, And Scoundrels: The Dawn Of The Automobile In America. SAE International, 2004

2.12 Dennis Adler. Mercedes-Benz: 110 Years of Excellence. MotorBooks/MBI Publishing Company, 1995

2.13 Hector Mackenzie-Wintle. Renault. Sutton Pub. , 1998

2.14 Roy A. Church. The Rise and Decline of the British Motor Industry. Cambridge University Press, 1995

CHAPTER THREE
STRUCTURE OF MOTOR VEHICLE

3.1 VEHICLE STRUCTURE

A motor vehicle is usually consists of three main assemblies, i. e. engine, chassis and body. The typical vehicle structure is shown in Fig. 3-1.

The function of an engine is to transfer chemical energy from fuel burning to mechanical power. In modern motor vehicles, internal combustion engine of reciprocal piston type is widely used. It consists of cylinder block, piston-crank mechanism, valve timing mechanism, fuel supply system, cooling system, lubrication system, ignition system (for gasoline engine) and starting system[1].

The chassis is an assembly to accept the engine power, to make the motor vehicle run and to follow the driver's orders. It consists of the following systems.

The drive train or transmission system conveys the engine power to the road wheels. As shown in Fig. 3-1, it consists of clutch 6, transmission 7, propeller Shaft 8, final drive,differential 9 and axle shaft 10[2].

In order to mount all the systems of the motor vehicle at the proper positions, support the whole motor vehicle, make it adhere to the road surface, and prevent it from the road shock and vibration, a load-carrying system[3] is needed. In some books the system is named "running gear"[4]. It consists of the integrated body 17 and the sub-frame 5[5] to fix all the systems of the motor vehicle including front suspension 2[6], front wheel 3, rear suspension 10 and rear wheel 13.

The steering system makes the motor vehicle operate in the direction given by the driver. It consists of steering gear (connected with steering

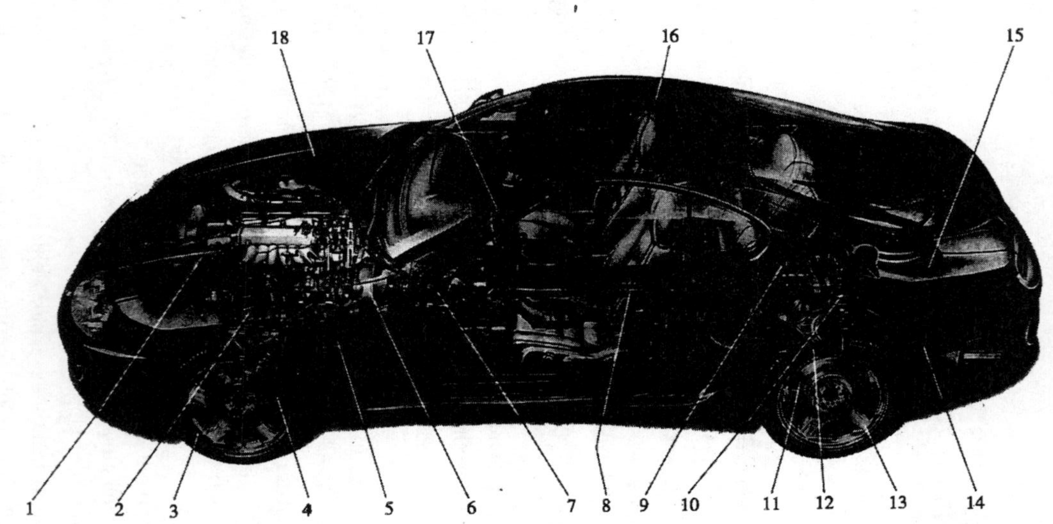

Fig. 3-1 Overall Structure of a Typical Car

1-engine; 2-front suspension; 3-front wheel; 4-front brake; 5-sub-frame; 6-clutch; 7-transmission; 8-propeller shaft; 9-final drive and differential; 10-rear suspension; 11-rear brake; 12-axle shaft; 13-rear wheel; 14-silencer; 15- fuel tank; 16- body; 17- steering wheel; 18- front end panels

wheel 16) and steering linkage[7]. Some of the motor vehicles have power steering system[8].

The braking system slows and stops the motor vehicle and ensures reliable parking[9] when the driver has left. It consists of the front brake 3, the rear brake 11, the control device and the energy supply device.

The body provides a place for the driver's operation and for the passengers and goods. It includes front end panels 15 and body shell 17, and it may also include cab and cargo carrying platform for the truck or other equipment for special job[10].

The overall structure or package [11] of motor vehicles may differ from each other to meet different requirements. According to the locations of the engine and the other systems, the overall structure of modern motor vehicles may be classified into 5 types (Fig. 3-2).

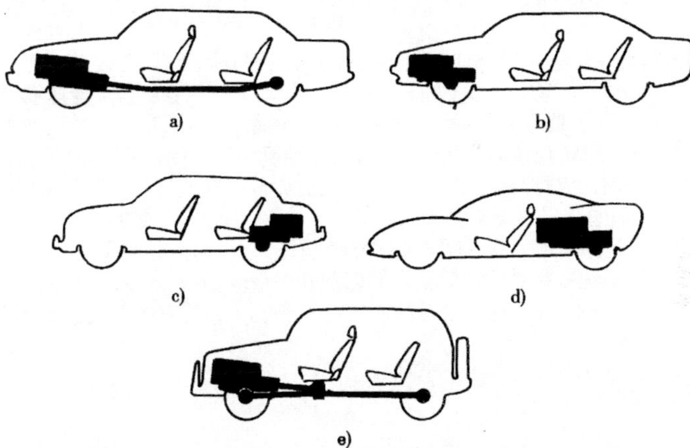

Fig. 3-2 Structural Types of Modern Motor vehicles
a) FR; b) FF; c) RR; d) MR; e) AWD

Front engine rear wheel drive (FR) is a traditional type. Most of the trucks, some cars and buses belong to this type.

Front engine front wheel drive (FF) is a type which is becoming popular in modern cars because of its compact structure, light weight, low floor and perfect handling stability at high speed[12].

Rear engine rear wheel drive (RR) is a current type for modern large and medium-sized buses because of its low interior noise and large interior room.

Middle engine rear wheel drive (MR) is a current type for sport cars and formula racing cars because a powerful and large engine is suitable to arrange behind the seat back of the driver and in front of the rear axle to achieve the best axle load distribution and high performances[13]. Some of the large and medium-sized buses also have a horizontal engine[14] under the middle of the floor.

All wheel drive (AWD) is a special type for high crossing performance vehicles[15] to equip a front engine and a transfer case[16] to split the power to all the road wheels.

本节注释：[1]它包括:机体、曲柄连杆机构、配气机构、供油系、冷却系、润滑系、点火系(汽油机用)和起动系。[2]如图3-1所示,传动系包括:离合器、变速器、传动轴、主减速器、差速器和半轴等。[3]承载系统；[4]行走系；[5]承载式车身和副车架；[6]前悬架；[7]转向器(与转向盘相连)和转向传动机构；[8]动力转向系统；[9]驻车；[10]它包括:车前板制件和车身壳体,还可包括货车的驾驶室和货箱以及用于专门作业的设备。[11]总体结构或总体布置；[12]在高速时很好的操纵稳定性；[13]中置发动机后轮驱动是跑车和方程式赛车流行的布置形式,因为强劲和尺寸大的发动机适于布置在驾驶员座椅靠背之后和后轴之前以便获得最佳轴荷分配和较高的使用性能。[14]卧式发动机；[15]全轮驱动是高通过性车辆的一种特有的形式；[16]分动器。

3.2 ENGINE

Engine is the source of power. In modern motor vehicles internal combustion engine is widely used. An internal combustion engine of piston type consists of the following systems: cylinder block, crank-connecting rod mechanism, valve timing mechanism, fuel supply system, cooling system, lubrication system, ignition system and starting system. A section view[1] of a typical gasoline engine of direct injection type[2] is shown in figure 3-3. In order to have a better understanding, it is advisable for the reader to analyze every component in this figure carefully.

The basic principle of the engine to develop power can be explained as

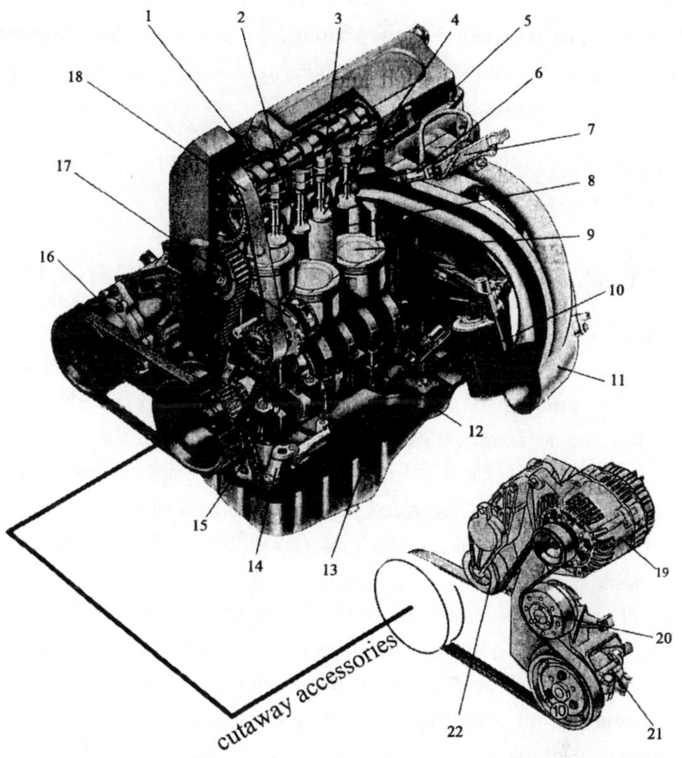

Fig. 3-3 Section View of A Typical Modern Car Engine

1-camshaft; 2-exhaust valve; 3-hydraulic tappet [3]; *4-intake valve; 5-cylinder head; 6-injector* [4]; *7-fuel rail* [5]; *8-cylinder block; 9-piston; 10-fuel filter; 11-intake manifold; 12-connecting rod; 13-oil sump; 14-oil pump; 15-crankshaft; 16-air conditioning compressor; 17-water pump; 18-timing belt; 19-alternator* [6]; *20-guide pulley* [7]; *21-power steering pump; 22-tensioner* [8]

follows, the gasoline and the air are mixed together to form a gas called combustion mixture[9] lighted by a spark in the cylinder to create high pressure to push the piston downward. Through the connecting rod, the piston pushes the crankshaft to rotate. The flywheel at the rear end of the crankshaft conveys the power to the clutch, the gearbox, the propeller shaft, the final drive, the differential one by one, and divides it to the left and right axle shafts and then to the left and right road wheels.

本节注释：[1]剖视图；[2]直喷式汽油发动机；[3]液力挺杆；[4]喷油器；[5]燃油分配管；[6]交流发电机；[7]导轮；[8]张紧轮；[9]可燃混合气。

3.2.1 *CYLINDER BLOCK AND PISTON-CRANK MECHANISM*

Cylinder block is the main support piece to fix various components of the engine. In the cylinder block there are some round holes called cylinders. The function of the cylinderis to guide the up and down movement of the piston and to form a closed chamber together with the cylinder head[1]. Cylinder block and cylinder head may be made of cast iron or cast aluminum[2]. The head is installed to the block by some studs and nuts[3] tightly. There is a piece of sealing material called gasket[4] between the head and the block.

An oil sump[5] is installed at the bottom of the cylinder block. It is a sheet metal stamping[6] and its function is to form a closed crankcase[7] and to hold the lubricating oil. There is also a piece of sealing gasket between the block and the oil sump tightened by some bolts[8].

The piston-crank mechanism is a device to change the linear motion into rotation. This mechanism includes the following parts, i. e. piston, connecting rod, crankshaft and flywheel. Explosion of the combustion mixture pushes the piston downward and drives the crankshaft rotate through the connecting rod. It is clear to see that the piston moves reciprocally, the connecting rod swings around the piston pin somewhat like a pendulum[9], and the motion of the crankshaft is pure rotation.

In Fig. 3-4, the upper moving limit of the piston is called the upper dead point[10] (UDP) and the space above UDP is called combustion chamber; the lower moving limit of the piston is called the lower dead point[11] (LDP) and the space above LDP is called overall volume of the cylinder[12]. The distance from UDP to LDP is called stroke[13] which is equal to twice the radius of the crankshaft. The volume in the cylinder between

UDP and LDP is called working volume[14] of the cylinder or swept volume (displacement[15]) of the piston. The ratio of overall volume to combustion chamber volume is called compression ratio and it means how many times the combustion mixture can be compressed when the piston moves from LDP to UDP[16].

In Fig. 3-5, piston 2 is usually made of aluminum by pressure

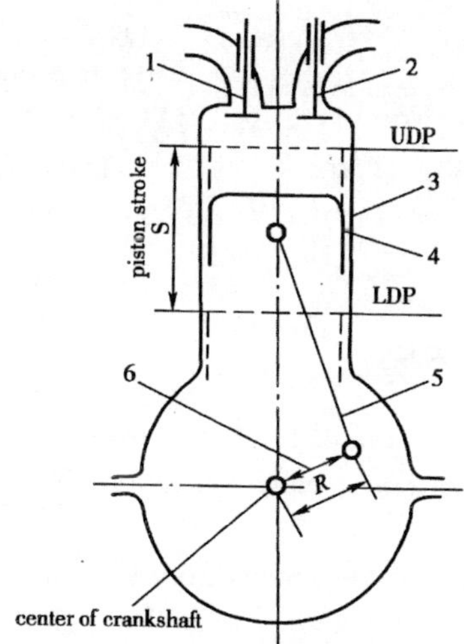

Fig. 3-4 Positions of Piston and Volumes of Cylinder
1-intake valve; 2-exhaust valve; 3-cylinder; 4-piston; 5-connecting rod; 6-crankshaft

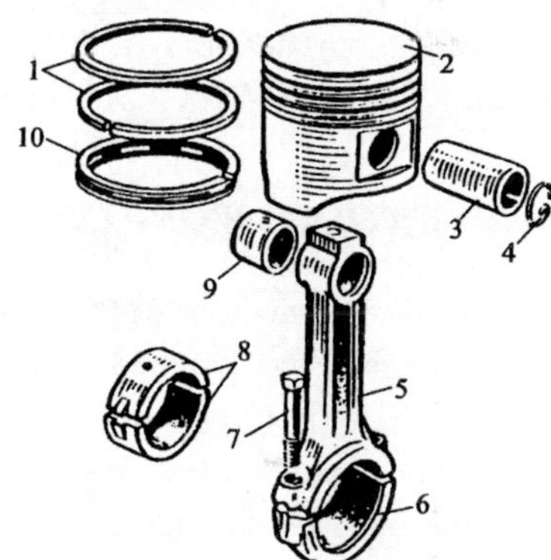

Fig. 3-5 Parts of Piston Group
1-compression rings; 2-piston; 3-piston pin; 4-stop ring; 5-connecting rod; 6-big end cap; 7-bolts; 8-bearing shells; 9-bronze sleeve; 10-oil ring

casting[17]. Clearance between the piston and the cylinder wall is sealed by two or three piston rings called compression ring[18] 1 installed in the grooves at the piston head. Below the compression rings there is an oil ring 10 to scrape the lubricating oil on the cylinder wall down to the oil sump. The piston pin 3 goes through the holes at the piston center part and through the bronze sleeve[19] 9 at the small end of the connecting rod 5 to connect the piston 2 and the rod together. There are two stop rings[20] 4 at each end of the piston pin to retain its axial position. The connecting rod 5 is made of forged steel[21], its big end is divided into two halves. The lower half 6 called big end cap[22] is fixed to the upper half by two bolts 7. Inside the big end there are two halves of bearing shells[23] 8 which are made of babbitt alloy[24].

本节注释：[1]气缸盖；[2]铸铁或铸铝；[3]螺柱和螺母；[4]衬垫；[5]油底壳；[6]冲压件；[7]曲轴箱；[8]螺栓；[9]连杆活像钟摆那样绕着活塞销摆动；[10]上止点；[11]下止点；[12]气缸总容积；[13]行程；[14]工作容积；[15]排量；[16]总容积和燃烧室容积之比称为压缩比，表示活塞从下止点到上止点时可燃混合气被压缩多少倍。[17]压铸；[18]气环；[19]青铜衬套；[20]卡环；[21]锻钢；[22]连杆（大头）盖；[23]轴瓦；[24]巴比合金。

3.2.2 *ENGINE WORKING PROCESS*

The basic principle of the working process of the four stroke[1] gasoline engine was founded by a German engineer Nikolas Otto. The four stroke cycle is described as follows.

Intake stroke[2] (Fig. 3-6a): As the piston moves from UDP to LDP, the intake valve opens and the exhaust valve closes. Through the intake valve the combustion mixture is drawn into the cylinder. As the piston reaches LDP, the intake valve closes and the intake stroke ends.

Compression stroke[3] (Fig. 3-6b): With the rotation of the crankshaft, the piston moves from LDP to UDP, both the intake and exhaust valves close and thus the trapped mixture is compressed by the piston. The volume reduction of the mixture is just equal to the compression ratio mentioned above.

Working stroke[4] (Fig. 3-6c): As the compression stroke ends and the piston reaches UDP, a spark comes from the top of the cylinder and lights the mixture to create high temperature and high pressure. The expanded gas pushes the piston downward and work is done. Besides, a part of the energy gathered in the flywheel can be the motive power of the engine during the other strokes.

Exhaust stroke[5] (Fig. 3-6d): As the piston reaches LDP, the working stroke ends and the exhaust valve opens. Then the piston moves upward and pushes the burnt gas outside the cylinder through the exhaust valve.

Four strokes of intake, compression, working and exhaust make up a complete cycle of the engine.

As the exhaust stroke ends, a cycle completes and the next cycle begins, i. e. another four strokes continue and repeat. During one cycle of the engine the piston reciprocates twice and the crankshaft makes two revolutions (720°).

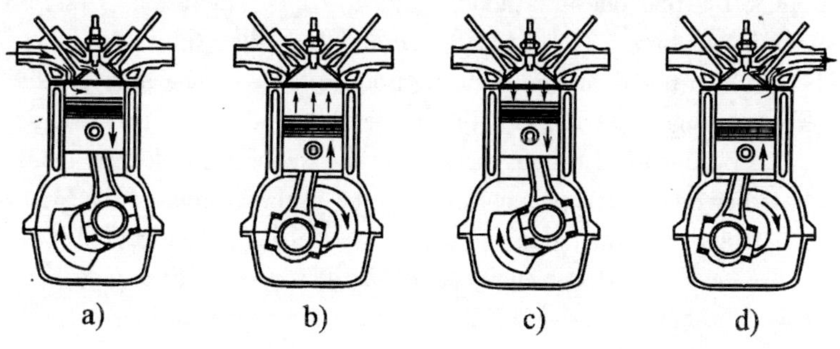

Fig. 3-6 Four Stroke Cycle

a) intake stroke; b) compression stroke; c) working stroke; d) exhaust stroke

本节注释：[1]四冲程；[2]进气行程；[3]压缩形行程；[4]做功行程；[5]排气行程。

3.2.3 *MULTI-CYLINDER ENGINE*

In the engine equipped with only one cylinder (single cylinder engine), every interval between two working strokes is 720°of the crankshaft rotation. Obviously, a single cylinder engine is far from smooth and a large flywheel is required to overcome such shortcoming. If the number of cylinders increases, the interval between two working strokes will reduce, for example every interval for a four cylinder engine is 180°of the crankshaft rotation, six cylinder engine 120°and eight cylinder engine 90°. The more the number of cylinders, the smoother the engine runs. The dimension of the flywheel becomes smaller too.

In the multi-cylinder engine the arrangement of the cylinders includes two common types, i. e. linear type and V type. For a linear type engine, the arrangement of cylinders is in one line. For a V type engine the arrangement of the cylinders is in two lines and the angle between the central planes of the left line and right line cylinders is like "V" shape. The nomination of every cylinder, for a linear engine, it is 1st, 2nd, 3rd… from the front to the rear one after another; for a V type engine, it is 1st, 3rd, 5th… (odd numbers[1]) on the left line and 2nd, 4th, 6th…(even numbers[2]) on the right line from the front to the rear one after another.

The working order of the cylinders, early or late, is called firing order[3]. In order to distribute the load to the cylinder block, the crankshaft and the other engine components evenly, the working order of the front and rear or left and right cylinders should be symmetrical. The examples of firing order are: for four cylinder engine 1-3-4-2, for six cylinder engine 1-5-3-6-2-4 and for V8 engine 1-8-4-3-6-5-7-2. The working order of four cylinder engine is given in table 3-1.

Working Order for Four Stroke Engine Table 3-1

Rotation angle of crankshaft	0° ~ 180°	180° ~ 360°	360° ~ 540°	540° ~ 720°
The first cylinder	Working	Exhaust	Intake	Compression
The second cylinder	Exhaust	Intake	Compression	Working
The third cylinder	Compression	Working	Exhaust	Intake
The fourth cylinder	Intake	Compression	Working	Exhaust

本节注释：[1]奇数；[2]偶数；[3]发火顺序。

3.2.4 *ENGINE CHARACTERISTICS*[1]

Working volume (displacement) V is equal to the sum of the volume of the cylinders and can be calculated by the formula:

$$V = \frac{\pi}{4} D^2 S i \times 10^{-6} \qquad (L)$$

Where: D——diameter of the cylinder (mm);

S——piston stroke (mm);

i——number of the cylinders.

Effective torque[2] T_e is the torque output by the engine through the flywheel.

Effective power[3] P_e is the power output by the engine through the flywheel.

The relationship of the effective power , effective torque and crankshaft revolving speed is expressed by the formula:

$$P_e = T_e \frac{2\pi n}{60} \times 10^{-3} = \frac{T_e n}{9550} \quad (\text{kW})$$

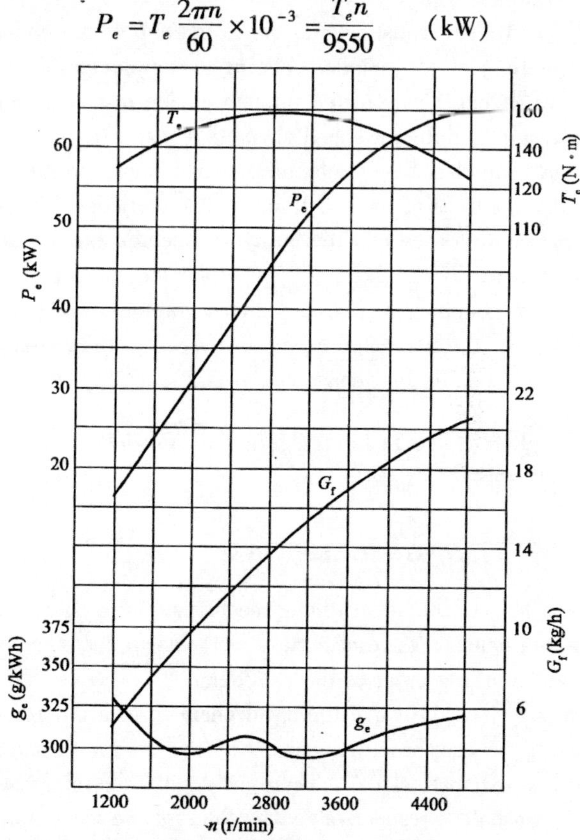

Fig. 3-7 Full Throttle Characteristics of a Typical Gasoline Engine

Where: T_e——effective torque (Nm);

n——crankshaft revolving speed (rpm).

Specific fuel consumption[4] g_e is the amount of fuel consumption (Unit is g) as the engine develops 1kW within 1h. It is calculated by:

$$g_e = \frac{G_f}{P_e} \times 10^3 \qquad (\text{g/kW} \cdot \text{h})$$

Where: G_f——fuel consumption of the engine within one hour (kg/h);

P_e——effective power (kW).

Engine speed characteristics[5] is the expression of the change of power, torque and specific fuel consumption relating to the change of crankshaft revolving speed. It can be measured through engine test. Different throttle[6] opening may result in different speed characteristics. The most important is the full throttle characteristics[7] measured at maximum throttle opening.

Lying on the curves of the full throttle characteristics, the maximum power, the maximum torque and the minimum specific fuel consumption at certain crankshaft revolving speeds are important targets to express the engine performance. For example, in Fig. 3-7 the maximum power is 65 kW at the speed of 4800 rpm, the maximum torque is 157Nm at the speed of 3000 rpm and the minimum specific fuel consumption is 292 g/kW · h.

本节注释：[1]发动机特性；[2]有效转矩；[3]有效功率；[4]燃油消耗率(或比油耗)；[5]发动机速度特性；[6]节气门；[7]外特性(节气门全开)。

3.2.5 *VALVE TIMING MECHANISM*

The main task of the valve timing mechanism is to open and close the intake valve and exhaust valve at certain moments in accordance with the firing order and working order of the cylinders.

Fig 3-8 describes the valve timing mechanism of a three cylinder engine. The engine has three cylinders, each cylinder with one intake valve[1] and one exhaust valve[2]. There are totally six valves operated by six cams on the camshaft[3] respectively. The force of the valve springs can keep the valves close. Because the cams are at different rotation angles (see table 3-3), the exact moment of each cam to open the corresponding valve (overcome the valve spring force) through the rocker arm[4] is different from each other. The camshaft 2 is driven by the crankshaft 10 through the timing belt[5] 5 and two timing gears[6] 1 and 9. The number of teeth of gear 1 is twice that of gear 9. Therefore, as the crankshaft makes two revolutions, the camshaft does one revolution only.

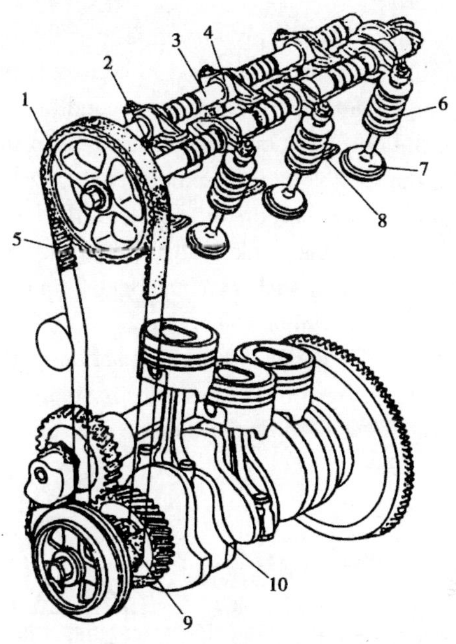

Fig. 3-8 Valve Timing Mechanism of Typical Car Engine

1-timing gear on camshaft; 2-camshaft; 3-rocker arm shaft; 4-rocker arm; 5-timing belt; 6-valve spring; 7-intake valve; 8-exhaust valve; 9-timing gear on crankshaft; 10-crankshaft

Positions of Cams for Three Cylinder Engine Table 3-2

	The first cylinder	The second cylinder	The third cylinder
Intake cam	0°	240°	120°
Exhaust cam	270°	150°	30°

本节注释：[1]进气门；[2]排气门；[3]凸轮轴；[4]摇臂；[5]正时传动带；[6]正时齿轮。

3.2.6 *FUEL SUPPLY SYSTEM FOR GASOLINE ENGINE*

The main task of the fuel supply system is to make up a combustion mixture of considerable concentration[1] and to convey it into the cylinder according to the requirements for different work conditions. Besides, the system has to drive the burnt gas out from the engine to the atmosphere.

Most cars are equipped with an electronic fuel injection (EFI) system[2] to replace the old mechanical carburetor[3] system. In the new system the injector[4] sprays the fuel to the intake valve directly to overcome the shortcomings in the old system such as: imperfect formation of the combustion mixture and non-uniform charging.

As shown in Fig. 3-9, under the drawing action of the piston during the intake stroke, the outside fresh air rushes into the intake manifold 5 through the air cleaner 7. At the same time the electric fuel pump 14 drives the

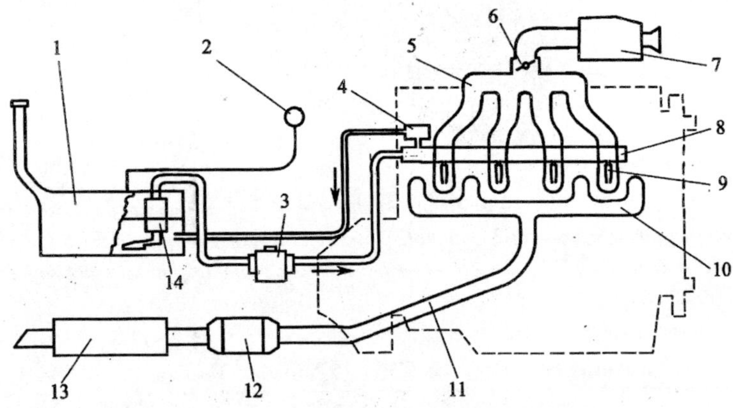

Fig. 3-9 Fuel Supply System of EFI Engine

1-gasoline tank; 2-fuel gauge; 3-fuel filter; 4-fuel pressure regulator; 5-intake manifold; 6-throttle; 7-air cleaner; 8-fuel rail; 9-injector; 10-exhaust manifold; 11-exhaust pipe; 12-catalytic converter; 13-muffler; 14-electric fuel pump

gasoline from the tank 1 through the filter[5] 3 and the fuel rail[6] 8 to the injector 9. As the intake valve opens, the injector 9 sprays the gasoline to the air flow to form an air-fuel combustion mixture. Excess fuel returns to the gasoline tank 1 through the fuel pressure regulator[7] 4. The throttle 6 actuated by the accelerator pedal controls the air flow. The burnt gas is driven out to the atmosphere through the exhaust manifold 10, the exhaust pipe 11 and the muffler (silencer)[8] 13. For low exhaust noise, the muffler 13 reduces the speed of the exhaust gas by splitting it into many minute flows to eliminate impulse and shock. Before the muffler, some of the engines have a catalytic converter[9] 12 to reduce harmful emissions.

In the EFI system signals such as engine speed, throttle opening, coolant temperature, quantity and temperature of air flow and exhaust gas temperature collected by the sensors[10] are transmitted to the electronic control unit (ECU) to make up a perfect combustion mixture suitable to all the work conditions of the engine.

Gasoline is the light component (small molecule hydrocarbon[11]) refined by distillation or cracking[12] of petroleum and its density is 0.66 ~ 0.75 g/cm^3. Anti-knock property[13] is the most important performance target of gasoline which refers to the ability to avoid detonation[14] or knock[15] in the cylinder during combustion. Detonation is the phenomenon of abnormal burning and some sounds like metallic knock can be heard from the cylinder. It would result in engine overheat, exhaust smoke, high fuel consumption and low power output. Selection of high anti-knock property gasoline is advantageous for the engine to increase compression ratio for high efficiency.

Anti-knock property of gasoline is evaluated by the research octane number (RON) [16]. The higher RON the gasoline has, the better its anti-knock property. The figure of RON indicates the percentage of isooctane in the mixture of isooctane and normal heptane[17]. For example, the anti-knock property of the 90# gasoline is equivalent to that of the mixture of 90% isooctane and 10% normal heptane. RON of isooctane is 100 (the best anti-knock property) whereas RON of normal heptane is 0 (the worst anti-knock property). In order to increase anti-knock property, an agent of tetraethyl lead[18] may be added into gasoline. Because the burnt emission of tetraethyl lead is harmful, lead gasoline is prohibited in many countries nowadays.

本节注释: [1]一定浓度的可燃混合气; [2]电控燃油喷射系统; [3]化油器; [4]喷油器; [5]滤清器; [6]燃油分配管; [7]燃油压力调节器; [8]消声器; [9]催化转化器; [10]传感器; [11]小分子烃; [12]分馏或裂化; [13]抗爆性; [14]爆燃; [15]敲缸; [16]研究辛烷值; [17]辛烷值的数字表示异辛烷和正庚烷的混合物中异辛烷百分比是多少。[18]四乙基铅。

3.2.7 *FUEL SUPPLY SYSTEM FOR DIESEL ENGINE*

Diesel (or diesel oil) is the component heavier (Hydrocarbon molecule is larger) than gasoline and kerosene during the process of distillation or cracking and its density is 0.86 g/cm^3. The brand of diesel is expressed by condensation point[1]. For example -10# diesel means its condensation point -10℃. Therefore, selection of diesel should be suitable to different ambient temperature in different seasons, especially in winter.

Because of higher viscosity and worse volatile property[2], diesel cannot be atomized to a uniform mist like that of gasoline in the carburetor. Therefore, the structure and operation principle of diesel engine is quite different from gasoline engine. Operation differences of the diesel engine from the gasoline engine may be described as follows. In the intake stroke air (not mixture) is drawn into the cylinder only; in the compression stroke air is compressed to a higher ratio to obtain higher temperature, and in the working stroke diesel is sprayed into the cylinder by high pressure to form misty particles ignited by the hot air.

Flaming property[3] is an important target of diesel and refers to the ability to catch fire easily at a considerable temperature. It is evaluated by the cetane number[4]. According to the national standard cetane number should not be less than 45.

As shown in Fig. 3-10, by the action of the supply pump[5] 6 diesel flows from the fuel tank 1 and through the filter 3 to the injection pump[6] 7. In the intake stroke, the outside air is drawn into the cylinder through air cleaner 15 and the intake manifold 16. In the working stroke, under the action of the plunger[7] in the injection pump high pressure diesel is sprayed into the combustion chamber 10 through the high pressure pipe 9 and the nozzle[8] 11. In the exhaust stroke, the burnt gas is driven to the atmosphere through the exhaust pipe 12.

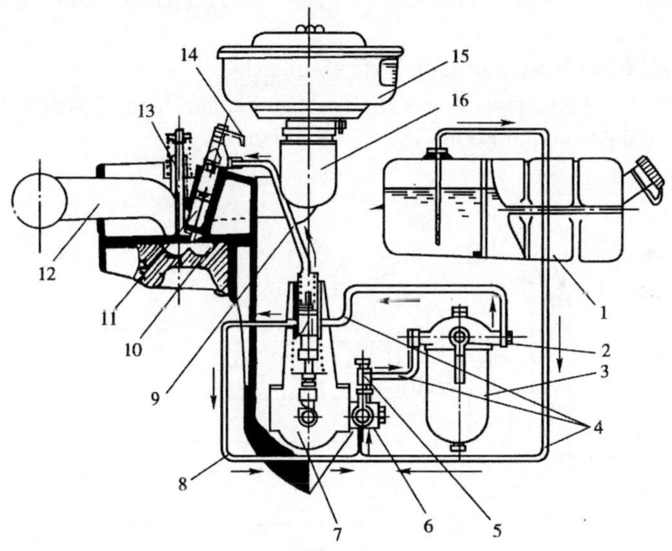

Fig. 3-10 Fuel Supply System of Diesel Engine

1-diesel tank; 2-bleed valve; 3-diesel filter; 4-low pressure pipe; 5-manual supply pump; 6-supply pump; 7-injection pump; 8-recycle pipe; 9-high pressure pipe; 10-combustion chamber; 11-nozzel; 12-exhaust pipe; 13-exhaust valve; 14-drain pipe; 15-air cleaner; 16-intake manifold

本节注释：[1]凝点；[2]较高的粘度和较差的挥发性；[3]发火性；[4]十六烷值；[5]输油泵；[6]喷油泵；[7]柱塞；[8]喷油器。

3.2.8 *COOLING SYSTEM*

During the working stroke, high temperature up to 2000℃ could happen in the cylinder. It may cause the parts in direct contact with cylinder block, cylinder head, piston and valve to expand and jam or make troubles such as abnormal burning and lubricant dilution. The main task of the cooling system is to bring the heat from the high temperature parts to outside atmosphere and to maintain normal working temperature for the engine. The cooling system consists of two structural types, i. e. water cooling system[1] and air cooling system[2].

Fig. 3-11 shows a cooling system circulated by engine power. Under the action of the water pump driven by the engine crankshaft through V-belt[3], water circulates as the arrows show in the figure.

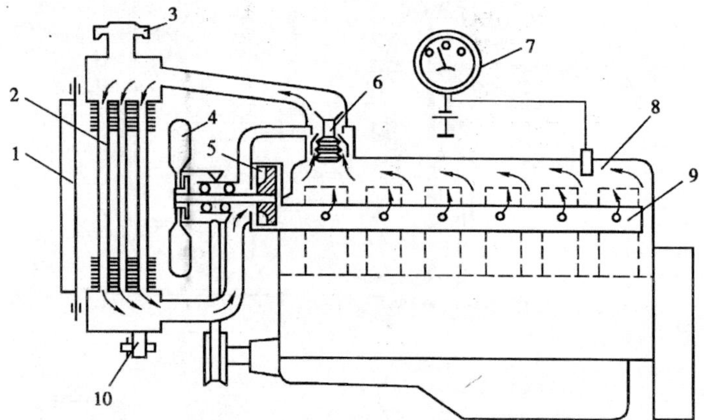

Fig. 3-11 Water Cooling System Circulated by Engine Power
1-shutters; 2-radiator; 3-radiator cap; 4-cooling fan; 5-water pump; 6-thermostat; 7-water temperature gauge; 8-water jacket; 9-distribution pipe; 10-drain cock

Every cylinder is surrounded by water jacket[4] 8, and water flows from the thermostat[5] 6 to the radiator 2. The function of the radiator is to bring the heat in the circulating water out to the atmosphere by the help of the cooling fan 4 behind it. In front of the radiator there are shutters[6] 1 to control the flow quantity of the air through the radiator. If the temperature is too low, the thermostat 6 closes the path to the radiator, and the water flows to the water pump 5 through the bypass and then returns to the water jacket. A drain cock[7] 10 is located at the lowest bottom of the system to drain the water. In a very cold winter, anti-freezing coolant[8] is added into the water to lower the freezing point[9].

The principle of air cooling system is to make high speed cold air flow through the cylinder block and cylinder head to remove heat. In order to increase the radiation area, a lot of radiating fins are cast on the cylinder block and cylinder head[10].

本节注释：[1]水冷系；[2]风冷系；[3]V形传动带(三角皮带)；[4]水套；[5]节温器；[6]百叶窗；[7]放水龙头；[8]防冻冷却液；[9]冰点；[10]在气缸体和气缸盖上铸造出许多散热片。

3.2.9 *LUBRICATION SYSTEM*

The main task of the lubrication system is to supply the lubricant[1] to the contact surface of the moving parts to reduce friction and abrasion[2]. Moreover, it can remove the abrasive particles, cool the friction surfaces and prevent them from corrosion.

The main lubricant of the lubrication system is oil. Brands of the oil are divided into classes expressed by English alphabets. The expression of the first alphabet "S" refers to oil used in the gasoline engine and "C" refers to diesel engine. Classes A, B, C, D, E, F, G and H express the performance levels. The level of the latter alphabet is higher than the former. There are six classes SC, SD, SE, SF, SG and SH of local made[3] oil for gasoline engine and five classes CC, CD, CD-Ⅱ, CE and CF-4 for diesel engine.

There are two types of lubrication in the engine, pressure lubrication and splash lubrication[4]. The former type is to force the oil through the passages to the important friction surfaces of high load and high speed while the latter type is to splash the oil to the exposed, low load and low speed parts. In Fig. 3-12, the oil pump 9 driven by the camshaft draws the oil from the oil sump and the suction filter[5] 16 and forces it through the primary filter[6] 11 to those parts including master oil passage[7] 4, crankshaft main bearing[8] 7, big end bearing of connecting rod[9] 6, camshaft bearing[10] 5, rocker arm shaft[11] 1 etc. The crankshaft turns rapidly and splashes the oil to those parts including cylinder wall, piston pin, cam and tappet[12].

As the engine is working, the gasoline vapor or burnt gas may leak to the

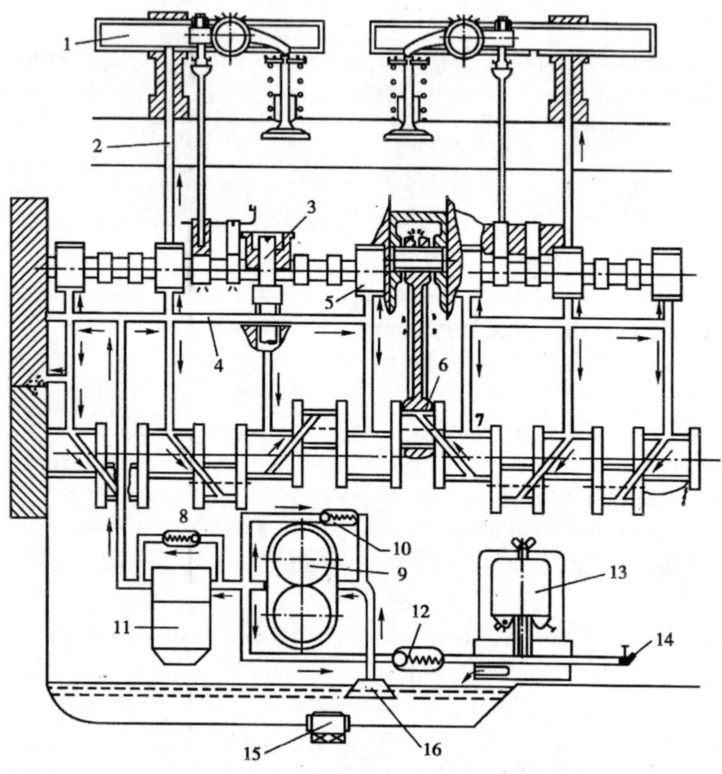

Fig. 3-12 Flow Chart of Engine Lubrication

1-rocker arm shaft; 2-upper oil passage; 3-oil pump shaft; 4-master oil passage; 5-camshaft bearing; 6-big end bearing of connecting rod; 7-crankshaft main bearing; 8-bypass valve[13]; *9-oil pump; 10-oil pressure adjusting valve; 11- primary filter; 12-relief valve*[14]; *13- secondary filter*[15]; *14-drain valve; 15-magnetic drain plug*[16]; *16-suction filter*

crankcase and spoil the oil. Therefore, ventilation is required to drive the vapor and gas outside from the crankcase. The way of ventilation is to connect a pipe from the crankcase to the intake path of the carburetor and remove the vapor and gas by the help of vacuum suction[17] during the intake stroke.

本节注释：[1]润滑剂；[2]磨损；[3]国产；[4]飞溅润滑；[5]集滤器；[6]粗滤器；[7]主油道；[8]曲轴主轴承；[9]连杆轴承；[10]凸轮轴轴承；[11]摇臂轴；[12]挺杆；[13]旁通阀；[14]减压阀；[15]细滤器；[16]磁性放油塞；[17]真空抽吸。

3.2.10 *IGNITION SYSTEM OF GASOLINE ENGINE*

The task of the ignition system is to ignite the mixture of gasoline and air at the beginning of the working stroke. The principle of ignition is to use high voltage (10000 ~ 15000V) breaking down the gap (0.5 ~ 1mm) between electrodes of the spark plug[1] to create sparks.

In Fig. 3-13, a traditional ignition system is shown. Every cylinder of the engine has one spark plug 6 and the ignition order[2] is the same as the firing

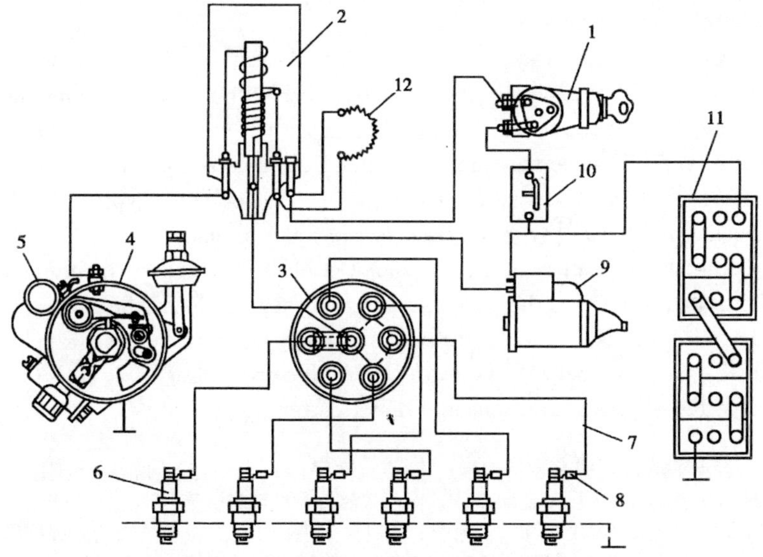

Fig. 3-13 Diagram of Ignition System of Six Cylinder Engine

1-ignition switch; 2-ignition coil; 3-distributor; 4-breaker; 5-condenser [11]; 6-spark plug; 7-high voltage wire; 8-damping resistance [12]; 9-starter; 10-ameter [13]; 11-storage battery; 12-atteched resistance

order mentioned in paragraph 3.2.3. One electrode of the spark plug connects the distributor[3] 3 while another electrode grounds to earth. There is ceramic material between the electrodes to provide good insulation. The ignition coil[4] 2 is indeed a high voltage transformer[5] and the breaker[6] 4 is a break switch leading to spark. There is a rotating cam in the breaker. The number of the edges of the cam is just equal to the number of cylinders. As one of the edges rotates to the breaker arm and separates the platinum contact points[7], the primary coil[8] switches off and creates induction current[9], thus produces high voltage in the secondary coil[10] and spark in the plug.

The distributor 3 has a rotor arm[14] to connect the certain spark plug one by one according to the firing order. The distributor and the breaker share the same main shaft driven by the camshaft. As the camshaft makes one revolution, so does the main shaft.

An evident disadvantage of the traditional ignition system is that the ignition signals are generated by the breaker. Platinum contact points may be burnt by the spark jumping through their gap when they are separated. In modern engines, some new ignition signal generators of non-contact structure[15] such as magnetic pulse type[16], Hall effect[17] type and photoelectric effect[18] type are used to avoid the trouble.

The storage battery 11 is the source of electricity and an ignition switch 1 is needed to operate the whole system. A generator feeds the storage battery to replenish the consumed electric energy. In modern motor vehicles, a three-phase alternator[19] is provided. A silicon rectifier[20] is used to change the alternative current into direct current.

本节注释：[1]火花塞的电极；[2]点火次序；[3]分电器；[4]点火线圈；[5]变压器；[6]断电器；[7]白金触点；[8]一次绕组；[9]感应电流；[10]二次绕组；[11]电容器；[12]阻尼电阻；[13]电流表；[14]分火头；[15]无触点结构的点火信号发生器；[16]磁脉冲式；[17]霍尔效应；[18]光电效应；[19]三相交流发电机；[20]硅整流器。

3.2.11 *STARTING SYSTEM*

The internal combustion engine cannot start itself. A starting system is required to provide enough suction force to make up the combustion mixture and to let the engine pass through the non-power strokes such as intake, compression and exhaust. The speed to ensure successful start for the engine is called starting speed. It is about 50 ~ 70 rpm for gasoline engine and about 150 ~ 300 rpm for diesel engine.

The starter 9 (Fig. 3-13) is a DC motor, its switch is in serial connection[1] with the ignition switch 1. As the driver turns the key in the ignition switch step by step, the switch of the starter is on. At this time the electro-magnetic control device drives the small gear on the main shaft of the starter to mesh with the ring gear on the flywheel, thus makes the crankshaft rotate. When the engine begins to run stably, the switch of the starter should be off and the return spring pushes the small gear back to separate it from the ring gear on the flywheel.

The storage battery is the source to supply electric power to the starter as well as all the other electric equipments (headlamp[2], windshield wiper[3], electric horn, radio and electronic control device).

3.2.12 *OPERATION PRINCIPLE OF TWO STROKE ENGINE*

Unlike the four stroke engine, a working cycle of the two stroke engine consists of two strokes only. That is, the piston reciprocates once and the crankshaft makes one revolution (360°).

As shown in Fig. 3-14, on the cylinder wall of the engine there are three ports. The intake port 1 connects the carburetor. Fig. b is the beginning of the intake process. The combustion mixture begins to come into the crankcase through port 1 and then to the combustion chamber through the transfer port[4] 3. In Fig. a, the piston closes all the three ports and continues to move upward and at this time the compression process begins. Fig. c is the end of the compression process, where a spark jumps into the cylinder and the working process begins. Fig. d is the end of the working process and the beginning of the exhaust process, where the burnt gas begins to rush out through the exhaust port 2 and the new mixture begins to come into the combustion chamber through the transfer port 3. As the piston continues to move a little downward, both port 2 and port 3 open. At this time the pressure at the port 3 is greater than the pressure at the port 2, i.e.

the fresh mixture is capable to drive the burnt gas out from the cylinder and the former replaces the latter.

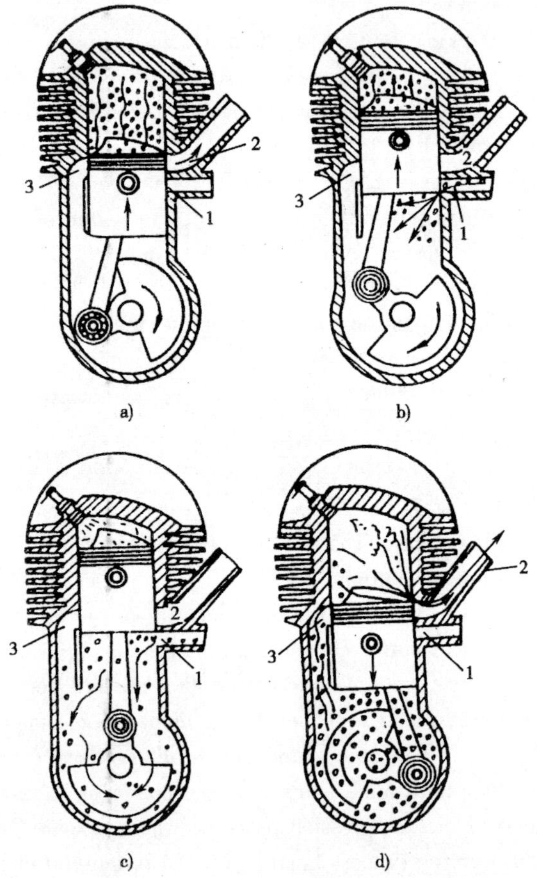

Fig. 3-14 Operation Diagram of Two Stroke Gasoline Engine
1-intake port; 2-exhaust port; 3-transfer port

In the two stroke engine one working cycle happens in one revolution of the crankshaft. Theoretically the power of a two stroke engine with the same volume and same speed should be twice the power of a four stroke engine, but practically only 1.5 ~ 1.6 times. Two stroke engine has advantages such as simple structure (without valve timing mechanism) and light weight (high liter power[5]), therefore it is widely used. On the other hand, the largest disadvantage of the two stroke engine is that it is impossible to drive the burnt gas outside thoroughly. Moreover, part of the fresh mixture is easier to escape outside when both port 2 and port 3 open. Therefore, harmful emissions[6] of the two stroke engine are more than the four stroke engine.

两节注释: [1]串连; [2]前照灯; [3]风窗刮水器; [4]扫气口; [5]升功率; [6]有害排放。

3.2.13 *ROTARY ENGINE*

Rotary engine[1] has a triangular piston and the way of the piston rotating in the cylinder is quite different from the reciprocal piston. Because of the fact that a German engineer named Felix Wankel invented the rotary engine, the engine is also called Wankel engine[2]. It was the German firm NSU that developed a car equipped with a rotary engine and began to introduce it to the market first in 1964. In 1967 the Japanese Mazda Company began to put the cars of rotary engine in batch production[3].

In Fig. 3-15, the main feature of the motion of the rotary engine is as follows. The center of the triangalar piston (or rotor) O_2 circulates on the orbit around the center of the crankshaft O_1 and at the same time the triangalar piston rotates around the center O_2 itself. As the piston circulates and rotates, the inner ring gear centering at O_2 meshes with the fixed gear centering at O_1. The ratio of the number of teeth of the ring gear to that of the fixed gear is 3:2. The motion relation mentioned above makes the piston corners move on a trajectory, i.e. the shape of the cylinder wall, like the figure "8".

It is clear that the piston divides the cylinder into three chambers. In Fig. 3-15a) chamber Ⅰ intakes the combustion mixture, chamber Ⅱ compresses the mixture and chamber Ⅲ is at the end of the working stroke and begins to exhaust. In Fig. 3-15b) chamber Ⅰ is on the midway of intake stroke, a spark jumps into chamber Ⅱ and the working stroke begins whereas chamber Ⅲ is on the midway of exhaust. In Fig. 3-15c) chamber Ⅰ compresses the mixture, chamber Ⅱ is on the midway of the working stroke and chamber Ⅲ is in the transferring state[4], i.e. both intake and exhaust ports open.

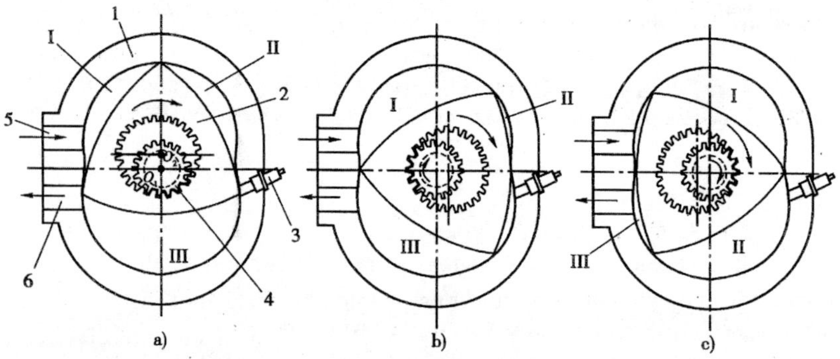

Fig. 3-15 Operation Diagram of Rotary Engine
1-cylinder block; 2-triangular piston (rotor); 3-spark plug; 4-crankshaft; 5-intake port; 6-exhaust port

During one revolution of the piston (rotor), the engine does work three times and all the chambers complete a four stroke cycle. The center of the crankshaft is O_1 and the center of the crankpin is O_2. The revolving speed of the crankshaft is three times as the revolving speed of the piston.

本节注释: [1]转子发动机(旋转活塞式发动机); [2]汪克尔发动机; [3]批量生产; [4]扫气状态。

3.3 CHASSIS

3.3.1 *CLUTCH*

The function of a clutch is not only to connect (or engage), but also to disconnect (or disengage) the engine with the drive train to meet the requirements for operation. As mentioned above, the engine cannot start under load. When the engine is to start, it should be disconnected from the drive train. After the engine starts and runs stably, it is possible to connect the drive train. Besides, the engine should be disconnected from the drive train before gear shifting and be connected the drive train after gear shifting.

The clutch relies on friction to transmit power, i. e. friction between its driving parts and driven parts. According to the principle of common physics, there must be a normal force built up by spring to press both the driving parts and the driven parts together.

Fig. 3-16 shows a typical diaphragm spring clutch[1] which is widely used in modern cars, also in light and medium trucks and buses. The engine flywheel 1 connects the rear end of the crankshaft and transmits power. The rear surface of the flywheel and the front surface of the pressure plate[2] 3 are the friction surfaces of the driving parts. In the figure, parts from number 3 to number 12 are mounted on the clutch cover[3] 10 and rotate together with the cover. The clutch cover is mounted on the flywheel by six bolts. All the above parts serve as the driving parts

There are two friction linings[4] mounted on both front and rear surfaces of the driven disc[5] by some rivets[6]. The linings serve the driven disc as the friction surfaces. The flywheel 1 and the pressure plate 3 grip the driven disc 2 tightly by the pressure of a diaphragm spring 6. This time power transmits from the engine to the driven disc and then to the input shaft of the gearbox through the spline hub[7] of the driven disc.

To disconnect the engine power from the gearbox the driver's left foot has to step on the clutch pedal, pushes the release sleeve and release bearing[8] 13 forward through a hydraulic device, then the release sleeve and release bearing pushes the center of the diaphragm spring 6 and the periphery of the diaphragm spring draws the pressure plate 3 rearward, thus releases the driven disc 2.

In order to prevent the drive train from sudden pulling and trembling, it is necessary to emphasize that the engagement of the clutch should be smooth and stable. Therefore, the driver has to relax his left foot on the pedal slowly

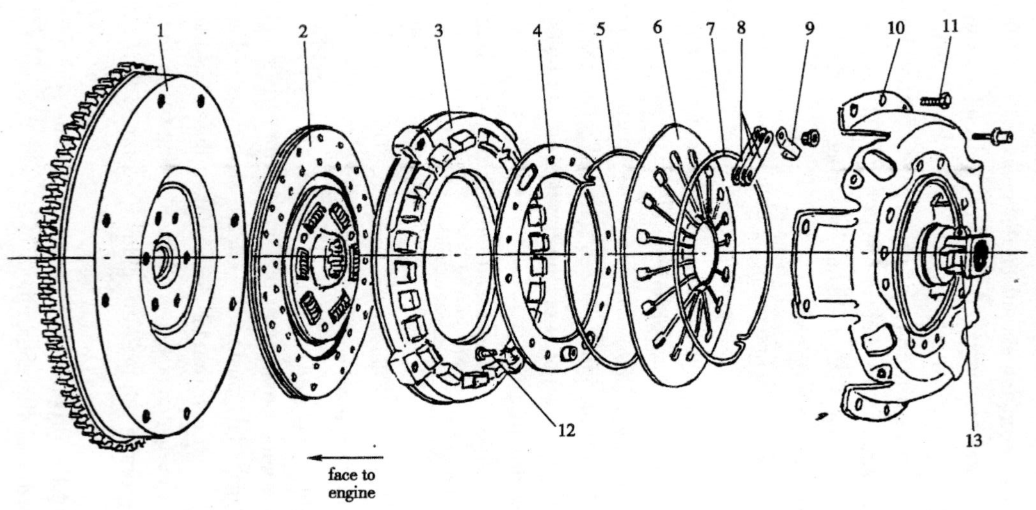

Fig. 3-16 Parts Of Diaphragm Clutch

1-engine flywheel; 2-driven disc; 3-pressure plate; 4-support ring; 5 and 7-wire ring; 6-diaphragm spring; 8-torque transfer plates; 9-release claw; 10-clutch cover; 11-bolt; 12-rivet; 13-release sleeve and release bearing and then the release sleeve and release bearing 13 is pulled rearward till its original position by a return spring[9]. The driver's action results in the pressure plate 3 increasing pressure on the driven disc 2 gradually, that is, slip between the driving and driven surfaces falls down gradually till zero, thus the clutch picks up the engine power smoothly.

In addition, another important function of the clutch is to prevent the transmission system from overload. When the torque in the transmission system becomes greater than the limit of the torque for the clutch to transmit, the driving and driven parts of the clutch would slip from each other.

To reduce and absorb vibration and impulse in the drive train, there is a vibration damper[10] including circular arranged springs and damping plates[11] at the center of the driven disc of the clutch.

本节注释: [1]膜片弹簧离合器; [2]压盘; [3]离合器盖; [4]摩擦衬片; [5]从动盘; [6]铆钉; [7]花键毂; [8]分离套筒和分离轴承; [9]复位弹簧; [10]减振器; [11]阻尼片。

3.3.2 *TRANSMISSION*

The main function of the transmission or gearbox is to enlarge the range of traction force and the range of velocity at the driving wheels. As shown in Fig. 3-7, the speed range of the typical engine is 1000 to 4800 rpm, that is, the maximum speed is 4.8 times of the minimum speed. But in practical operation for a common motor vehicle, the maximum velocity is more than 100 km/h and minimum velocity less than 4 km/h, which is at least 25 times difference. Evidently, a gearbox is needed to enlarge the engine speed range at least 5 times.

Definition of the gear ratio[1] or transmission ratio is the ratio of the number of teeth of the driven gear to the driving gear. When motion is transmitted from one gear to another, teeth of both gears should come into mesh one by one and any tooth is impossible to break through. For example, the driven gear has 20 teeth and the driving gear has 10 teeth, then the gear ratio is 2:1. In other words, when motion is transmitted from the driving gear to the driven gear, torque increases one time and speed reduces one time.

The shifting principle of the gearbox is to match the gears of different teeth in some pairs. To shift gear means another pair of gears to replace the former.

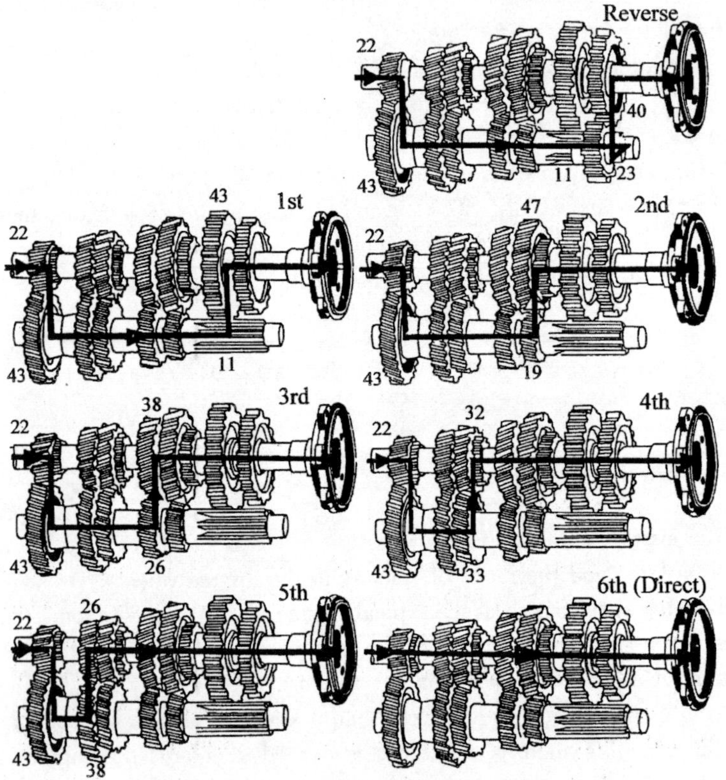

Fig. 3-17 Transmission Paths of Six Speed Gearbox
(Digits near each gear are the number of teeth)
Transmission ratio: 1st 7.640; 2nd 4.834; 3rd 2.859; 4th 1.895; 5th 1.337; 6th 1.000; reverse 7.107

Fig. 3-17 describes the transmission paths of different gears in a six speed gearbox. The gearbox of a FR motor vehicle has three shafts: input shaft[2] or clutch shaft, output shaft[3] or main shaft and counter shaft[4].

The input shaft and the output shaft are on the same straight line and the counter shaft is parallel to them. In the figure, the gear on the upper left corner is connected with the input shaft and there is a hole drilled in this gear. The front end of the output shaft extends into the hole and is supported by a needle bearing[5]. That is, except the input gear, all the gears behind it (on the right side) are on the output shaft. Transmission paths from 1st gear to 5th gear[6] are: at first the pair of gears at the front (the left side on the Figure) transmits power from the input shaft to the counter shaft and then from the counter shaft to the output shaft through the pair of gears at the rear (the right side on the Figure). Therefore the transmission ratio of the FR gearbox is equal to the product of two ratios of two pairs of gears. For example:

Transmission ratio of the 1st gear is $\frac{43}{22} \times \frac{43}{11} = 7.640$; the 5th gear is $\frac{43}{22} \times \frac{26}{38} = 1.337$. In Fig. 3-17, 6th gear is called the direct gear[7], i. e. the input shaft and the output shaft are locked together and the power goes from the input shaft to the output shaft directly, without going through the gears. This time the transmission ratio equals 1.

Because the internal combustion engine does not reverse, a reverse gear[8] is provided in the gearbox. A gear is added between the gears on the countershaft and on the output shaft, thus makes the output shaft reverse, see the upper right diagram in Fig. 3-21.

Transmission ratio of the reverse gear is $\frac{43}{22} \times \frac{23}{11} \times \frac{40}{23} = 7.107$.

The FF transmission is simpler than the FR transmission and has two shafts, i. e. input shaft and output shaft parallel to each other. In the FF transmission power transmits through one pair of gears only.

Fig. 3-18 shows a structure of lateral arranged engine[9], the gearbox is on the left side of the engine and the drawing of engine and clutch is not given. Power goes from the engine and the clutch to the input shaft 7 and then to the output shaft 3 through a pair of gears. The pinion gear of the final drive[10] is on the right end of the output shaft. Power transmits from

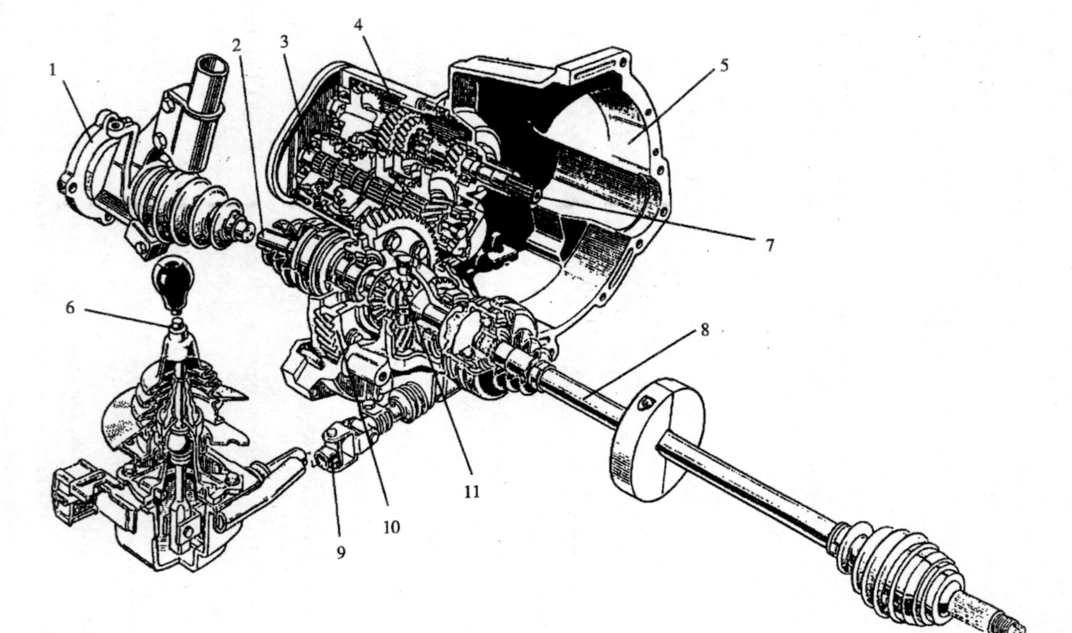

Fig. 3-18 Transaxle of Typical FF Car

1-left steering knuckle[13]; *2-left drive shaft; 3-output shaft of gearbox; 4-gearbox; 5-clutch housing*[14]; *6-shifting lever*[15]; *7-input shaft of gearbox; 8-right drive shaft; 9-control shaft of shifting*[16]; *10-final drive; 11-differential*

the output shaft to the left and right wheels through the ring gear of the final drive[11] 10 , the differential 11, left and right drive shafts 2 and 8. In the figure, the input shaft has 5 gears and they are (from right to left): 1st, reverse, 2nd, 3rd, 4th gears[12]. The output shaft also has 5 gears to match with the gears on the input shaft respectively.

In modern motor vehicles synchronizer[17] is widely used in the gearbox to promote shifting. At the moment of shifting synchronizer can make the speed of the driving parts become the same with the speed of the driven parts to prevent them from impact and noise, therefore the life of gears can be increased.

Fig. 3-19 is the lock ring type synchronizer[18] widely used in modern

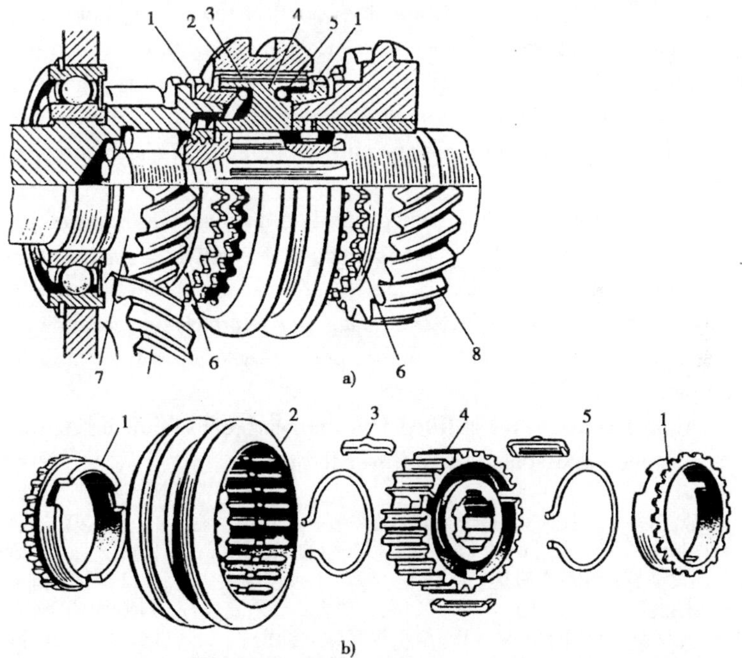

Fig. 3-19 Lock Ring Type Synchronizer

a) Assembled; b) Dissembled

1-bronze lock ring; 2-sliding sleeve; 3-sliding piece[22]; 4-spline hub; 5-ring spring; 6-outer ring gear; 7-gear on input shaft; 8-3rd gear on output shaft

cars. When shifting gear, the driver controls the shifting lever to push the sliding sleeve[19] 2 of the synchronizer (in the direction of left or right in the figure). The inner gear of the sliding sleeve moves to the outer ring gear 6 of the gear 7 or gear 8. In this case the gear (7or 8) transmits power through the sliding sleeve and the spline hub 4 to the main shaft (output shaft).

Near both the front and rear ends of the synchronizer there is a bronze lock ring[20] 1. Its inner friction cone[21] matches the outer friction cone of the gear 7 or 8. If there is speed difference between the driving and driven parts, the outer and inner cones slip from each other to make the lock ring limit the movement of the sliding sleeve. Friction between both cones reduces the speed difference, that is, makes the speed of the driving parts and the speed of the driven parts become the same gradually. As the speed of the driving parts equals to the speed of the driven parts, there is not any friction force to limit the movement of the sliding sleeve. This time the sliding sleeve 2 passes the lock ring 1 and meshes with the outer ring gear 6 to complete shifting.

There is a set of shifting device installed on the gearbox cover including shifting lever, shifting forks[23], striking rods[24], self-lock device[25] and interlock device[26]. The self-lock device ensures the sliding sleeve of the synchronizer working in correct positions. The interlock device allows one striking rod to move only and therefore prevents two gears from mesh in the same time.

Certain amount of oil is filled into the gearbox to lubricate the parts. The gears rotate and splash the oil over the parts.

本节注释：[1]速比；[2]输入轴(又称第一轴)；[3]输出轴(又称第二轴)；[4]中间轴；[5]滚针轴承；[6]由第一档至第五档的传递路线；[7]直接档；[8]倒档；[9]横置发动机；[10]主减速器小齿轮；[11]主减速器大齿轮；[12]一档、倒档、二档、三档、四档齿轮；[13]左转向节；[14]离合器壳；[15]变速杆；[16]换档操纵轴；[17]同步器；[18]锁环式同步器；[19]滑动齿套(啮合套)；[20]青铜锁环；[21]内摩擦锥面；[22]滑块；[23]换档拨叉；[24]换档拨叉轴；[25]自锁装置；[26]互锁装置。

3.3.3 *TRANSFER CASE*

A transfer case can be found in an all wheel drive motor vehicle. Its function is to distribute the power to all the drive axles. Besides, there is a low gear in the transfer case to provide enough traction to overcome difficult road conditions.

As shown in Fig. 3-20, the transfer case 7 is located behind the gearbox

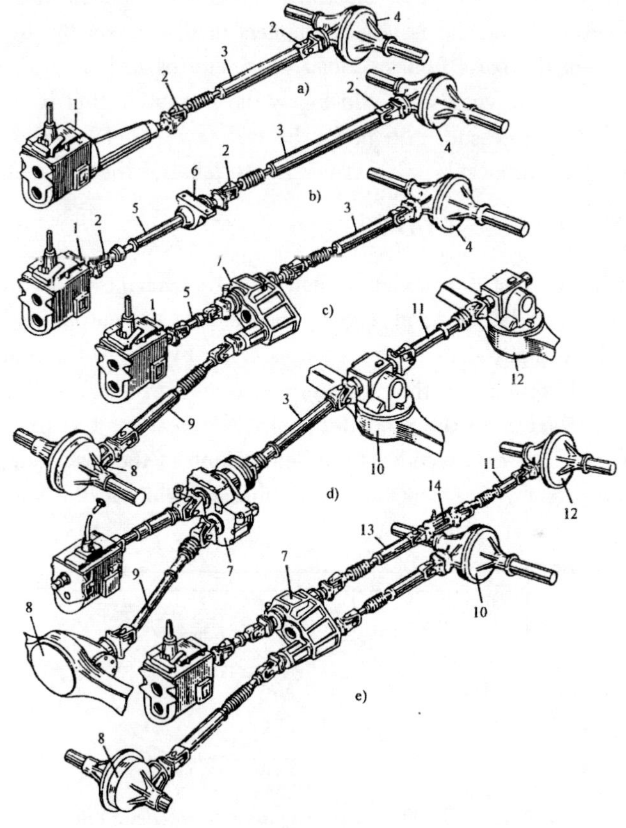

Fig. 3-20 Transfer Case and Propeller Shaft

1-gearbox; 2-universal joint; 3-main propeller shaft; 4-drive axle; 5-intermediate propeller shaft; 6-central support bearing; 7-transfer case; 8-steering drive axle; 9-propeller shaft to front axle; 10-middle drive axle; 11-propeller shaft to rear axle; 12-rear drive axle; 13-intermediate propeller shaft to rear axle; 14-central support bearing of propeller shaft to rear axle

1 and transmits the power to all the drive axles through propeller shafts.

In the transfer case there are three to four shafts and some gears to transmit power in different directions (front or rear) and different revolving directions (clockwise or counter-clockwise). Besides, the transfer case has high gear and low gear and is able to connect or disconnect the front axle.

To prevent the parts from overload when shifting to low gear, the operation of the transfer case should follow the regulation that before shifting to low gear, it is necessary to connect the front axle; and before disconnecting the front axle, it is necessary to take off the low gear.

3.3.4 *PROPELLER SHAFT*

The main task of the propeller shaft is to transmit power between two shafts at different positions and angles, for example the output shaft of the gearbox and the input shaft of the drive axle. In Fig. 3-20 there are propeller shafts installed between gearbox, transfer case and drive axles. Fig. 3-21 is the operation diagram of the propeller shaft. The gearbox 1 is fixed on the frame and the drive axle 4 follows the deformation of the leaf spring to move up and down. In this case both the transmitting angle and the length of the propeller shaft are changing.

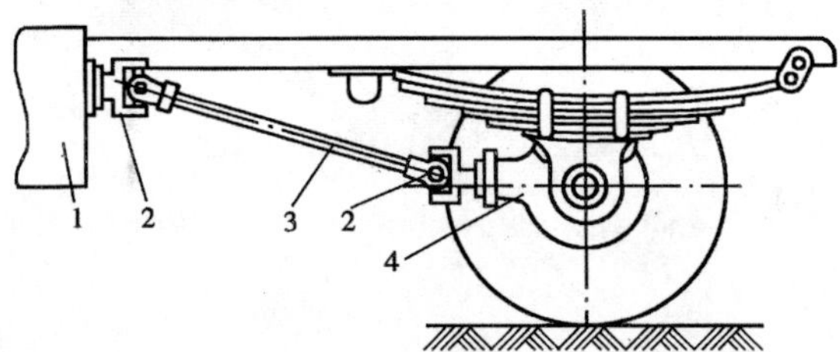

Fig. 3-21 Operation Diagram Of Propeller Shaft
1-gearbox; 2-universal joint; 3-propeller shaft; 4-drive axle

Universal joint (U-joint)[1] is used to solve the problem of angle change. Fig. 3-22a) is the most popular Cardan type (cross type) U-joint[2]. The cross or spider 2 consists of two shafts perpendicular to each other. One shaft connects to the driving fork 1 and the other connects to the driven fork 4. There are four needle bearings 3 on the four ends of two shafts. This structure permits the axis of the driving fork 1 to lie at an angle to the axis of the driven fork 4. During the process of rotation the plane where the cross lies on is swinging fore and aft. In this case the instant angular velocity of the driving fork is not equal to that of the driven fork, and therefore this type of universal joint is called the U-joint of inconstant angular velocity[3].

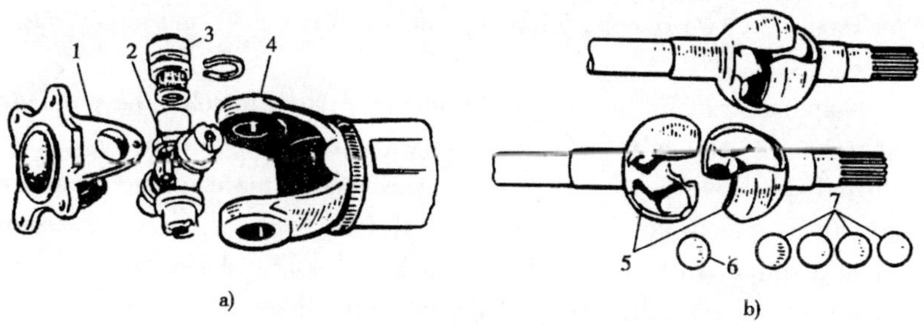

Fig. 3-22 Universal Joints

a) Cardan type U-joint; b) Weiss type U-joint (constant angular velocity)
1-driving fork; 2-cross; 3-needle bearing; 4-driven fork; 5-driving and driven forks; 6-central steel ball; 7-power transmitting balls

To solve the problem of inconstancy two U-joints of cross type are used. In Fig. 3-21, as the power transmits from the output shaft of the gearbox 1 to the propeller shaft 3 through the first U-joint, the instant angular velocity of the latter is not the same as the former. As the power transmits through the second U-joint, because of the principle of reverse symmetry[4] the instant angular velocity of the input shaft of the drive axle 4 is not equal to that of the propeller shaft 3 but equal to that of the output shaft of the gearbox 1.

Fig. 3-22b) is Weiss type U-joint[5]. It is a type of constant velocity U-joint. In this joint the driving fork has the same shape as the driven fork, and power transmits through four steel balls 7. A central steel ball 6 is provided to hold all the parts in position. No matter what angle is between the driving fork and the driven fork, the plane of four balls is in the half angle position. Therefore, the angular velocity of the driving fork is equal to that of the driven fork all the time.

For the FF cars, the drive shaft has to transmit power to the front wheel at different steering angle. Having better performance than Weiss type U-joint, Rzeppa type (ball and cage type) U-joint[6] is widely used in most of the FF cars. The structure has six steel balls and a retainer (cage) [7] between the driving part (inner race[8]) and the outer part (housing with outer race[9]). Two Rzeppa joints are for one drive shaft and totally four for a FF car.

A spline structure is used in the propeller shaft to solve the problem of length change. The spline structure is the coupling of two parts, the spline shaft and spline sleeve[10]. They are somewhat like the coupling of an inner gear with long teeth and an outer gear with long teeth. As power transmits through a spline structure, the spline shaft and spline sleeve can slide from each other to change the length of the propeller shaft.

本节注释：[1]万向节；[2]十字轴式万向节；[3]等角速万向节；[4]反对称原理；[5]球叉式万向节；[6]球笼式万向节；[7]保持架或隔离罩(球笼)；[8]内滚道；[9]带有外滚道的壳体；[10]花键轴和花键套。

3.3.5 *DRIVE AXLE*

A drive axle includes final drive, differential, axle shafts[1] and axle housing.

As seen in Fig. 3-7, the engine speed is too high and the engine torque is too small to connect the road wheel directly. There must be a set of gears called final drive to reduce the engine speed and increase the engine torque. As given in Fig. 3-20, the power transmitting direction from the gearbox to the drive axle is longitudinal, but after the final drive the transmitting direction becomes lateral. A pair of bevel gears[2] is used to change the transmitting direction. For the lateral arranged engine (see Fig. 3-18), the final drive is equipped with a pair of spur gears[3] and it is not necessary to change the transmitting direction.

The task of a differential is to transmit power and to make the left and right road wheels possible to operate at different speeds. When the motor vehicle is steering, the path for the outer wheel on the curved road is longer than that for the inner wheel and the speed of the outer wheel is greater than the inner wheel.

A planetary gear system[4] is widely used in most of the differentials and it includes left side gear[5] 4, planetary pinions[6] 6, pinion shaft[7] 5, differential housing[8] 7 and right side gear 8 (Fig. 3-23a). Power goes from the final drive pinion 1 to the final drive ring gear 3. The differential housing 7 is mounted on the ring gear 3 and therefore turns together with it. Then the power transmits to the pinion shaft 5, the planetary pinions 6 and to the left and right side gears 4 and 8. When the motor vehicle is going along a straight road, the planetary pinions 6 turn together with the differential housing 7 (orbit motion[9]) and do not rotate on the planetary shaft 5 (rotary motion[10]), thus the speed of the left side gear n_L is equal to the speed of the right side gear n_R (see Fig. 3-24a). When the motor vehicle is going along a curved road, the planetary pinions not only do orbit motion, but also rotary motion, thus make the left side gear and the right side gear possible to

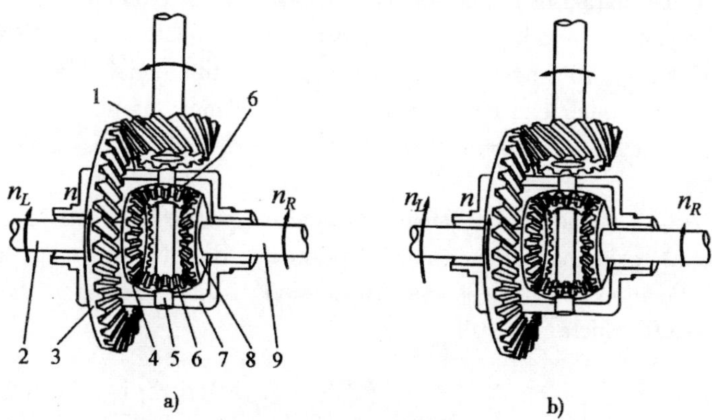

Fig. 3-23 Structure of Differential

a) straight driving; b) right turning

1-final drive pinion; 2-left axle shaft; 3-final drive ring gear; 4-left side gear; 5-pinion shaft; 6-planetary pinions; 7-differential housing; 8-right side gear; 9-right axle shaft turn at different speed (Fig. 3-23b).

The main feature of a common planetary differential is equal distribution of the torque to left and right road wheels at any time. For example, if the torque transmitted to the final drive ring gear is 100 N · m, the torque distributed to each left and right road wheel is 50 N · m. If one wheel is on slippery surface (for example icy road), traction force on this side is limited by rather small adhesive force. In this case, traction force on the other side is also as small as this side, the motor vehicle may not develop enough traction to overcome all the resistances. Therefore, a phenomenon can be seen quite often that one wheel on slippery surface may spin quite fast and the other wheel even on good road surface is too weak as the former to drive the motor vehicle.

In order to overcome such shortcoming of the common planetary differential, a special structure of anti-skid differential (ASD) [11] is used to lock one axle shaft with the differential housing together or to increase friction between the left and the right parts, that is, to change the situation of equal distribution of torque for the common planetary differential.

The task of an axle shaft is to transmit the power from the differential to the road wheel. The inner end connects with the differential side gear by spline and the outer end connects with the wheel hub. As mentioned above the axle shaft for a FF car is also called the drive shaft and is provided with U-joints.

The task of the axle housing is to hold the parts (final drive, differential, axle shaft etc) in correct positions. Besides, an integrated axle housing (equipped with dependent suspension) is able to support the weight of the motor vehicle.

本节注释：[1]半轴；[2]锥齿轮(伞齿轮)；[3]圆柱齿轮；[4]行星齿轮系；[5]半轴齿轮；[6]行星齿轮；[7]行星齿轮轴；[8]差速器壳；[9]公转；[10]自转；[11]防滑差速器。

3.3.6 *STEERING SYSTEM*

The function of a steering system is to make the motor vehicle operate on the direction given by the driver.

Fig. 3-24 shows the structural components of a typical steering system equipped with a steering gear of re-circulating ball type[1]. For this type there are some balls between the threads[2] of the steering screw[3] and the steering nut[4]. In order to reduce friction between the screw and the nut there are some balls re-circulating from the end to the front of the threads through a guide tube[5]. As the driver turns the steering wheel 8 (for example left turn), this action is transmitted through the steering shaft[6] 7, U-joints 5 and steering drive shaft[7] 6 to the steering screw 4. As the steering screw 4 turns, the steering nut 3 slides along its axis. Some teeth are at the bottom of the steering nut 3 and mesh with the teeth on the sector shaft[8] 2. A pitman arm[9] 9 connects to the outer end of the sector shaft 2 and transmits the action to the drag link[10] 10 and then to the knuckle

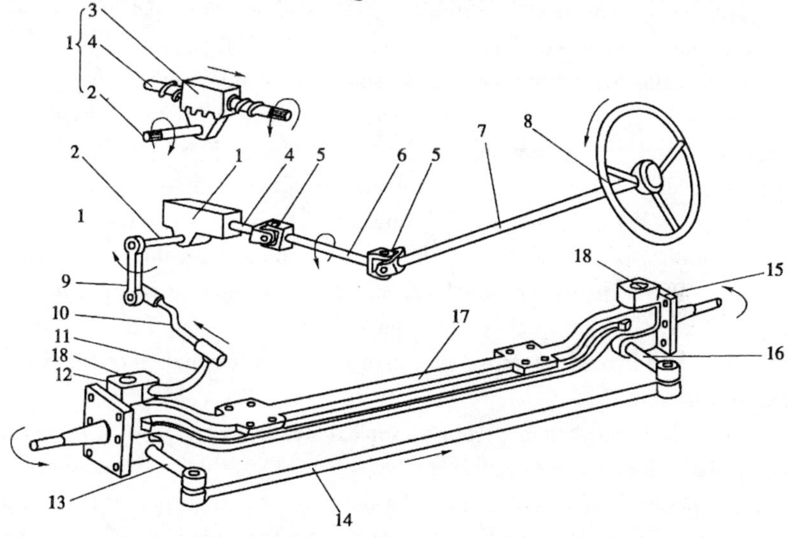

Fig. 3-24 Steering System of a Typical Truck

1-steering gear; 2-sector shaft; 3-steering nut; 4-steering screw; 5-U-joints; 6-steering drive shaft; 7-steering shaft; 8-steering wheel; 9-pitman arm; 10-drag link; 11-knuckle arm; 12-left steering knuckle; 13-left steering arm; 14-tie rod; 15-right steering knuckle; 16-right steering arm; 17-front axle beam; 18-king pins

arm[11] 11. The action of the knuckle arm turns the steering knuckle[12] 12 around the king pin[13] 18 mounted on the axle beam[14] 17. Motion of the left steering knuckle 12 transmits to the right steering knuckle 15 through the left steering arm[15] 13, the tie rod[16] 14 and the right steering arm 16. The left and right road wheels are installed on the left and right knuckles respectively and turn together with them. Nearby arrows express the motion directions of the components.

When the motor vehicle is steering, the inner wheel on the curved road turns greater than the outer wheel. If the inner steering knuckle is linked to the outer steering knuckle by a parallelogram[17] linkage, they will turn at the same angle. Obviously, a parallelogram does not meet the requirement of the angular difference between the inner knuckle and the outer knuckle. Therefore the linkage must be a trapezoid[18], that is, the length of the tie rod 14 is shorter than the distance between the left and right king pins.

Most of the modern cars use a steering gear of rack and pinion type[19]. This type of steering gear is advantageous by its simple structure, light weight and good road sensation[20]. Because independent suspension is quite common in modern cars, the tie rod should be divided into two parts 11 and 4 (see Fig. 3-25). The length of the tie rods 11 and 4 is equal to the length of the control arms 17 and 14 and the tie rod is parallel to the control arm on each side. When the motor vehicle is steering, the steering wheel 9 makes the pinion rotate. The rotation of the pinion drives the rack 5 and the tie rods 11 and 4 to move laterally, and then turns the left and right steering arms and the knuckles.

Power steering system [21] (or power assisted system) is widely used in modern cars, heavy trucks and other types of motor vehicles. A power hydraulic pump driven by the engine is used to force high pressure oil to a power assisted cylinder through a control valve. The operation of the control valve and the flow of the power oil should keep pace with the steering angle and steering force of the steering wheel.

本节注释：[1]循环球式转向器；[2]螺纹；[3]转向螺杆；[4]转向螺母；[5]导管；[6]转向轴；[7]转向传动轴；[8]齿扇轴；[9]摇臂；[10]直拉杆；[11]转向节臂；[12]转向节；[13]主销；[14]前桥梁；[15]梯形臂；[16]横拉杆；[17]平行四边形；

[18]梯形；[19]齿轮齿条式转向器；[20]良好的路感；[21]动力转向系；[22]转向柱。

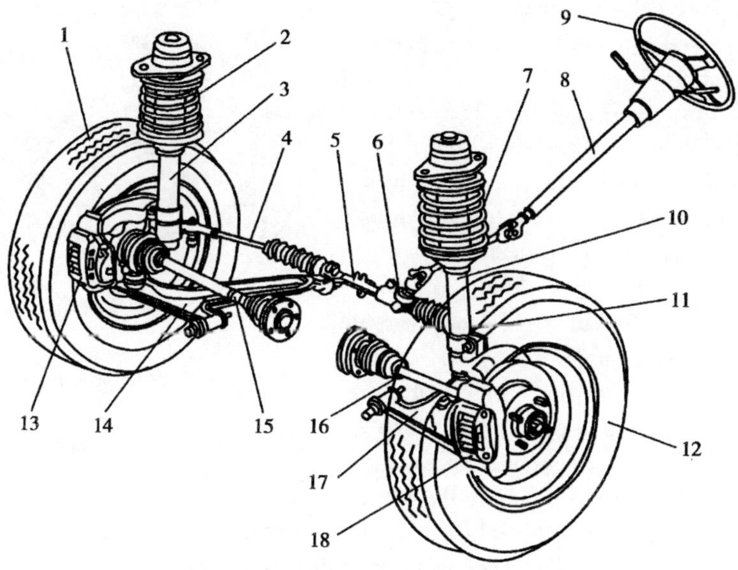

Fig. 3-25 Front Suspension and Steering System of a Modern Car

1-right road wheel; 2-right spring; 3-right strut and shock absorber; 4-right tie rod; 5-rack; 6-pinion; 7-left spring; 8-steering column[22]*; 9-steering wheel; 10-left strut and shock absorber; 11-left tie rod; 12-left road wheel; 13-right front brake; 14-right control arm; 15-right drive shaft; 16-left drive shaft; 17-left control arm; 18-left front brake*

3.3.7 *BRAKING SYSTEM*

The braking system is to slow and stop the motor vehicle and to ensure reliable parking[1]. By means of friction in the brake the road wheel of the motor vehicle can reduce speed and stop.

Fig. 2-26 is a drum brake[2]. The brake base plate[3] 3 is mounted on the steering knuckle of the front axle or on the rear axle housing. There is a wheel cylinder[4] 1 and two brake shoes[5] mounted on the base plate 3. The brake drum[6] 4 is mounted on the wheel hub[7] and turns together with the road wheel. When the brake is applied, pressure oil flows through the pipe (expressed by an arrow) to the wheel cylinder 1. There are two pistons at each end of the wheel cylinder. Either piston pushes the respective brake shoe 2 to turn around the pivot[8] 5. This action makes the shoes press against the brake drum 4. Because of friction between the shoes (immovable) and the drum (movable) rotation of the road wheel (together with the drum) slows down.

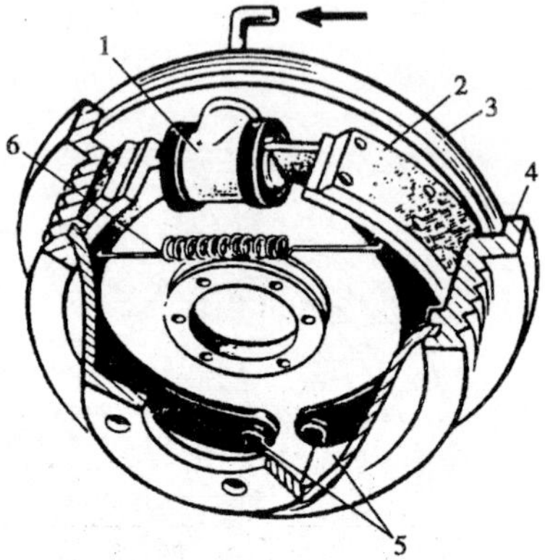

Fig. 3-26 Drum Brake
1-wheel cylinder; 2-brake shoe; 3-brake base plate; 4-brake drum; 5-pivots; 6-return spring

When the driver's right foot exerts force on the brake pedal, this action makes the master cylinder[9] press the oil to flow through the piping to the wheel cylinder. When the driver's foot releases the brake pedal, the return spring 6 pulls the brake shoes back to their original positions (to keep a small clearance from the brake drum). This time the oil flows from the wheel cylinder back to the master cylinder through the piping.

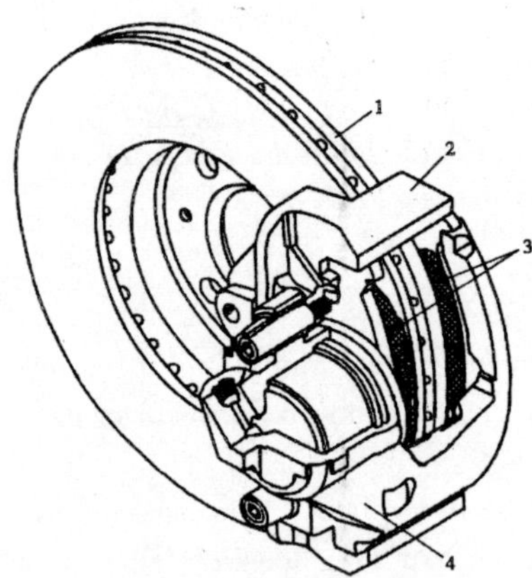

Fig. 3-27 Disc Brake
1-rotor (disc); 2-caliper support; 3-friction linings; 4- caliper body

From Fig. 3-26 it is evident that the brake drum packs almost all the parts in a small space and difficulty of bringing heat outside may be a large shortcoming of the drum brake.

Fig. 3-27 is the structure of a disc brake[10]. A rotor or disc[11] 1 is mounted on the wheel hub and rotates together with the wheel. A caliper body[12] 4 is installed on the caliper support[13] 2. There are a pair of friction pads 3 and a cylinder in the caliper body. When the driver's foot steps the brake pedal, oil from the master cylinder flows to the caliper cylinder[14]. A piston pushes the pads to grip the rotating rotor. Friction between the pads and the surfaces of the rotor makes the wheel slow down. Because the rotor is exposed to the outside air, disc brake has many advantages such as: good heat dissipation, fast recovery of braking effect after getting wet, automatic adjustment etc.

For the braking system is much related to the operation safety, a motor vehicle should be equipped with several sets of brakes such as operation brake[15], parking brake[16] and auxiliary brake[17]. In order to avoid all the wheel cylinders losing brake effect out of oil leakage in the piping, a braking system of dual circuit[18] is necessary for modern motor vehicles. Each circuit connects two wheels only, not four wheels. If one circuit or piping is broken, another is still effective.

Hydraulic system[19] is widely used in the braking system of cars, light trucks and light buses. In the hydraulic system, the master cylinder pumps the oil to the wheel cylinders. Usually the hydraulic system is incorporated with a vacuum booster (vacuum power assister)[20] to increase the driver's pedal force on the master cylinder.

Pneumatic system[21] is widely used in the braking system of medium and heavy trucks and buses. An air compressor[22] driven by the engine supplies the compressed air to a reservoir[23]. A control valve[24] actuated by the brake pedal distributes the compressed air from the reservoir to all the brake chambers[25] near the wheels and reduces the speed of the motor vehicle.

As the wheels set on road areas of different adhesive conditions or the weight distribution may be different on the wheels from each other, the brake forces acting on the wheels may be different too. In this case, braking effect of the motor vehicle may reduce or the motor vehicle may lose directional stability. In modern motor vehicles, an advanced system of electronic brake-force distribution (EBD)[26] is developed to solve the problem. The EBD system can adjust the oil pressure in each wheel cylinder respectively to meet the requirement of brake force.

本节注释；[1]驻车；[2]鼓式制动器；[3]制动器底板；[4]轮缸(分泵)；[5]制

动蹄；[6]制动鼓；[7]轮毂；[8]支承销；[9]主缸(总泵)；[10]盘式制动器；[11]制动盘；[12]制动钳体；[13]制动钳支架；[14]制动钳油缸；[15]行车制动器；[16]驻车制动器；[17]辅助制动器；[18]双管路制动系统；[19]液压系统；[20]真空助力器；[21]气压系统；[22]空气压缩机；[23]贮气筒；[24]控制阀；[25]制动气室；[26]电控制动力分配系统。

3.3.8 *SUSPENSION*

A suspension is a system which locates between the frame (or integrated body) and the axle (or the wheel) to connect them and to transmit forces. Types of suspension may differ from each other, but all of them may consist of three components including elastic element[1], shock absorber[2] and guiding mechanism[3].

The function of an elastic element is to cushion the road shock. Two types of elastic element are quite common: leaf spring[4] and coil spring[5]. Leaf spring is formed by a group of elastic steel pieces of different length (Fig. 3-28). The front and rear ends of the upper two pieces are rolled up to form spring eyes[6] 1. The central part of the leaf spring is clamped on the axle housing by two U-bolts[7]. A central bolt 4 is used to hold the pieces in position and the spring clips 2 are used to keep the pieces close together. From the principle of mechanics, it is clear to see that the bending moment[8] is the largest at the central part of the leaf spring and is smallest at both ends. Therefore the central part of the leaf spring is the thickest and both ends are the thinnest.

A coil spring is made of a long elastic steel bar. Compared with the leaf spring, the coil spring has the advantage of light weight and little space and is widely used in modern cars.

A torsion bar[9] is an elastic steel bar, its one end is fixed on the frame and the other end is mounted on the control arm. The road wheel is installed on the other end of the control arm. As the road wheel jounces and rebounds[10], the torsion bar twists over and over again.

An air spring[11] is a hollow chamber filled with compressed air. Compression and expansion of the air play the role of elastic action.

Jounce and rebound of the road wheel causes reciprocal vibration of the

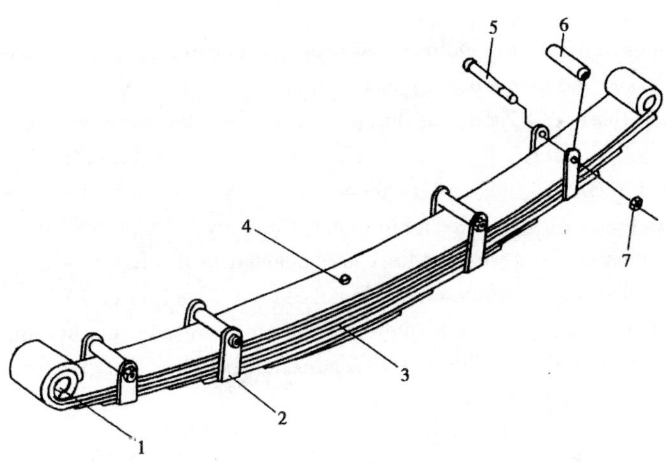

Fig. 3-28 Leaf Spring

1-spring eye; 2-clip; 3-elastic pieces; 4-central bolt; 5-clip bolt; 6-sleeve; 7-nut

elastic element. In order to improve comfort, shock absorbers should be incorporated in the suspension system. The shape of a shock absorber is like a telescopic container filled with oil. The shock absorber compresses and extends just like the elastic element does. This time oil in the absorber is forced to flow through the small holes reciprocally to cause resistance and to damp the vibration. Damping resistance[12] of the shock absorber is small during the compression stroke to avoid a hard jounce to the occupants, and is large during the extension stroke to reduce vibration.

A guiding mechanism is a linkage to transmit forces and to guide the up and down motion of the wheel along a certain trajectory. There are various types of guiding mechanism, and some times the suspension systems are named after the guiding mechanisms such as, single control arm type[13], double wishbone type[14], longitudinal swing arm type[15], strut type[16] etc. Fig. 3-25 shows the suspension system of McPherson type[17]. The guiding mechanism includes a strut (10 and 3) and a lower control arm (17 and 14) on each side. Either strut consists of a shock absorber and a coil spring (7 and 2).

Suspension systems include two main categories, dependent suspension system[18] and independent suspension system[19]. In the dependent suspension there is a rigid axle to connect the left and right wheels together, and the motion of one wheel would affect the motion of the other wheel. As shown in Fig. 3-29a) the upward motion of one wheel would make the other wheel together with the axle incline, and the body inclines too. In the independent suspension each wheel is connected to the frame through an independent linkage. As shown in Fig. 3-29b) the motion of one wheel would not affect the other wheel and therefore the structure can improve the quality of ride and comfort and also increase adhesion between tire and road.

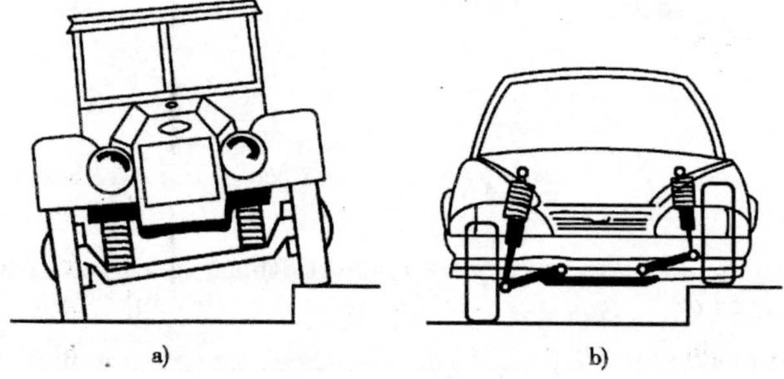

Fig. 3-29 Dependent Suspension and Independent Suspension
a) dependent suspension; b) independent suspension

The suspension system of some modern cars is equipped with an intelligent system[20] controlled by electronic device. The intelligent system is able to adjust the stiffness[21] of the elastic element and the damping resistance of the shock absorber to remove shock and vibration effectively. Moreover, the system is able to adjust the body height from the ground too. When the car drives on the rough road or even makes a sharp steer, the occupants would not feel uncomfortable because the body is able to keep leveling[22].

本节注释：[1]弹性元件；[2]减振器；[3]导向机构；[4]钢板弹簧；[5]螺旋弹簧；[6]卷耳；[7]U形螺栓；[8]弯矩；[9]扭杆；[10]车轮上下跳动；[11]空气弹簧；[12]阻尼力；[13]单摆臂式；[14]双横臂式；[15]纵摆臂式；[16]滑柱式；[17]麦弗

逊式悬架；[18]非独立悬架系统；[19]独立悬架系统；[20]智能系统；[21]刚度；[22]保持水平状态。

3.3.9 *WHEEL AND TIRE*

The task of wheel and tire is to support the weight of the motor vehicle, to cushion the road shock, to transmit forces such as traction force and braking force by adhesion to the road, and to increase crossing performance by the special tire pattern[1].

The rim[2] is the round part of the wheel to install the tire. The hub[3] is the central part of the wheel to install the wheel on the axle. The spoke[4] is the part of the wheel to connect the rim and the hub. They can be made by sheet steel stampings or by pressure casting of aluminum alloy[5]. The wheel made of aluminum alloy can reduce one third of the weight and moment of inertia compared to sheet steel stamping[6].

Fig. 3-30 is the structure of a common bias ply tire[7]. The outside is the rubber layer including tread or crown[8] 3, shoulder[9] 2 and side wall[10] 4. Some groves are cut on the tread to improve tire performance, they are called pattern. The cord[11] 1 is the important part of the tire to withstand load and is made of several plies of fabric strings including nylon strings or steel wires. Direction of the strings in a common bias ply tire inclines at an angle with the central line of the tread. The strings on one ply inclines to the left and the other to the right. The number of plies is even number and the left and right inclining plies overlap one another[12]. There is a cushion layer[13] 5 between the tread and the cord to strengthen the periphery of the tire and to prevent the cord from separation with the tread. All the above components are called tire carcass[14]. The rubber tube[15] 6 is a closed space to be filled with air and a bleed valve[16] is needed. There is a protector[17] 7 between the tube and the rim.

Radial tubeless tire[19] is widely used in most of the modern cars, light trucks and buses. Direction of the cord strings in a radial tire is radial, that is, perpendicular to the central line of the tread[20] (Fig. 3-31). The appearance of the tubeless tire is similar to the tube-type tire. On the inner wall of the tubeless tire a sealing layer of rubber is incorporated. Radial tire

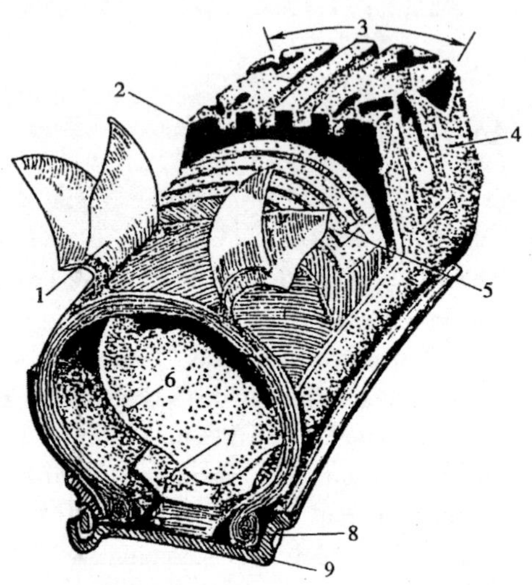

Fig. 3-30 Structure of Common Bias Ply Tire

1-cord; 2-tire shoulder; 3-tread (crown); 4-side wall; 5-cushion layer; 6-tube; 7-protector; 8-bead [18]; *9-rim*

has many advantages such as light weight, small moment of inertia, low rolling resistance, high duty, low cost, low probability of leakage and burst etc. Therefore radial tire is much better than bias ply tire.

Nomination of a tire is used to express its specifications[22]. There are two common kinds of nominations. The first kind is the nomination of common low pressure tires, for example 9.00-20. As shown in Fig. 3-32, the figure 9.00 is the nominal profile width (in.) of tire[23] B and the figure 20 is the nominal diameter (in.) of rim d. The second kind is the nomination of radial tire, for example 185/70SR14. The figure 185 is nominal profile width (mm) of tire B; the figure 70 is nominal height-width ratio of tire profile[24] H/B; the alphabet S is speed level code[25] (see Table 3-4), the alphabet R refers to radial structure and the figure 14 is nominal diameter (in.) of rim d.

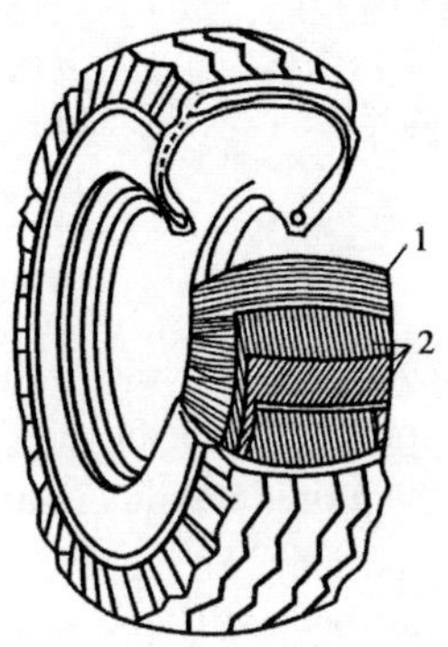

Fig. 3-31 Radial Tire
1-cord; 2-belted layer [21]

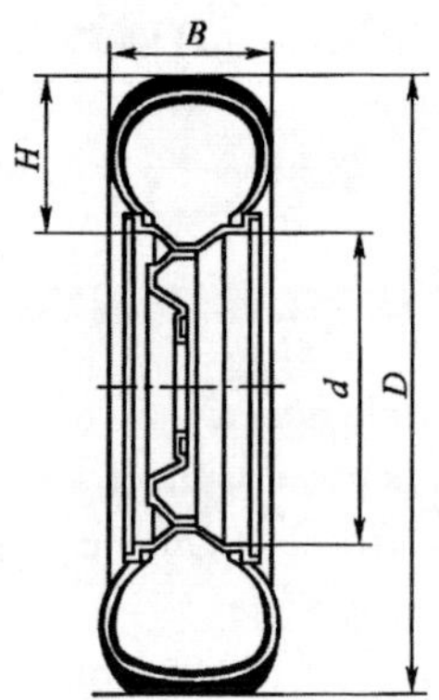

Fig. 3-32 Expression of Tire Nomination

Tire Speed Level Code Table 3-4

Code	Maximum Speed (km/h)	Code	Maximum Speed (km/h)
J	100	R	170
K	110	S	180
L	120	T	190
M	130	U	200
N	140	H	210
P	150	V	240
Q	160	X	>240

Low profile is the trend of tire development, i. e. the height-width ratio becomes smaller and smaller. The smaller the ratio is, the better the handling stability will be. For example, the height-width ratio was nearly 100% fifty years ago, 80% thirty years ago and is 70% ~60% nowadays.

本节注释: [1]轮胎花纹; [2]轮辋; [3]轮毂; [4]轮辐; [5]铝合金压铸件; [6]与钢板冲压件相比,铝合金制成的车轮可减少三分之一的重量和转动惯量。[7]普通斜交轮胎; [8]胎冠(胎面); [9]胎肩; [10]胎侧; [11]帘布层; [12]帘布层的数目是偶数并且左倾斜层和右倾斜层交替叠合。[13]缓冲层; [14]外胎; [15]橡胶内胎;

[16]气门；[17]垫带；[18]胎圈；[19]子午线无内胎轮胎；[20]子午线轮胎帘布层帘线的方向是径向,亦即垂直于胎面中心线；[21]带束层；[22]轮胎命名用以表达其规格；[23]轮胎名义断面宽度；[24]轮胎断面名义高宽比；[25]速度级别代码。

3.3.10 *WHEEL ALIGNMENT*

Wheel alignment[1] is to position the wheels so that they roll reasonably on the road surface without scuffing and slipping[2] under all operation conditions. Wheel alignment is essential to handling stability, safety, fuel economy and tire life.

In a modern motor vehicle the wheels are not really perpendicular to the road surface but at proper angles. Five angles or parameters are needed for correct wheel alignment: caster[3], camber[4], steering axis inclination[5], toe[6] and tracking[7]. These parameters of wheel alignment can be checked on a test rig called four-wheel aligner[8].

Caster is the forward or rearward tilt angle γ of the steering axis or kingpin axis on the side view of the motor vehicle[9]. As shown in Fig. 3-33a), suppose the wheel deviates to the right by interference, the reaction force y of the ground to the wheel is opposite the centrifugal force. Because of the angle γ, the force y has an arm l to the steering axis. The force y and the arm l form a return moment[10] to correct the deviation of the wheel.

Camber is the inward or outward tilt angle α of the wheel (Fig. 3-33b) on the front view of the motor vehicle[11]. The reasons for camber are: to let the wheel perpendicular to the road crown[12] and to load the inner bearing of the wheel on the knuckle spindle[13].

Steering axis inclination is the inward tilt angle β of the steering axis on the front view of the motor vehicle. Steering axis inclination can reduce the arm c on the ground (Fig. 3-33b) thus reduce the resistant moment and make the steering easier. As shown in Fig. 3-33c), suppose the wheel turns 180 degrees, it seems that the wheel presses into the road. Actually the road is too hard to press down, in other words, the turning of the wheel lifts the motor vehicle up to a higher position. In this case, the gravity of the motor vehicle would force the motor vehicle to return down to the original lower position. Therefore, steering axis inclination aids directional stability by forcing the wheel to return to the original straight ahead position.

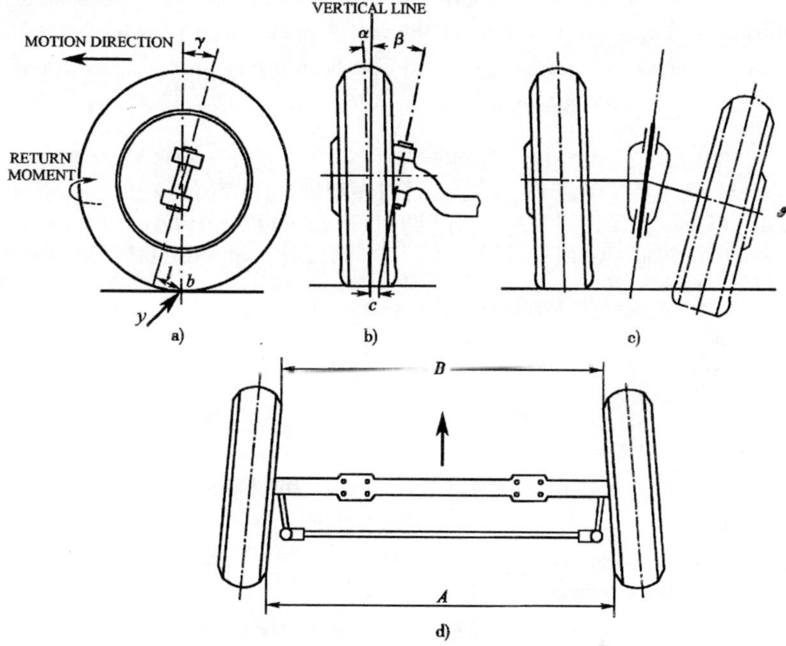

Fig. 3-33 Wheel Alignment

As shown in Fig. 3-33d), toe is the difference between the distance *B* measured from the front of the left wheel to the front of the right wheel and the distance *A* measured from the rear of the left wheel to the rear of the right wheel. Toe-in[14] means that *B* is shorter than A, and toe-out[15] means that *B* is longer than *A*. For a rear wheel drive motor vehicle, resistant forces tend to make the front wheels toe-out, therefore the toe setting should be toe-in ($B < A$); whereas for a front wheel drive motor vehicle, traction forces tend to make the front wheels toe-in, therefore the toe setting should be toe-out ($B > A$). Incorrect toe is much concerned with bent or damaged steering parts.

Tracking means the rear wheels should follow the tracks[16] of the front wheels. A new motor vehicle does not have tracking problem. Because of collision or damage of the parts of the frame, body, axle housing, suspension or wheel, inharmonious motion of the wheels may happen and lead to poor handling, excess fuel consumption and tire wear[17].

本节注释：[1]车轮定位；[2]拖刮和滑动；[3]转向轴线后倾；[4]车轮外倾；[5]转向轴线内倾；[6]前束；[7]随辙；[8]称为四轮定位仪的试验台；[9]汽车的侧视图；[10]回正力矩；[11]汽车的前视图；[12]道路(横断面)的鼓形；[13]使转向节枢轴上车轮内侧的轴承加载；[14]正前束；[15]负前束；[16]车辙、轨迹；[17]由于行走系统零件(车架、车身、桥壳、悬架或车轮)的碰撞或损坏，几个车轮的运动可能不协调而导致操纵性能变坏、油耗增加和轮胎磨损。

3.3.11 *FRAME*

The frame of a motor vehicle is the base to install all the systems and components at proper positions and to bear all the loads from them.

Fig. 3-34 is a typical frame of longitudinal type or ladder type[1]. It consists of two side rails[2], several cross members[3] and some brackets[4] welded or riveted together[5]. It is advised readers should analyze this figure carefully and to found the positions of the brackets of every system.

本节注释：[1]边梁式或梯子式车架；[2]纵梁；[3]横梁；[4]托架；[5]焊接或铆接在一起；[6]保险杠；[7]发动机前悬置托架；[8]挂钩；[9]驾驶室前悬置托架；[10]货箱；[11]拖钩；[12]副簧。

3.4 BODY

Body provides place for the driver's operation and for the passenger and goods. It includes body shell[1], doors, windows, front end panels[2], seats, ventilation, heating, air-conditioning devices etc. For trucks and special utility motor vehicles body includes platform or other special equipments also.

3.4.1 *BODY SHELL AND FRONT END PANELS*

Body shell is the base to install all the body systems. It usually refers

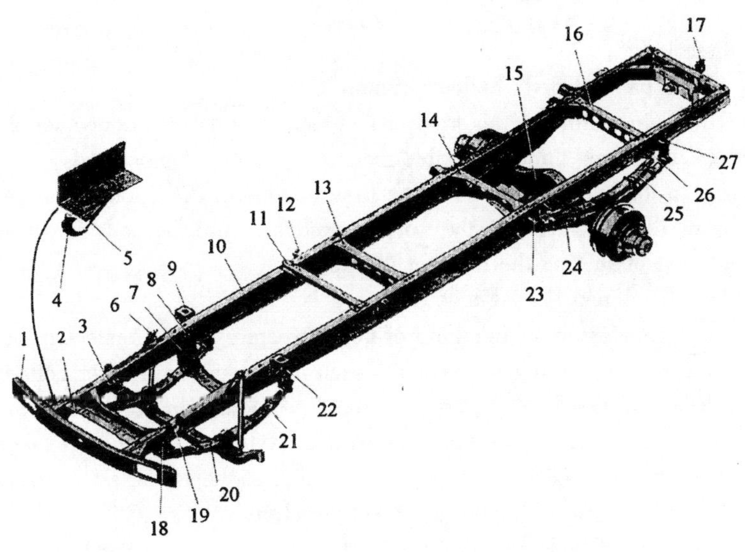

Fig. 3-34 A Typical Truck Frame

1-bumper [6]; 2-front cross member (radiator support); 3-bracket of engine front mounting [7]; 4-trailing hook [8]; 5-spring lock of hook; 6-bracket of shock absorber; 7-cross member of engine rear mounting; 8-bracket of engine rear mounting; 9-bracket of cab front mounting [9]; 10-side rail; 11-cross member of cab rear mounting; 12-platform [10] front bracket; 13-central cross member (central bearing support of propeller shaft); 14-front cross member of rear leaf spring; 15-rear axle; 16-rear cross member of rear leaf spring; 17-tow hook [11]; 18-front bracket of front leaf spring; 19-bracket of steering gear; 20-front axle; 21-front leaf spring; 22-rear bracket of front leaf spring; 23-front bracket of rear leaf spring; 24-rear main spring; 25-auxiliary spring [12]; 26-bracket of auxiliary spring; 27-rear bracket of rear leaf spring

to the structure formed by longitudinal, lateral, vertical support elements and panels welded on them. Most of the bus bodies have evident frame structure, but cars and truck cabs do not. Body shell also includes isolation layers of noise, heat and vibration and coatings of anti-corrosion and sealing.

According to the way of load carrying[3], body shells can be classified into three kinds:

(1) Separated Body-Frame Structure[4]

The main feature of this kind of body structure is the connection of the body and the frame through flexible mountings such as rubber pads or springs. In this case the frame is the base to support the whole motor vehicle and bears all the loads from the working systems. And the body is not taken into account of sharing the loads of the frame.

(2) Combined Body-Frame Structure[5]

The main feature of this kind of body structure is the connection of the body and the frame through stiff joints such as welded, riveted or bolted connections. In this case the frame is the base to support all the systems and bears most part of the loads from the working systems. The body is taken into account of helping the frame and sharing a part of the loads.

(3) Integrated or Monocoque Body Structure[6]

This kind of body structure has no frame. In this case the body is the base to install all the systems and bears all the loads from them.

In order to get rid of the rather heavy frame, almost all the cars and most of the buses choose the integrated body structure. Because the cab occupies only a small part of the whole length of the truck, it is impossible to use integrated body structure. For those motor vehicles without a complete body framework (such as convertibles[7]) it is difficult to choose integrated body structure. Some of the local made buses always use the combined body-frame structure because the chassis (together with the frame) and the body are made by different manufacturers and it is easier to weld them together.

Fig. 3-35 is a typical integrated body shell of a family car. After careful consideration the structural parts are grouped together by flanged edge or lap welding in a particular order[8]. At last the body shell is made up by rear floor assembly, left and right side panel assembly, front floor and cowl assembly and roof assembly[9] to form a perfect space structure.

The body shell of separate body-frame structure is similar to that of the integrated body structure. Their differences are: the former is weaker, panel thickness and structural section size[23] are smaller. Besides, the latter has a front end structure welded by left and right front side rails, left and right

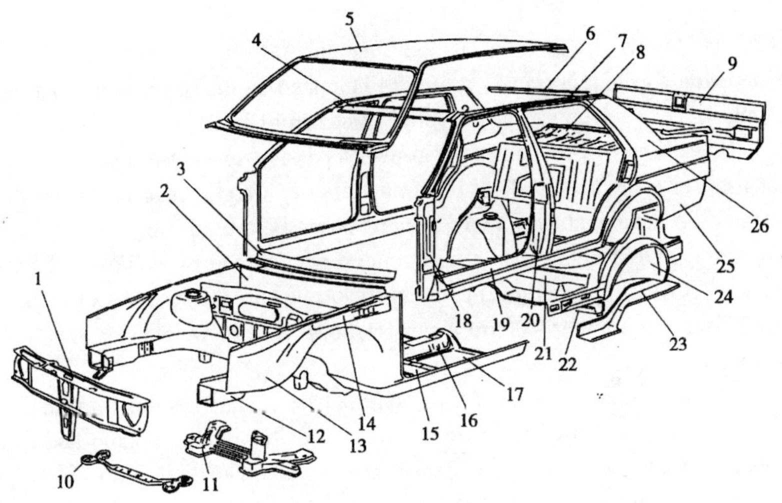

Fig. 3-35 Typical Integrated Body Shell of a Family Car

1-radiator support; 2-dash board (fire wall) [10]*; 3-cowl upper panel* [11]*; 4-front windshield frame upper brace* [12]*; 5-roof; 6-rear windshield upper brace; 7-roof rail* [13]*;8-package tray panel* [14]*; 9-rear end panel* [15]*; 10-front cross member; 11-sub-frame; 12-front side rail* [16]*; 13-front fender apron* [17]*; 14-fender apron reinforced brace; 15-front seat cross member; 16-floor tunnel* [18]*; 17-front floor; 18-front pillar* [19] *(A-pillar); 19-rocker panel (side sill)* [20]*; 20-center pillar (B-pillar); 21-rear floor; 22-rear floor cross member; 23-rear side rail; 24-rear wheel house panel* [21]*; 25-rear fender (quarter panel)*[22]*; 26-rear pillar (C-pillar)*

front fender aprons and radiator support, but the former has not.

Almost all the truck cabs belong to the separate body-frame structure and are connected to the frame through three or four elastic mountings. The structural sections, the formation of panels and the manufacturing process of the cab are much similar to those of the car body but are simpler than those of the latter.

Most of the buses look like the shape of regular square boxes, therefore have a complete body framework. On the early days of the history, the bus body was formed by the special body manufacturer and installed on a readymade[24] chassis frame, therefore belonged to the separate body-frame structure. The advantage of this kind of structure is the possibility of installing different bus bodies on a given chassis frame. Because the body is not used to share the loads of the frame, heavy weight must be the remarkable disadvantage. Many modern buses belong to the integrated body structure. The structure has a truss underbody instead of a thick and heavy frame[25]. All the structural members including the skin panels share the load and affect one another to form a perfect body of light weight and high stiffness.

Motor vehicle body of normal control type[26] has several front end panels welded or bolted together to provide shelter for the engine and front wheels. Front end panels of a typical car are given in Fig. 3-36. The upper panel of radiator support 3, left lamp support 6, right lamp support 4, left fender apron 9 and right fender apron 2 with their reinforcements[27] 5, 8, 10, 11 and 15 are welded together to form a strong base of the front end. The bottom of the base is welded to the front cross member and the front side rails of the underbody and the rear of the base is welded to the dash board of the body shell. The left and right fenders 7 and 1 are installed to the base through some screws and are easy to take off when they are damaged in the collision accident. The engine hood[28] consists of the outer panel 14 and the inner panel 13 and is fixed to the dash board by two hinges 12. The front of the hood is locked to the upper panel of the radiator support through a safety latch[29].

本节注释：[1]车身壳体；[2]车前板制件；[3]承载方式；[4]非承载式车身(车身车架分开式结构)；[5]半承载式车身(车身车架结合式结构)；[6]承载式车身(整体式车身结构)；[7]敞篷汽车；[8]经过慎密的考虑后，采用翻边或搭接的焊接方式将构件按一定的顺序组装。[9]后地板总成、左右侧围总成，前地板和前围总成以及顶盖总成；[10]前围板；[11]前围上盖板；[12]前风窗框上横梁；[13]上边梁；[14]包裹架；[15]后围板；[16]前纵梁；[17]前档泥板；[18]地板通道；[19]前立柱(A柱)；[20]门槛；[21]后轮罩；[22]后翼板；[23]结构断面尺寸；[24]现成的；[25]这种结构具有一个桁架式底板以取代粗大笨重的车架；[26]长头式；[27]加强件；[28]发动机罩；[29]发动机罩安全锁钩。

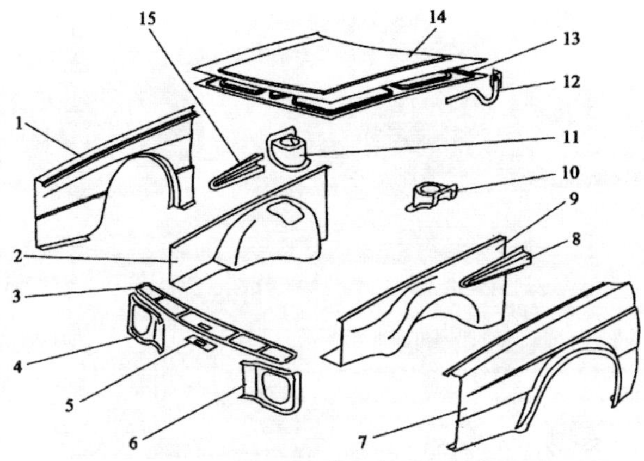

Fig. 3-36 Front End Panels of a Typical Car

1-right fender; 2-right fender apron; 3-upper panel of radiator support; 4-right lamp support; 5-reinforced panel of engine latch; 6-left lamp support; 7-left fender; 8-upper reinforced brace of left fender apron; 9-left fender apron; 10-reinforced seat of left suspension upper mounting; 11-reinforced seat of right suspension upper mounting; 12-engine hood hinge; 13- inner panel of engine hood; 14-outer panel of engine hood; 15-upper reinforced brace of right fender apron

3.4.2 *DOORS, WINDOWS, THEIR ACCESSORIES AND SEALING*

Door is an important assembly of body. Fig. 3-37 shows types of doors sorted by their opening ways. The front-hinged door[1] is safe and widely used because it can be closed by head-on air pressure as the motor vehicle is running. The rear-hinged door[2] is quite rare because it is not safe and can be opened by head-on air pressure if it is not locked surely. The up-hinged door[3] is widely used as the back door (also called "hatch back") of the car or the light bus, and sometimes it is used in low motor vehicles. The sliding door[4] is widely used in the body sidewall. Its outstanding advantage is the possibility to open fully when the distance between the sidewall and the obstacle is rather small. The folding door[5] and the outside swinging door[6] are widely used in medium and large buses.

Fig. 3-38 shows the structural components of a car door. Door inside

Fig. 3-37 Door Types

1-rear-hinged door; 2-front-hinged door; 3-up-hinged door; 4-sliding door; 5-folding door; 6-outside swinging door

panel 4 is the support base for all the components and parts including window glass 3, its guide channels[7] and window regulator[8], door lock 6 and its inside handle 8, door hinge 19, door check[9] 17 and door inside trim board[10] 7. In new car models, there are some control buttons such as 10, 11, 14, 15 and 18 on the driver's door inside trim board. The door outside panel 1 is also mounted on the door inside panel, and the door lock outside handle 5 is mounted on the door outside panel.

Curved glass is usually used to make the front and rear windshields of the motor vehicle because of its beautiful shape and good visibility. The windshield of most modern cars is stuck on the window frame by special glue. For natural ventilation, the side window can be regulated up and down or fore and aft. There are sealing strips between the regulated window and its guide channels. Some of the side windows are smoked colored[14] and have heat isolation layer to prevent the interior from hot sunshine and to make the interior atmosphere gentle and comfortable. In the bus of perfect ventilation, heating and air-conditioning, the side windows cannot be opened to improve

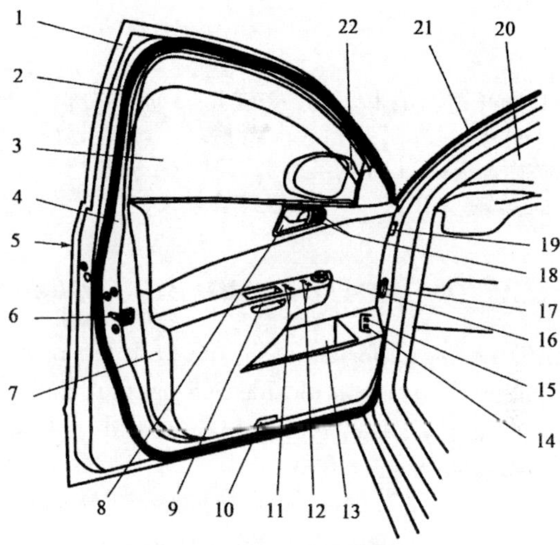

Fig. 3-38 Components of the Driver's Door

1-door outside panel; 2-door weather strip [11]; 3-window glass; 4-door inside panel; 5-door lock outside handle; 6-door lock; 7-door inside trim board; 8-door lock inside handle; 9-door pull [12]; 10-illuminating light; 11-window regulating buttons of rear doors; 12-window regulating buttons of front doors; 13-document pocket; 14- control button of deck lid lock [13]; 15- control button of fuel tank lock; 16-adjusting button of exterior rear view mirror; 17-door check; 18-central control buttons of four door locks; 19-door hinge; 20-front windshield; 21-weather strip of front windshield; 22-exterior rear view mirror

sealing performance.

In modern cars, sunroof[15] becomes more and more popular. When the sunroof and other windows open, the body interior opens to the outside environment and is similar to a convertible body[16] to let the passengers enjoy the warm sunshine and fresh air in wonderful seasons. The sunroof not only can increase interior illumination, but also is an effective structure of natural ventilation. According to different requirements, the sunroof can partially or fully open or close to provide an excellent function of all weather

body structure.

本节注释:[1]顺开式车门; [2]逆开式车门; [3]上掀式车门; [4]滑移式车门; [5]折叠式车门; [6]外摆式车门; [7]导轨、导槽; [8]玻璃升降器; [9]车门限位器; [10]车门内护板或内饰板; [11]密封条; [12]门拉手; [13]行李箱盖锁; [14]指茶色玻璃; [15]太阳车顶或遮阳顶窗; [16]敞篷式车身。

3.4.3 *VENTILATION, HEATING AND AIR-CONDITIONING*

Ventilation is necessary for taking in the fresh air to the interior and driving the air polluted by carbon dioxide and harmful emission from the engine outside. In cold weather, the fresh air should be heated to provide the interior with suitable temperature.

The operation principle of the heating system is to heat the air flowing through a radiator and to conduct it to the interior. The radiator is connected with the engine cooling system and heat comes from the engine cooling water.

The main principle of the refrigeration cycle[1] goes like this: the first step, to lower the pressure so as to make the refrigerant[2] change from liquid to gas, i. e. to evaporate and absorb heat; the second step, to increase pressure and to cool the refrigerant so as to make it reduce[3] to the original liquid state, i. e. to condense and disperse heat.

Fig. 3-39 shows a combined installation of ventilation, heating and air-conditioning. Under the pressure of the compressor 4 driven by the engine crankshaft through a V-belt, the circulation path of the refrigerant (expressed by thin arrows) is as follows: The first step, it flows from the storage tank[4] 2 through the expansion valve[5] 7 which lowers its pressure and increases its volume to become gas state, and then the refrigerant evaporates in the evaporator[6] 12 and absorbs heat, i. e. lowers the temperature of the surrounding air. The second step, the refrigerant from the evaporator flows through the compressor 4 to increase pressure, goes through the condenser[7] 3 in front of the engine radiator to cool up, i. e. to reduce to liquid state, and returns to the storage tank 2. Under the action of the blower 10, fresh air comes from the air duct 1 into the system, and then flows from the filter

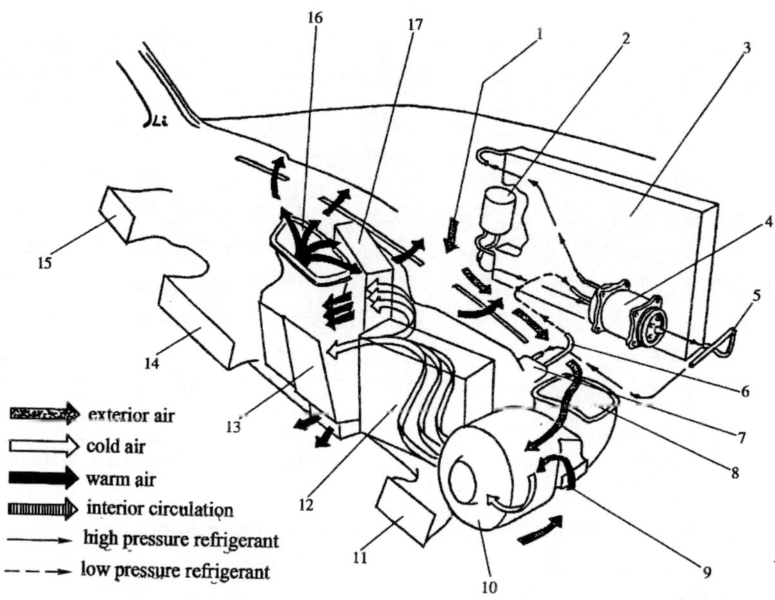

Fig. 3-39 Combination Appliance of Ventilation, Heating and Air-conditioning of a Typical Car

1-air duct; 2-storage tank; 3-condenser; 4-compressor; 5-high pressure pipe; 6-sucking pipe; 7-expansion valve; 8-filter port; 9-inlet port for interior circulation; 10-blower; 11-right outlet; 12-evaporator; 13-distribution box; 14-central outlet; 15-left outlet; 16-defrosting outlet port; 17-radiator

port[8] 8 through the evaporator 12 and the radiator 17 to the distribution box[9] 13. In a cold season, cooling water of the engine can be conducted to the radiator 17 to heat the air. The distribution box can lead the warm air through the outlet port[10] 16 to the windshield for defrosting[11] or through the outlets 11, 14 and 15 to warm the interior. The blower 10 can also let the interior air enter the system through the inlet port 9 to form an interior circulation. When both the heating and the refrigerating systems stop working, the fan 10 can also make the outside air flow through the interior and then conduct it outside to form compulsory ventilation[12].

本节注释：[1]制冷循环；[2]制冷工质；[3]还原；[4]贮液罐；[5]膨胀阀；[6]蒸发器；[7]冷凝器；[8]过滤口；[9]分配箱；[10]出口；[11]除霜；[12]强制通风。

本章参考文献

3.1 陈家瑞. 汽车构造 上、下册 第五版. 北京:人民交通出版社, 2006

3.2 细川武志. 魏朗 译. 汽车构造图册. 北京:人民交通出版社, 2005

3.3 黄余平. 汽车构造教学图解. 北京:人民交通出版社. ,2005

3.4 蒋兴阁. 中外汽车构造图册 发动机分册(一). 长春:吉林科学技术出版社, 1995

3.5 孙存真,王占歧. 中外汽车构造图册 底盘分册(一). 长春:吉林科学技术出版社, 1995

3.6 J. E. Duffy. Modern Automotive Technology. The Goodheart-Willcox Company Inc, 1994

3.7 Tom Newton. How Cars Work. Black Apple Press, 1999

3.8 Don Knowles, Jack Erjavec. Automotive Engine Performance. Delmar Publishers, 2000

3.9 Don Knowles, Jack Erjavec. Manual Transmission and Transaxles. Delmar Publishers, 2000

3.10 Don Knowles, Jack Erjavec. Automotive Suspension and Steering system. Delmar Publishers, 2000

CHAPTER FOUR
OPERATION OF MOTOR VEHICLE

4.1 BASIC OPERATION PRINCIPLE

In order to make a motor vehicle run, two requirements must be met: enough traction force or traction pulling to overcome various resistant forces and enough adhesion between wheels and ground to ensure maximum traction for the motor vehicle[1].

4.1.1 *REQUIREMENT FOR TRACTION*

Resistant forces include rolling resistance, air resistance and gradient resistance[2]. Rolling resistance is caused by tire deformation and road surface deformation; air resistance is caused by the interaction between the motor vehicle and the surrounding air; gradient resistance is caused by the component of the gravity of the motor vehicle along the direction of the slope surface[3].

Engine power is transmitted through the transmission system to the road wheel, resulting in a force F_0 acting on the ground at the contact area between the wheel and the ground. At the same time the ground exerts to the motor vehicle a reaction force F_t equal to F_0 and in the opposite direction (Fig. 4-1). F_t is called the traction force to make the motor vehicle move.

Motion of the motor vehicle is a complicated process of interaction between the traction force and the resistant forces. As the traction force is greater than the sum of the resistances, the motor vehicle moves from still to start, or increases speed (accelerates). With the increase of speed, air resistance increases quickly until the sum of resistances equals to the traction force, which results in new balance at a higher constant speed. As the

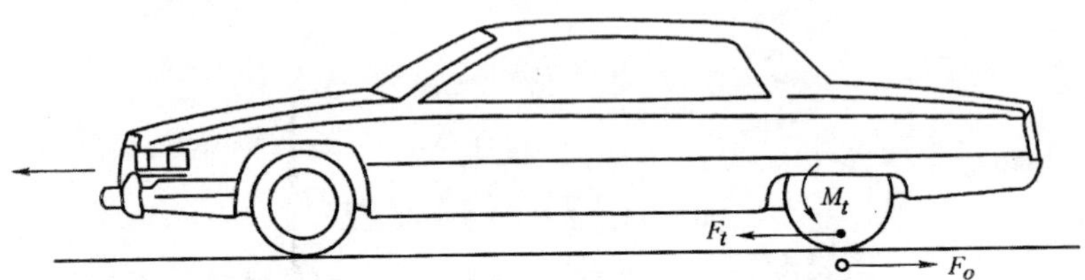

Fig. 4-1 The Cause of Traction force

This figure describes F_t *and* F_0 *acting on different objects, but actually they lie on the same straight line.*

traction force is less than the sum of the resistances, the motor vehicle decreases speed (decelerates), and even stops. To maintain the motion of the vehicle, the driver needs to increase the engine output or to shift a lower gear[4] to obtain more traction force.

4.1.2 *REQUIREMENT FOR ADHESION*

The maximum traction force depends on the maximum engine torque and the lowest gear on the one hand; and the maximum traction force is limited by the adhesion between the tire and the ground on the other hand.

When the motor vehicle is moving on a dry and hard road surface, adhesion depends on the magnitude of the friction force between the tire and the road surface. According to the principle of common physics, when a normal pressure force[5] is given, there must be a maximum amount of static friction between two objects. As the drive force becomes greater than this maximum amount, two objects begin to slide from each other. The same reason applies to the motion of the motor vehicle, as the traction force becomes grater than the maximum static friction force between the tire and the road surface, the road wheel begins to skid and spin. Therefore, on the even, dry and hard road surface, the maximum traction force developed by the motor vehicle cannot be grater than the maximum static friction force between the tire and the road surface.

When the motor vehicle is moving on the soft soil, adhesion depends not only on friction between the tire and the soil, but also on the tire projections pressing into and grabbing the soil[6]. Skid occurs only when both the friction becomes less and the grabbed soil is cut off.

Adhesion is defined by two factors: friction between tire and ground surface and interaction between tire projections and grabbed soil. The maximum resistance determined by adhesion against skid of tire is called adhesive force, which is a limitation of the maximum traction force developed by the motor vehicle. The magnitude of adhesive force depends on the normal pressure force acting on the drive wheels (called the adhesive gravity, i. e. that part of distribution of the whole motor vehicle gravity to the drive axle[7]), and also depends on the conditions of the tire and the ground surface. On muddy and snowy roads, the adhesive force is much lower than that on the dry and hard road surface, thus skid is easier to occur. The reason is that the mud and snow are rather easy to cut off and also too wet to maintain high friction. The vehicle has to slow down and even stop because traction force is limited by too small adhesive force.

There are some effective ways to increase adhesive force, such as to use tires of high crossing performance pattern[8], to install anti-slip chain on the tire[9], and to choose all wheel drive (AWD) vehicle. The AWD vehicle can use the whole vehicle gravity as adhesive gravity which is greater than that of the part wheel drive vehicle because the latter can only use the part of the whole vehicle gravity distributed to the drive axle[10].

两节注释：[1]为了使汽车行驶,必须满足两个先决条件:第一,汽车必须发出足够的驱动力以克服各种阻力;第二,在车轮和地面之间必须有足够的附着性能以保证汽车发挥最大的驱动性能;[2]阻力包括滚动阻力、空气阻力和坡道阻力。[3]汽车重力沿坡面方向的分力；[4]换入较低的档位；[5]正压力；[6]压入和抓住土壤的轮胎凸起部位；[7]称为附着重力,亦即全车重力分配到驱动桥那部分；[8]高通过性花纹的轮胎；[9]在轮胎上安装防滑链；[10]全轮驱动车辆可利用全车重力作为附着重力,它大于部分车轮驱动的车辆的附着重力,因为后者仅能利用全车重力分配到驱动桥那部分。

4.2 VEHICLE PERFORMANCES

Operation performances are some targets to evaluate how much the motor vehicle can meet the requirements in practical use. Operation performances include traction performance, fuel economy, braking performance, handling stability, ride and comfort[1], crossing performance, safety, reliability and durability. Because of the variety of practical use, the requirements for various motor vehicles are different from each other. For example, a popular family car emphasizes the requirement for fuel economy while a racing car emphasizes the requirement for traction performance and fuel economy is less important. Therefore, to evaluate a particular type of motor vehicle, various factors concerned must be considered comprehensively and dialectically.

4.2.1 *TRACTION PERFORMANCE*

Traction performance of a motor vehicle can be evaluated by three targets, i. e. maximum velocity, acceleration time and maximum gradient ability[2].

Maximum velocity is the highest speed developed by the motor vehicle on horizontal, dry and smooth road surface covered by asphalt or cement. It can be determined by engine revolving speed, transmission ratio and radius of the road wheel. To a particular road design, important parameters such as continuous velocity and maximum velocity should be given.

Acceleration ability of the motor vehicle is usually measured by the acceleration time from still to a particular velocity (for example 100km/h) or to a particular driving distance (for example 400m). Good acceleration ability means the motor vehicle has good overtaking ability[3], i. e. good maneuverability[4] in crowded traffic flow. This target has great influence on the average operation velocity[5].

Gradient ability is measured by the greatest slope for the motor vehicle to overcome when shifting to the lowest gear and on good road surface. It should not be less than 30% (16.7°) for common motor vehicles, and even more for all wheel drive vehicles in various road conditions.

两节注释：[1]平顺性和舒适性；[2]最大爬坡能力；[3]超车能力；[4]机动性；[5]平均行驶速度。

4.2.2 *FUEL ECONOMY*

Fuel economy is evaluated by fuel consumption in a given mileage, or driving mileage in a given amount of fuel. The evaluation target in China is how many liters of fuel has been consumed in the mileage of 100km (L/100km), in the United States it is how many miles the motor vehicle can drive in one gallon of fuel consumption (MPG).

Fuel economy of a motor vehicle depends on both internal factors and external factors. Internal factors refer to the structure and the parameters of the motor vehicle itself such as a high fuel efficiency engine, a transmission system matching the engine perfectly, light weight and low air resistance. External factors refer to road and traffic conditions, weather and the driver's skill.

Because various factors may affect fuel economy, test methods of fuel consumption are quite different from each other. There are fuel consumption at a given constant velocity on horizontal, straight and good road surface, average fuel consumption in city traffic situation and combined fuel consumption in various road conditions.

4.2.3 *BRAKING PERFORMANCE*

Braking performance is evaluated by three targets, i.e. braking effect, braking constancy and directional stability of braking[1].

Braking effect is measured by braking distance (m) or braking deceleration (m/s^2) at a given initial speed on horizontal and good road surface. For example, according to the regulation issued by the National Traffic Administration, with a given initial speed of 30km/h braking distance should not be longer than 6 m for any cars, 7 m for any light trucks and 8 m for any medium-sized trucks. Braking performance is much concerned with the structure of components and parts in the braking system, and also the structure of tires.

Braking constancy means whether braking effect can be maintained during serious braking process. Serious braking at high speed or continuous braking while going down a long slope may result in overheating of the brake parts, sometimes more than 600℃ due to serious friction. This phenomenon is called fading of braking effect or heat fading. High quality friction material, improvement of brake structure and cooling method are helpful to increase braking constancy. By good ventilation, braking constancy of disc brake[2] is better than drum brake[3].

Directional stability of braking means the ability to keep the correct direction without yaw, side slip or even loss of steering control during the braking process. If a motor vehicle lost its directional stability, accidents such as crash, driving out of the road or falling down the cliff would happen.

As the motor vehicle is braking, the rolling speed of road wheel would slow down gradually and might stop revolving (lock[4]). Because of inertia, the motor vehicle continues to move forward and the wheels begin to slide. If the front wheels locked, the motor vehicle would lose steering control; and if the rear wheels locked, side slip would occur. As the traction force is equal to the adhesive force, the wheel begins to slide, or in other words, as the traction force is equal to the adhesive force, the wheel stops rolling and starts to lock. It is evident that wheel lock has great influence on directional stability of braking. In order to avoid wheel lock, a special electronic anti-lock device needs to be incorporated into the braking system and this system is called the anti-lock braking system (ABS)[5].

本节注释：[1]制动效能,制动效能的恒定性和制动时的方向稳定性；[2]盘式制动器；[3]鼓式制动器；[4]抱死；[5]防抱死制动系统。

4.2.4 *HANDLING STABILITY*

Handling stability includes two aspects, i. e. the stability of the motor vehicle to follow the direction given by the driver and the stability for the motor vehicle to keep from the interference[2] of various external forces.

Handling stability is very complicated. There are quite a lot interfering factors such as centrifugal force, lateral slop, side wind, evasive sharp steer[1] and different adhesion of tires. The structure and parameters of the motor vehicle such as the structure of the steering system, wheel alignment[2], the structure of the suspension, the structure of tire and the overall parameters also have effect on handling stability. Therefore, during the motor vehicle design process, comprehensive study to interfering factors concerned and careful selection of structural parameters should be given to obtain perfect handling stability.

本节注释：[1]避险急转弯；[2]车轮定位。

4.2.5 *RIDE AND COMFORT*[1]

Ride quality refers to the ability of a motor vehicle to isolate vibration caused by uneven road. Vibration stimulated by uneven road would lead to fatigue[2] of driver, less comfort of passengers and damage of goods, and also shorten the life of the components of the motor vehicle. Elastic tire, suspension system and seat cushion[3] of the motor vehicle can isolate the vibration to a small range to meet the requirements for comfort.

Except ride quality, the requirements for comfort also consist of isolation of noise, ventilation[4], control of interior temperature and moisture[5], etc (see table 4-1).

Comfortable Factors and Their Limits Table 4-1

Factors	Comfortable	Uncomfortable	Harmful
Deceleration(m/s^2)	0~3	3~4	>4
Vibration (cm)	0.2~2	2~15	>15
Noise (dB)	45~65	65~120	>120
Hot (℃)	22~27	27~43	>43
Cold (℃)	18~15	15~0	<0
Moisture (%)	70~30	30~15	<15
Ventilation (m^3/min)	0.6~0.35	0.35~0.14	<0.14
CO Concentration[6] (%)	0~0.01	0.01~0.03	>0.03
CO_2 Concentration (%)	0.03~3	3~10	>10

本节注释：[1]平顺性和舒适性；[2]疲劳；[3]坐垫；[4]通风；[5]湿度；[6]浓度。

4.2.6 *CROSSING PERFORMANCE*

Crossing performance or off-road performance is the ability to cross bad roads and to overcome obstacles (such as steep slope, stage[1] and trench[2]) under certain payload and at a given speed. Vehicles driving through battlefield, forest and mine yard require high crossing performance. When those vehicles are on the soft terrain[3], rolling resistance is much greater and adhesive force is much smaller than on the dry and hard road surface. Therefore, the motor vehicle should be provided with special structure to meet the two requirements mentioned before, for example, more powerful engine, all wheel drive, low gear in the transfer case, low air pressure and wide profile tires[4].

Geometric parameters of the motor vehicle should meet the requirement to cross irregular terrain without blockage at its front end, underbody and rear end (Fig. 4-2). The motor vehicle should have enough ground clearance[5] to straddle over road projections. Besides, the motor vehicle may be able to stride over the trench (Fig. 4-3).

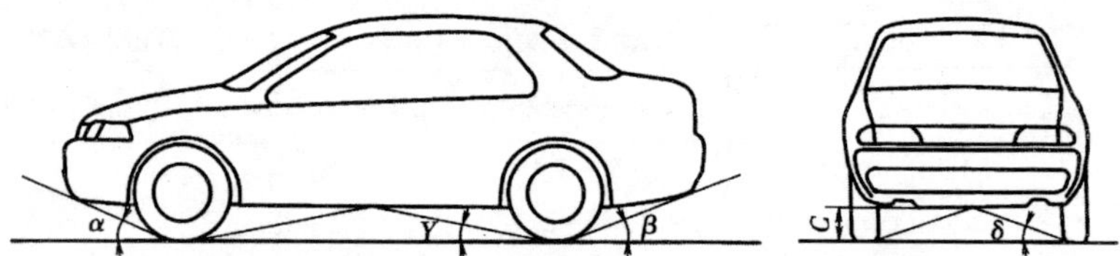

Fig. 4-2 Geometric Parameters of Crossing Performance

α-approach angle[6]; β-departure angle[7]; C-ground clearance; γ-longitudinal ramp angle[8]; δ-lateral ramp angle[9]

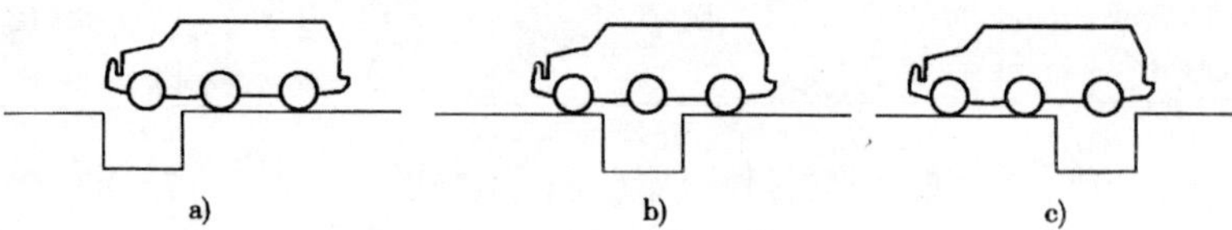

Fig. 4-3 Stride over the Trench

本节注释：[1]台阶；[2]壕沟；[3]松软地带；[4]低压和宽断面轮胎；[5]离地间隙；[6]接近角；[7]离去角；[8]纵向通过角；[9]横向通过角。

4.2.7 *SAFETY*

Safety means the ability to avoid collision accident and to lighten the accident result of people injury or reduce damage as the accident happens. Collision accident is the collision of the motor vehicle with pedestrians, non-motor vehicles, obstacles or other motor vehicles, including rollover of the motor vehicle itself or fire and burnt injury caused by fuel leakage.

Safety includes active safety and passive safety[1]. Active safety refers to the ability to avoid collision accident, such as braking performance, tire performance, steering agility, visibility and illumination. Passive safety refers to the ability to lighten the accident result of people injury or object damage as the accident happens, such as bumper[2], safety cage[3], safety seat belt, air bag and safety glass.

Figure 4-4 describes the impacts of the motor vehicle and the occupant in an accident. Figure a) describes the instant when the motor vehicle is just in contact with the barrier. At this moment the velocity of the motor vehicle has not decreased yet and the deformation of the motor vehicle is zero. Figure b) describes the moment when the velocity of the motor vehicle has reduced and the occupant still keeps moving at the original velocity because of inertia, which leads to relative displacement and relative velocity between the occupant and the motor vehicle. As the velocity of the motor vehicle continues to reduce, relative velocity becomes greater. Figure c) describes the moment when the occupant continues to rush forward and the relative displacement

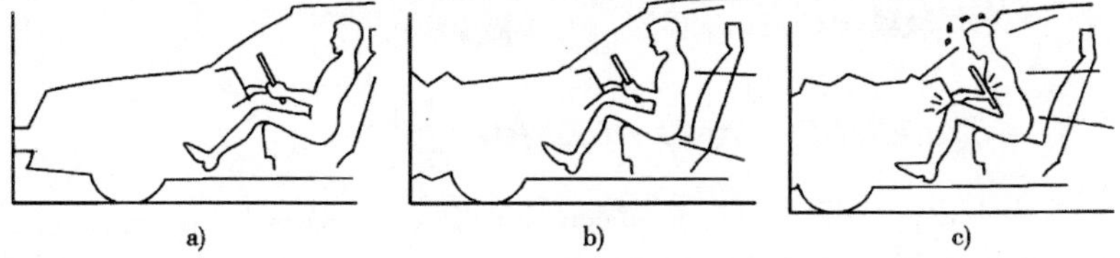

Fig. 4-4 Collision Process of the Motor vehicle and the Occupant

may be limited by the interior objects such as steering wheel, instrument panel[4] and windshield[5] in front. That is to say, another impact of the occupant with an interior object happens, it is called "the second impact[6]".

It is evident that the first impact (motor vehicle-barrier) does not cause injury directly, whereas the second impact (occupant-interior object) does. Because the distances between different parts of the occupant's body and different objects are not equal, the exact moments of the second impact do not happen at the same time. The second impact of knee-lower part of the instrument panel may happen first, and then the occupant's chest-steering wheel impact may happen, at last the occupant's head-windshield impact may happen. The later the second impact happens, the greater the relative velocity will be, which results in more serious injury.

The collision process of the motor vehicle is quite short, it is about 0.1 second from the beginning of the contact to the end of motor vehicle deformation. The process of the occupant's second impact is a little shorter than the process of the first impact. If the rush of the occupant's body was restrained by the safety seat belt, the second impact and injury would not happen. Air bag can inflate fully in a very short period of 0.05 second and fill the space between the occupant and the interior objects to provide soft cushion thus to prevent injury.

Automotive safety is a very important issue concerning the loss of life and property and therefore has gained serious attention of all the countries to spare no expense and effort[7] on the research work and effective measures.

本节注释：[1]主动安全性和被动安全性；[2]保险杠；[3]车身安全构架；[4]仪表板；[5]挡风玻璃；[6]第二次碰撞；[7]不惜金钱和人力。

4.2.8 *RELIABILITY AND DURABILITY*

Reliability is the ability to accomplish a required task in a certain period and under normal conditions. If a component of the motor vehicle does not meet the performance requirement in a certain period, it is called "trouble[1]" or "unreliable". Troubles include the following situations: out of order, instable operation or low performance. Troubles may consist of two types, i. e. suddenly happening and gradually fading[2]. Some of the troubles of the components can be removed by maintenance while others cannot and need to have parts replaced.

The period of a component from the beginning of normal work till discard is called the operation life[3]. It may be calculated by working period or operation mileage of the motor vehicle. Both definitions of reliability and durability are quite similar, but reliability concerns troubles whereas durability concerns operation life.

本节注释：[1]故障；[2]突发和渐衰；[3]使用寿命。

4.3 MOTORING[1]

A driver must understand the motor vehicle very well. The simplest way is to read the operation manual[2] carefully. Even for a driver of rich experiences, it is advisable to review the operation manual again and again, not to lay it aside.

4.3.1 *CONTROLS AND GUAGES*

When you sit at the driver's position, the first thing in contact with may be the steering wheel to determine the direction of the motor vehicle. On the right side of the steering wheel is the shifting lever to change speed and traction force of the motor vehicle. The nearby is the hand brake (parking brake) lever. There are three pedals in the foot well[3] of the floor, i. e. the accelerator on the right to control the engine speed (notice: Fully release of the accelerator does not mean that the fuel supply of the engine is off. It is only the situation of idle engine rotation or called idle fuel supply), the brake pedal at the center to slow down and stop the motor vehicle and the clutch pedal on the left to connect or disconnect the engine with the transmission system. The accelerator and the brake pedal are controlled by your right foot and the clutch pedal is controlled by your left foot.

The control switches include ignition and starting switch opened by the key, lamp switch, high beam (main beam) and low beam (dim light) switch of the headlamps[4], windshield wiper switch, windshield washer switch, switches for ventilation, heating and air conditioning, and switches for radio and CD player.

The gauges include speedometer and mileage recorder[5], tachometer[6], engine coolant temperature gauge (water temperature gauge)[7], fuel gauge, oil pressure gauge, ammeter, air pressure gauge (in the motor vehicle equipped with pneumatic braking system), etc. Almost every gauge has its warning signal light[8]. Besides, there are indicators such as turning indicator[9] and braking signal light (Fig. 4-5).

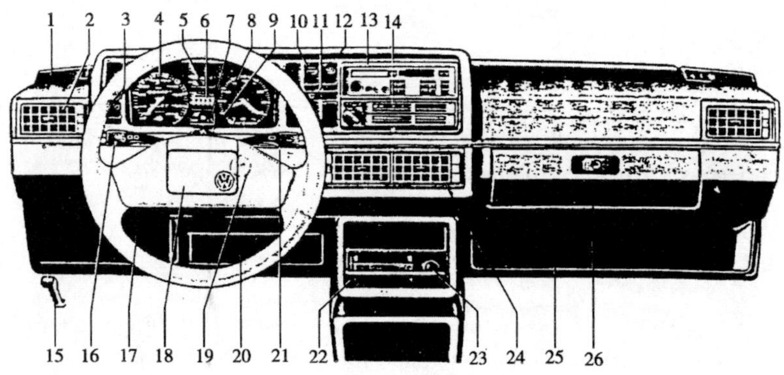

Fig. 4-5 Controls and Gauges

1-loud speaker lid[10]; 2-left outlet; 3-lamp switch and illumination adjustment button for instrument panel; 4-speedometer and mileage recorder; 5-engine coolant temperature gauge; 6-warning signal lights; 7-fuel gauge; 8-clock; 9-warning signal switch for emergency; 10-switch for rear window defrosting; 11-parking signal light; 12-switch for fog lamps[11]; 13-radio and CD player; 14-switches of air conditioner; 15-handle to open the engine hood; 16-handle of turning indicator and main-low beam change[12]; 17-fuse box; 18-horn button[13]; 19-ignition and starting switch (also lock of steering wheel); 20-document box; 21-windshield wiper and washer control lever; 22-ash tray[14]; 23-cigarette lighter; 24-middle outlet; 25-shelf; 26-glove box[15]

It is very important for a driver not only to get familiar with the positions and actions of the above controls and gauges, but also to understand their operation principle.

本节注释: [1]汽车驾驶; [2]行车手册(说明书); [3]搁脚空间; [4]前照灯远光和近光开关; [5]车速表和里程表; [6]发动机转速表; [7]发动机冷却液温度表(水温表); [8]警报信号灯; [9]转向指示灯; [10]扬声器盖; [11]雾灯开关; [12]远近光切换; [13]喇叭按钮; [14]烟灰盒; [15]手套箱(杂物箱)。

4.3.2 *PREPARATION FOR DRIVING*

Good preparations before driving are very important ways to avoid troubles and accidents. They are as follows.

(1) Check all the certificates[1] for driving.

A new motor vehicle needs to go to the traffic management department to examine its performances, and apply for a set of number plates[2] and operation certificates. A qualified driver should carry license[3].

(2) Check the condition and pressure of the tires.

This is an item very easy to be neglected. If the tire pressure is abnormal, lots of troubles would occur. It is especially important for high speed driving on freeway.

(3) Check the engine oil.

Pull out the dip stick[4] and check if the oil level is within the marks given on the stick.

(4) Check the coolant in the radiator and the opening of the shutter[5].

(5) Check the fuel gauge to see if the fuel is enough.

(6) Check to see if the braking system is effective.

(7) Check to see if the steering system is firm and reliable.

(8) Check to see if the lights and electric equipments are normal.

(9) Check to see if the controls are active and effective.

(10) Check the other necessary items given in the owner's operation manual.

本节注释: [1]证件; [2]汽车号牌; [3]随身携带驾驶执照; [4]机油尺; [5]百叶窗开度。

4.3.3 *BASIC OPERATIONS*

4.3.3.1 STARTING

Check the manual to learn how to best start the motor vehicle. Make sure the hand brake (parking brake) is on before you start the engine. If the vehicle has a manual transmission, it must be at neutral gear and in some vehicles the clutch must be depressed. For a vehicle equipped with an automatic transmission, you must put the shifting lever at "P" (parking).

Put the key into the ignition switch and turn it to start the engine. At the same time the right foot steps on the accelerator to supply the engine with fuel. In some of the new models, the eletro-magnetic key is plugged into the ignition switch to open the circuit and then it serves as a button to start and stop the engine[1]. As the engine begins to start and then runs stably, your right foot can be removed from the accelerator to let the engine run idly. Steps to start the motor vehicle are as follows.

(1) Release the hand brake

If the motor vehicle is on a slope, the hand brake should be released a little later to prevent the motor vehicle from slipping down the slope.

(2) The left foot presses the clutch pedal and the right hand puts the shifting lever at the first gear (at "D" or "L" for automatic transmission).

(3) Release the clutch pedal gradually and press the accelerator to increase the engine speed.

As the motor vehicle begins to move slowly, you need to make sure nobody or nothing nearby would be hit.

4.3.3.2 SHIFTING

The purpose of shifting is to change the speed and traction force of the motor vehicle to meet different road conditions. Every gear of the motor vehicle is suitable for a particular speed range only. To accelerate the motor vehicle needs to shift to a higher gear whereas to decelerate the motor vehicle needs to shift to a lower gear. Before shifting gear, the driver should step down the clutch pedal to disconnect the engine from the drive train. After a particular gear is selected, the driver should release the clutch pedal to connect the engine with the drive train again.

Table 4-2 indicates the speed ranges of a car at different gears. Its engine speed range is from the minimum (idle speed) 850 rpm to the maximum 5 000 rpm. Suppose the car needs to drive at 30 km/h, the engine speed is 4 053 rpm at the first gear, and 2 416, 1 613, 1 133 rpm at the second, third and fourth gear respectively. As we know, the faster the engine rotates, the more fuel it consumes. This is because more engine rotations mean more working cycles and every cycle needs fuel supply. Therefore, one of the operation rules is, at any time the driver must select a higher gear as possible.

Maximum and Minimum Speed at Different Gears of the Car Charade Table 4-2

	Engine speed (rpm)	Car Operation speed(km/h)			
		1st gear	2nd gear	3rd gear	4th gear
Maximum	5000	37.0	62.1	93.0	132.4
Minimum	850	6.3	10.6	15.8	22.5

The shifting lever of the automatic transmission normally has five positions. They are P-R-N-D-L which means parking, reverse gear, neutral gear, drive gear and low gear respectively. When the car is moving ahead, the shifting lever is at "D". In this situation, the automatic transmission is able to select a proper gear according to the information of speed, acceleration and accelerator position[2], and it is unnecessary for the driver to shift gear. In this case, the car has no clutch pedal (Notice: this does not mean the car has no clutch). Therefore, the new traffic regulation in China allows a handicap person without left leg to apply for a license[3].

两节注释：[1]在一些新车上，用电磁钥匙插入点火开关打开电路，然后它作为按钮去起动和关闭发动机。[2]根据速度、加速度和加速踏板的位置信息去选择合适的档位；[3]允许没有左腿的残疾人申请驾驶执照。

4.3.3.3 SPEEDING

Speeding[1] means to drive beyond the speed limit set by regulations or road signs[2]. The best way not to speed is to know how fast you are going.

Check the speedometer often. People are not very good at judging how fast they are going. It is easy to be traveling much faster than you think. This is especially true when you leave faster roads and drive on much slower roads.

Follow the speed limit signs. Pay attention to them for your safety.

本节注释：[1]超速；[2]道路标志。

4.3.3.4 COASTING

Coasting[1] is a way to save fuel. To put the shifting lever at neutral position and disconnect the engine may let the motor vehicle go ahead by its inertia or down the slope by the weight itself. At this time the driver frees the accelerator and the engine is at the idle situation possible to save fuel. If you pay attention to the operation manner of a bus driver, you would find the driver taking the measure of starting-accelerating (shifting to high gear)-coasting-braking-stopping between two bus stops[2]. The driver's operation manner forms lots of reciprocal working cycles from stop to stop.

For those motor vehicles equipped with pneumatic braking system, special attention should be paid to the air pressure gauge because the engine at idle speed for a long time would lead to low braking pressure and poor braking.

Never stop the engine during coasting because the air compressor and the pump of the power steering system (They are driven by the engine) do not work this time.

本节注释：[1](依靠惯性)滑行；[2]在两个公共汽车站之间采取起步—加速(换入高档)—滑行—制动—停车的措施。

4.3.3.5 BACKING[1]

Press down the clutch pedal and put the shifting lever at reverse position. If the motor vehicle is moving ahead, it is necessary to stop it before changing to the reverse gear.

When you back up, it is hard for you to see behind your vehicle. Try to do as little backing as possible. In a shopping center, try to find a parking space you can drive through, so you can drive forward when you leave. Where backing is necessary, here are some hints[2] that will help you back up your vehicle safely.

(1) Check behind your vehicle before you get in. Children or small objects behind the trunk[3] cannot be seen from the driver's seat.

(2) Place your right arm on the back of the seat and turn around so that you can look directly through the rear window. Do not depend on your interior or exterior mirrors as you can not see directly behind your vehicle.

(3) Back slowly, your vehicle is much harder to steer while you are backing.

(4) Whenever possible use a person outside the vehicle to help you back up.

本节注释: [1]倒车; [2]提示; [3]汽车行李箱。

4.3.3.6 STEERING

The correct posture[1] to handle the steering wheel is both hands should be on opposite sides of the steering wheel, i. e. left hand between 8 and 10 o'clock and right hand between 2 and 4 o'clock positions. The driver would feel some resistance on the steering wheel transmitted from the road. It is called "road sense"[2] which makes the driver feel safe, i. e. feel not losing control.

Look well down the road and on both sides of the road, not just at the road in front of your vehicle. Watch at traffic situations where you will need to steer or slow before you get to them. This way, you have time to steer smoothly and safely.

Before turning a sharp corner, signal the turning indicator and then turn the steering wheel using the "hand-over-hand" technique. Usually you should decelerate your motor vehicle (shift to a lower gear) while on a sharp steer. When you complete a turn, straighten out the steering wheel by hand.

本节注释: [1]姿势; [2]路感。

4.3.3.7 BRAKING, STOPPING AND PARKING

As your right foot presses the braking pedal, your motor vehicle would slow down or stop. According to the requirement of deceleration, your foot may press lightly or hard.

You must check behind your vehicle whenever you slow down. This is very important when you slow down quickly or at points where a driver would not expect you to slow down, such as private driveways or parking spaces. Be alert so that you know well ahead of time when you will have to stop, otherwise you will make it harder[1] for drivers behind you to stop without hitting you.

Try to avoid panic stops[2] by seeing events well in advance. It is important to keep proper space with the other motor vehicles[3]. Stopping suddenly is dangerous, which could cause the road wheels to lock and slip. Especially on a slippery icy surface, you should be very careful and should not press the pedal hard to prevent the road wheels from locking.

When you want to stop your motor vehicle temporarily, you should signal the right turning indicator and then slow down, drive to the roadside and stop.

When you want to park you motor vehicle, you should let it stop at a proper place and shift to neutral gear first, then pull the hand brake on, and shut down the engine at last. Check the doors and windows if they are closed and locked reliably before you leave.

本节注释：[1]不易判定；[2]慌忙停车；[3]与其他汽车保持恰当距离。

4.3.3.8 SEEING WELL

Most of what you do in driving depends on what you see. To be a good driver, you need to see well. The reason of a large percent of crashes is failing to see what is happening. You must look down the road, to the sides and behind your vehicle and be alert for unexpected events. At night and at other times when it is hard to see, you must use your headlights.

You must be alert to what is going on around you. Many crashes occur because drivers do not pay enough attention to their driving. Do not take your eyes off the road for more than a few seconds at anytime. If you need to look at a map, pull safely off the road before you try to look at it. Do not try to read the map while you are driving. In many crashes with motorcycles, bicycles and pedestrians, drivers reported that they looked but did not see them.

Don't make phone call when the vehicle is in motion. Even with "hands free" equipment, conversing on a phone or radio takes your attention away from driving and can cause you to be less likely to notice a dangerous situation. According to the statistic figure, phone call accidents are more than alcohol accidents[1]. Do not drive with head or earphones that cover or go in both ears. These are illegal[2] and make it hard to hear emergency horns or sirens.

Look to the sides-As other vehicles or pedestrians may cross or enter your path anytime, you should look to the sides to make sure no one is coming. This is especially true at intersections and railroad crossings.

Intersections[3] are any place where traffic merges or crosses. They include cross streets, side streets, driveways and shopping center or parking lot entrances. Before you enter an intersection, look to both the left and right for approaching vehicles and/or crossing pedestrians. If stopped, look to both the left and right just before you start moving. Look across the intersection before you start moving to make sure the path is clear all the way through the intersection and you will not block it if you have to stop.

As you approach any railroad crossing slow down and look up and down the tracks to make sure a train is not coming. Do not assume that a train is not coming even if you have never seen one at that crossing before. Assuming that a train is not coming is one of the leading causes of fatalities at railroad crossings. Make sure there is room for your vehicle on the far side before you cross the tracks[4].

Besides watching traffic ahead of you, you must check traffic behind you. You need to check more often when traffic is heavy. This is the only way you will know if someone is following too closely or coming up too fast and will give you time to do something about it. It is very important to look for vehicles behind you when you change lanes, slow down, back up or drive down long or steep hill.

本节注释：[1]打电话出事故比饮酒出事故更多；[2]非法的；[3]道路交叉；[4]通过轨道之前要判定较远的一侧有足够的车位。

4.3.3.9 CHANGING LANES

Whenever you want to change lanes[1], you must check that there are no vehicles in the lane you want to enter. This means you must check for traffic to the side and behind your vehicle before you change lanes. Changing lanes includes changing from one lane to another, merging onto a roadway from an entrance ramp[2] and entering the roadway from the curb[3] or shoulder[4]. When changing lanes, you should:

(1) Look in your outside and inside rear-view mirrors. Make sure there are no vehicles in the lane you want to enter. Make sure that nobody is about to pass you.

(2) Look over your shoulder in the direction you plan to move. Be sure no one is near the rear corners of your vehicle. These areas are called "blind spots"[5] because you cannot see them through your mirrors. You must turn your head and look to see vehicles in your blind spot.

(3) Check quickly. Do not take your eyes off the road ahead for more than an instant. Traffic ahead of you could stop suddenly while you are checking traffic to the sides, rear or over your shoulder. Also, use your mirrors to check traffic while you are preparing to change lanes, merge or pull onto the roadway. This way you can keep an eye on vehicles ahead of you at the same time.

(4) Check over your shoulder just before you change lanes for traffic in your blind spot. Remember to look several times if you need to.

(5) Check the far lane. Be sure to check the far lane, if there is one, as someone in that lane may be planning to move into the same lane you want to enter.

(6) Check for other road users. Remember that there are other road users such as motorcycles, bicycles and pedestrians that are harder to see than cars and trucks. Be especially alert when you are entering the roadway from the curb or driveway.

When going down a long or steep hill—Check your mirrors when you are going down hills or mountains. Vehicles often build up speed going down a steep grade. Be alert for large trucks and buses that may be going too fast.

本节注释：[1]更换车道；[2]匝道(立体交叉上下两层之间的连接道)；[3]路缘,人行道；[4]路肩；[5]盲点。

4.3.3.10 NIGHT DRIVING

It is much harder to see at night. Here are some hints you can do that will help you see better:

(1) Use your high beams whenever there are no oncoming vehicles. High beams let you see twice as far as low beams. It is important to use high beams on unfamiliar roads, in construction areas or where there may be people along the side of the road.

(2) Dim your high beams[1] whenever you come within about an one-block distance of an oncoming vehicle.

(3) Use your low beams when following another vehicle or when in heavy traffic[2].

(4) Use the low beams in fog or when it is snowing or raining hard. Light from high beams will reflect back[3], causing glare[4] and making it more difficult to see ahead. Some vehicles have fog lights that you should also use under these conditions.

(5) Do not drive at any time with only your parking lights on. Parking lights are for parking only.

If a vehicle comes toward you with high beams on, flash your headlights quickly a couple of times. If the driver fails to dim the lights, look toward the right side of the road. This will keep you from being blinded by the other vehicle's headlights and allow you to see enough of the edge of the road to stay on course[5]. Do not try to "get back" at the other driver by keeping your bright lights on. If you do, both of you may be blinded.

本节注释: [1]将远光变暗(变近光); [2]繁忙的交通; [3]反射回来; [4]刺眼; [5]留在原线路。

4.4 MAINTENANCE AND REPAIR

The purpose of maintenance[1] and repair is to keep the motor vehicle in good working conditions. Maintenance is to check and adjust the parts or assemblies whereas repair is to mend or replace the damaged or worn parts[2]. After a considerable period of driving, the motor vehicle may have some problems such as looseness, dirt, corrosion, deformation, wear, damage, etc. If small problems would not be dealt with earlier, they might result in serious problems. That is, a motor vehicle owner pays a little now for maintenance is better than he/she will pay much more tomorrow for repair. It is advisable for the owner to read the operation manual carefully and to visit service shops by the maintenance instructions given. A good service shop for the customers to go is the so called "4S dealer", i. e. sales, service, spare part and second hand[3], where they can have their motor vehicles maintained and repaired.

本节注释：[1]维护，保养；[2]损坏或磨损的零件；[3]所谓4S 经营商，即销售、售后服务、配件和二手货。

4.4.1 *MAINTENANCE*

Kinds of maintenances are classified by operation mileage of the motor vehicle. They are routine maintenance, 1 500 km maintenance or running-in maintenance[1], 7 500 km maintenance, 15 000 km maintenance and 30 000 km maintenance.

4.4.1.1 ROUTINE MAINTENANCE

Routine maintenance is daily work done by the driver. It includes cleaning the exterior, checking the safety devices, tightening the parts, inflating the tires[2], filling the motor vehicle with fuel, oil and liquids, etc.

两节注释：[1]磨合、走合保养；[2]使轮胎充气。

4.4.1.2 1 500 KM MAINTENANCE

Running-in means that the contact surfaces of two fitting parts[1] should rub each other for a considerable period to get rid of their sharpness or roughness. Then, the parts will match very well and run smoothly. Length of the running-in period is given by operation mileage, that is, from the beginning (0 km) to 1 500 km.

During this period, the motor vehicle should not work hard, i. e. not to operate at full speed, under full load or on bad roads.

After this period, it is advisable to send the motor vehicle to the service shop. Checking and adjusting are required, especially changing lubricating oil contaminated by abrasive particles[2].

本节注释：[1]两个相互配合的零件；[2]被磨出的微粒污染的润滑油。

4.4.1.3 7 500 AND 15 000 KM MAINTENANCES

Table 4-3 briefly describes the service items for a typical car after every 7 500 km and every 15 000 km operation mileage.

Service Items for a Typical Car Table 4-3

	○	(1) Check performance of lights, warning signals, indicators and horn.
	○	(2) Check windshield wiping and washing devices, fill with washing liquid if necessary.
	○	(3) Check clutch pedal stroke[1], adjust it if necessary.
△	○	(4) Check liquid of storage battery, fill it with distilled water[2] if necessary.
△	○	(5) Eye-check engine leakage (fuel, oil, lubricant, refrigerant[3]).
△	○	(6) Check coolant in the cooling system, adjust it and measure pressure if necessary.
	○	(7) Check V-belt tension[4], replace it if necessary.
	○	(8) Replace spark plugs, instead of long effect spark plugs[5] after 30 000 km.
	○	(9) Clean exterior of air-cleaner and replace cartridge[6].
		(10) Replace fuel filter.
△	○	(11) Lubricate door hinges and seat belts.
△	○	(12) Change engine oil.
	○	(13) Replace oil filter cartridge.
	○	(14) Check leakage and damage of corrugated pipe[7].
	○	(15) Eye-check leakage and damage of braking system.
		(16) Check damage of underbody protection layer[8].
	○	(17) Check damage of exhaust system.
	○	(18) Check clearance in tie rod ball joint and its firmness[9] and check dust cover.
	○	(19) Check damage of dust cover of propeller shaft.

△	○	(20) Eye-check leakage and damage of gear box.
△	○	(21) Check thickness of brake lining[10].
	○	(22) Check parking brake, adjust it if necessary.
	○	(23) Check depth of tire pattern[11] and tire pressure, inflate it if necessary.
	○	(24) Check level and quality of braking oil.
	○	(25) Check tightening torque of wheel bolt[12].
	○	(26) Check oil volume of central hydraulic system, fill it if necessary.
	○	(27) Check oil volume of power steering system, fill it if necessary, replace filter net.
	○	(28) Check ignition phase (advanced or retarded)[13], adjust it if necessary.
	○	(29) Check idle speed, adjust it if necessary.
	○	(30) Check carbon monoxide content[14] at engine idle speed, adjust it if necessary.
	○	(31) Check beam of headlamp[15], adjust it if necessary.
	○	(32) Drive car and check braking, parking, shifting, steering and air conditioning.
1 △ expresses the service item after every 7 500 km. 2 ○ expresses the service item after every 15 000 km. 3 All the above items should be carried out after every 30 000 km. 4 Every two years change braking oil and check brake warning system and braking booster[16].		

本节注释：[1]离合器踏板行程；[2]蒸馏水；[3]制冷工质；[4]V传动带的张紧度；[5]长效火花塞；[6]滤芯；[7]波纹管；[8]车身下部的保护涂层；[9]横拉杆球头的间隙及其紧固度；[10]制动衬片的厚度；[11]轮胎花纹的深度；[12]车轮螺栓的拧紧力矩；[13]点火相位(提前或滞后)；[14]一氧化碳成分；[15]前照灯的灯光；[16]制动助力器。

4.4.1.4 OTHER MAINTENANCES

After every 30 000 km, all the service items in table 4-3 should be carried out, including replacing fuel filter and checking damage of underbody protection layer. After every 45 000 km, clean the oil sump of the automatic transmission[1] and fill it with new oil.

Body services include cleaning, waxing, polishing and making-up with paint[2].

Tire services include inflation, dynamic balance[3], tire rotation[4], etc. If depth of the tire pattern is less than 1 mm, it should be replaced.

本节注释：[1]自动变速器的油底壳；[2]上蜡、抛光和补漆；[3]动平衡；[4]轮胎换位。

4.4.2 *REPAIR*

4.4.2.1 INSPECTION AND DIAGONOSIS[1]

After a long term operation, performances or technical conditions of a motor vehicle would not be as good as before. Parts would not fit each other very well because their shape has changed out of abrasion[2], heavy load and damage. Accident might happen if not to take measure to solve such problems. The best way is to send the motor vehicle to the service shop.

Before repair, inspection and diagnosis are needed. Inspection is to examine the performances of the motor vehicle by the measurement of some particular parameters[3]. Diagnosis is to analyze the inspection result and to find out the exact trouble cause.

Because of harsh working conditions such as high speed, heavy load and high temperature, engine parts are more likely to have problems and need to be checked firstly. Table 4-4 shows the parameters of the engine necessary for inspection and diagnosis.

Besides, components such as braking system, tire and steering system are also important because they are much concerned with safety. According to the statistic figures in table 4-5 given by German authority[19] of traffic management, 31.6% collision accidents come from tire ineffectiveness[20], 57.1% from braking system ineffectiveness and 3.8% from steering system ineffectiveness. These three items make up more than 90% accidents. Undoubtedly, they should be taken seriously[21] during processes of inspection and diagnosis.

Engine Parameters for Inspection and Diagnosis Table 4-4

Engine component	Parameters for inspection and diagnosis
Engine overall	Power Fuel consumption Concentration of harmful emissions[4] Vacuum in intake manifold[5]
Group of cylinder and piston	Pressure in cylinder during compression stoke Volume of gas leaking to crankcase[6] Ratio of gas leakage from cylinder[7] Abnormal sound in engine Engine oil consumption
Group of crankshaft and connecting-rod	Oil pressure in main oil passage[8] Abnormal sound in engine
Valve timing mechanism	Valve ascent[9] Timing phases[10]
Fuel supply system and exhaust cleaning device	Fuel consumption Air-fuel ratio[11] Concentration of harmful emissions
Lubrication system	Oil pressure Light penetration of oil[12] Amount of metal particles in oil
Cooling system	Coolant temperature Temperature difference between entrance and exit of radiator[13] Tension of fan V-belt[14]
Ignition system	Voltage and current in primary side circuit Voltage-drop in primary side circuit[15] Capacity of condenser[16] Closed angle and overlap angle of contact points[17] Ignition voltage Advanced angle of ignition Oscillogram of primary side voltage[18] Oscillogram of secondary side voltage
Starting system	Starting voltage Starting current Starting speed

Percentages of Collision Accidents Caused by Component Ineffectiveness Table 4-5

Component	Percentage of collision accidents
Tire	31.6
Braking system	57.1
Steering system	3.8
Front axle	0
Rear axle	1.4
Electric equipment	1.0
Body	1.0
Transmission system	3.4
Others	0.7

In a modern service shop there are quite a lot of advanced instruments and equipments for inspection and diagnosis. Being controlled by computers, they are intelligent[22], accurate, efficient and convenient. Many of them can examine the motor vehicle directly without disassembling any component off. The test results can be displayed, stored or printed. Some of the examples are engine universal inspector[23], engine leakage inspector, engine stethoscope[24], ignition timing gun[25], harmful emission analyzer, tester of braking performances[26], four wheel aligner[27], etc.

本节注释：[1]检测与诊断；[2]磨损；[3]测量一些规定的参数；[4]有害排放物浓度；[5]进气歧管真空度；[6]曲轴箱串气量；[7]气缸漏气率；[8]主油道机油压力；[9]气门升程；[10]配气相位；[11]空燃比；[12]机油透光率；[13]散热器进出口温差；[14]风扇的V传动带张紧度；[15]一次侧电路电压降；[16]电容容量；[17]触点的闭合角和重叠角；[18]一次侧电压示波图；[19]权威部门；[20]失效；[21]应予重视；[22]智能化的；[23]发动机综合检测仪；[24]发动机听诊器；[25]点火正时枪；[26]制动性能试验台；[27]四轮定位仪。

4.4.2.2 DISASSEMBLY AND REPAIR

Normally a motor vehicle can run the mileage of more than 100 thousand km without any repair. Some motor vehicles are even better and can run the mileage of more than 300 thousand km. Unfortunately, some motor vehicles can not due to early damage such as collision.

Repair includes running repair[1] and capital repair, also called major repair or heavy repair[2]. Running repair aims at a few particular components or parts which are detected ineffective, whereas capital repair aims at the whole motor vehicle which should be disassembled totally and many problems should be solved. Evidently, whether a motor vehicle or a component needs repair or not, can be determined by inspection and diagnosis.

Before repair, the component should be taken off from the motor vehicle and disassembled into parts. To take off some parts, special tools may be needed, for example, a spark plug socket[3], a bearing puller[4], a valve spring compressor[5], etc.

Oil or grease should be removed from the surfaces of the parts by a special kind of detergent. The main contents of this kind of detergent are sodium carbonate and sodium phosphorate[6]. To remove carbon deposit[7], a benzene-alcohol detergent[8] is used whereas to remove scale deposit[9], water solution with phosphoric acid[10] is used.

Some of the worn or damaged parts (normally small parts) can be replaced whereas some other parts are not simply discarded because they are rather expensive. The cylinder block is a typical example.

During capital repair, the cylinders should be bored and grinded[11] because they are not round out of abrasion, heat and corrosion after long term operation. That is, the diameter of the cylinder has been enlarged a little bit. In order to match the larger cylinder, a new piston of larger diameter is needed to replace the old one. In many motor vehicles, it may be cheaper to replace the old set of cylinder sleeves[12] with a new set than the cost of boring and grinding operations.

The body shell[13] may be another typical example. It is more expensive than the cylinder block. After a collision accident, the body shell may deform seriously. Its shape can be corrected by hydraulic pulling or hammering[14]. Some of the damaged panels may be cut off and replaced by the new ones through welding[15].

本节注释：[1]小修；[2]大修；[3]火花塞套筒；[4]轴承起拔器；[5]气门弹簧钳；[6]碳酸钠和磷酸钠；[7]积碳；[8]苯－酒精洗涤剂；[9]水垢；[10]含有磷酸的水溶液；[11]镗孔和磨削；[12]气缸套；[13]车身壳体；[14]液压拉拔或锤打；

[15]焊接。

4.5 TRANSPORTATION AND ROAD

4.5.1 *TRANSPORTATION*

Transportation is to carry persons and goods from one place to another by land, water, air and pipeline. Modern transportation tools include trains on the railway, automobiles on the highway, ships on water and airplanes in the air. Pipeline transportation is a kind of special transportation to make long distant transfer of flows, mainly oil and natural gas, through pipeline under pressure difference between two places. Compared with modern transportation tools, the quantity transported by man-powered or animal-powered vehicles and wind-driven ships is much less and therefore is not taken into account in the national statistic figures of transportation.

Transportation plays a very important role in national economy. With the development of economic construction and the change of social intercourse[1], requirements of the society for transportation quantity become more and more crucial, which leads to the rapid development of transportation. For a long time in China, transportation has not been enough to meet the requirements of the national economy and therefore it is so called a "bottle neck industry[2]" which jams the flow of economy. But on the other hand, development of transportation will make all trades and professions[3] thrive and it is so called the "leading industry[4]" to drive the national economy.

Evidently, transportation of a country is a huge and very complicated system. It needs to be considered from many aspects by carefully planning land, water and air routes and precisely arranging the amount of various transportation means.

For a long time in our country, the term "the great railway" is well-known, which means the quantity of railway transportation occupies the first place. However, from the national statistic figures in table 4-6, we can see that is not true. Quantity of railway transportation has reduced to the second place not only in transportation of people, but also goods. With the development of automotive industry and the improvement of highway network, quantity of highway transportation will keep on increasing and occupying the first place without doubt. Not only in China, but also in foreign countries, "the great railway" replaced by "the great highway" has become a truth.

Statistic Figures of China's Transportation in 2003 Table 4-6

Items / Ways	Transportation of Persons(%)		Transportation of Goods(%)	
	Quantity	Circulating Quantity[5]	Quantity	Circulating Quantity
Highway	91.1	54.5	77.1	14.0
Railway	7.1	36.5	12.3	30.2
Water	1.3	0.8	9.1	54.3
Airline	0.5	8.2	0.01	0.1
Pipeline	—	—	1.5	1.4
Total	100	100	100	100

本节注释：[1]社会交际；[2]瓶颈产业；[3]各行各业；[4]先导产业；[5]周转量。

4.5.2 *ROAD*

4.5.2.1 CLASSIFICATION OF ROADS

Road is the engineering facility for persons and vehicles to pass. Roads for motor vehicles have pavement and are classified into city roads, forest roads, factories and mines roads[1], country roads[2], etc.

Highway is the road to connect cities, villages and industrial bases. According to its traffic quantity and task, highway is graded into several technical classes. By the national standard, highway in China is graded into 5 classes, i. e. freeway[3], the first class, the second class, the third class and the fourth class. The highways served as traffic skeletons are called the arterial highways[4], and other highways of less importance are called feeder highways[5]. The highways of national political, economic and defensive importance are named the national trunk highways[6] or national highways[7].

The name of any national highway is expressed by a 3-digit figure. The first digit "1" refers to the highway centering at Beijing. The first digit "2" refers to the highway stretching from the south to the north (longitudinal direction). The first digit "3" refers to the highway stretching from the east to the west (lateral direction).

Fig. 4-6 is the cross section of a typical freeway, and its width is 26 m. It consists of a separator[8] of 4.5 m width and two carriage ways[9] of 7.5 m on each side. Every carriage way is formed by two lanes[10] of 3.75 m width. Outside the carriage way is the parking lane[11] of 2.5 m width, and outside the parking lane is the shoulder[12]. On each side of the separator and inside the shoulders, there are marginal strips[13] of 0.75 m respectively.

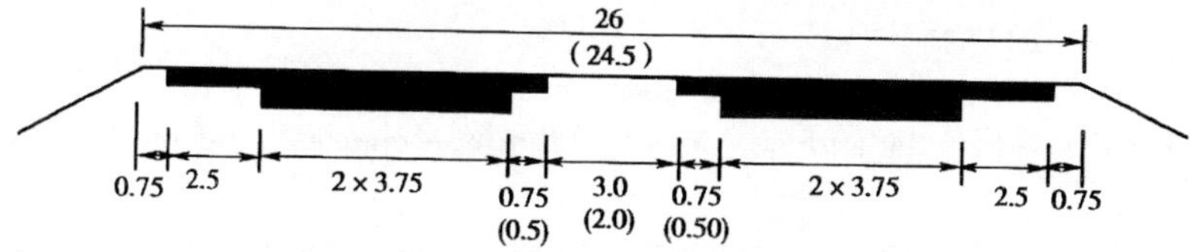

Fig. 4-6 Cross Section of Typical Freeway

The freeway or the first class highway is provided with 4 lanes, 1 separator and 2 parking lanes. The width of every part is determined by the following factors.

The width of a lane is 3.75 m on the plain terrain[14] and rolling terrain[15] (design speed [16] 120 or 100 km/h) or 3.5 m on the mountainous terrain[17] and the hilly terrain[18] (design speed 80 or 60 km/h). It is determined by the maximum width of the motor vehicle (the limit of 2.5 m by the national regulation) and the consideration of safety clearance between two motor vehicles at design speed.

The width of the separator is 4.5 m on the plain terrain and rolling terrain or 2.5 m on the mountainous terrain and the hilly terrain for the freeway. It is 3.5 m or 2.5 m respectively for the first class highway. It is determined by the safety clearance between two passing motor vehicles without influence on the driver's visual sensation.

The second class highway has no separator and no parking lane and is classified into two types. The first type is special for the operation of motor vehicles, and its width is 11 m on the plain terrain and the rolling terrain or 9 m on the mountainous terrain and hilly terrain. The second type is for ordinary use (mixed traffic[19]), and its width is 12 m or 8.5 m respectively.

The width of the third class highway is 8.5 m or 7.5 m respectively and the width of the fourth class highway is 6.5 m.

本节注释：[1]厂矿道路；[2]乡村道路；[3]高速公路(英国 motorway)；[4]干线公路；[5]支线公路；[6]国家干线公路；[7]国道；[8]分隔带；[9]行车道；[10]车道；[11]停车道；[12]路肩；[13]路缘带；[14]平原区域；[15]微丘区域；[16]计算行车速度(设计速度)；[17]山岭区域；[18]重丘区域；[19]混合交通。

4.5.2.2 ROAD PAVEMENT

The structural layers of the road pavement from the top to the bottom are composed by the surface course[1], the base course[2] and the bed course[3].

The surface course withstands the load of the vehicles and the corrosion of the natural factors. The top of the surface course is constructed by hard granular material[4] and combined materials[5] and therefore is called the wearing course[6]. Its function is to improve the rolling condition of the vehicle road wheels and to prevent the surface course from wear and thus to prolong the life of the surface course. The bottom of the surface course is so called the binder course[7] to link the surface course and the base course together and to decrease the influence of the cracks in the base course on the surface course.

The base course withstands the loads transferred from the surface course and evenly spreads the loads to the bed course and the lowest soil base[8].

Main functions of the bed course are to separate and drain water, to prevent the road from freezing and to improve the work condition of the base course.

According to the quality of the materials used on the surface course, road pavements are graded into four classes, i.e. the high type pavement[9], the sub-high type pavement[10], the intermediate type pavement[11] and the low type pavement[12].

The surface course of the high type pavement is made of cement concrete[13], bitumen concrete[14], regular block stones[15] or hot mixture of bitumen and broken stones (gravels)[16]. The surface course of the sub-high type pavement is made of bitumen filled with broken stones (gravels)[17], cold mixture of bitumen and broken stones (gravels)[18], semi-regular block stones[19], etc. The surface course of the intermediate type pavement is made of the combination of water (or mud) with broken stones (gravels)[20], irregular block stones[21], etc. The surface course of the low type pavement is made of granules[22] or mud strengthened by other materials[23].

The base course of the freeway or the first class highway is made of cement stable category[24], lime stable category[25], lime-industrial solid waste[26], bitumen mixture, etc. The base course of the highways under the second class can be made of the above materials, inlaid broken stones[27] or other proper local materials[28].

The bed course is usually made of water-stable rough granules[29] or other materials of stable category[30].

The freeway and the first class highway use the high type pavement. The second class highway uses the high type pavement or the sub-high type pavement. The third class highway uses the sub-high type pavement or the intermediate type pavement. The fourth class highway uses the intermediate type pavement or the low type pavement.

本节注释：[1]面层；[2]基层；[3]垫层；[4]坚硬的粒料；[5]结合料；[6]磨耗层；[7]联结层；[8]最底层土基；[9]高级路面；[10]次高级路面；[11]中级路面；[12]低级路面；[13]水泥混凝土；[14]石灰混凝土；[15]整齐石块；[16]热拌沥青和碎石(砾石)；[17]沥青灌碎石(砾石)；[18]冷拌沥青和碎石(砾石)；[19]半整齐石块；[20]水结或泥结碎石(砾石)；[21]不整齐石块；[22]粒料；[23]其他材料加固土壤；[24]水泥稳定类；[25]石灰稳定类；[26]石灰—工业废渣；[27]嵌入碎石；[28]其他适当的当地材料；[29]水稳定粗粒料；[30]其他稳定类材料。

4.5.2.3 ROAD INTERSECTION

A road intersection[1] refers to two or more than two roads to cut across each other at the same site. It includes the at-grade intersection[2] and the grade-separated junction[3]. On an at-grade intersection, passing of the motor vehicles on one road affects the passing on the other roads, which is easy to result in speed decrease, traffic accident and traffic jam. Therefore, it needs to be controlled by traffic lights[4]. Because the motor vehicles pass at different heights and do not affect each other, a grade-separated junction can increase speed and reduce traffic accident. It has many advantages but is not popular for its expensive cost.

Type and shape of road intersections may differ from each other. It is determined by traffic conditions and geographic environment, the common types may be cross intersection[5], T intersection and ring intersection[6]. Fig. 4-7 shows a clover-leaf junction[7], it has a grade-separated cross intersection linked by four loop ramps[8] and four outer oblique ramps[9]. A right turn needs to drive along the outer oblique ramp and a left turn needs to go through the cross intersection and then drive along the loop ramp.

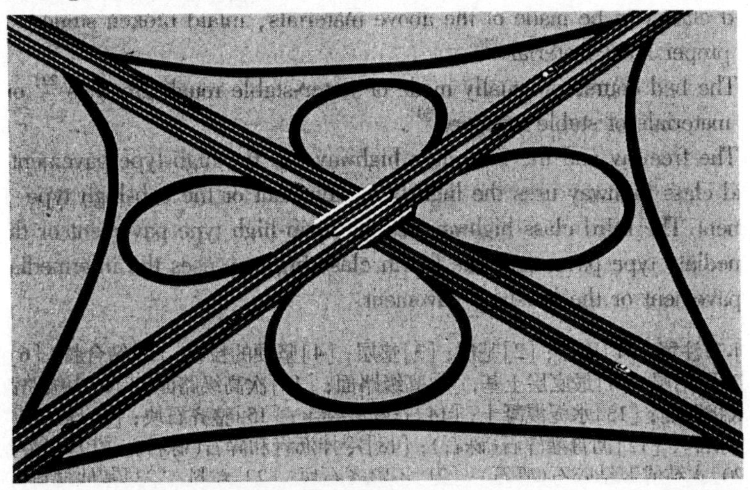

Fig. 4-7 Clover-Leaf Junction

本节注释:道路交叉; [2]平面交叉; [3]立体交叉; [4]交通红绿灯; [5]十字形交叉; [6]环形交叉; [7]首蓿叶形立体交叉; [8]环形匝道; [9]外侧斜叉匝道。

4.5.2.4 BRIDGE AND TUNNEL

Bridge is an engineering facility over a river, a lake, a valley or other obstacles. Many bridges have passed through quite long historic period and appeared in their glory[1]. The history of motor vehicle is not long, but influence of the bridges built for motor vehicles is much greater than that of the bridges in the long history because of their social effect, elegant appearance and skillful construction. For example, the United States is a country built up with perfect highway networks. There have been more then 500 thousand bridges for motor vehicles in this country.

Bridges vary in construction according to the gap they must span and their designed load. They may be classified into truss girder bridge[2], arch bridge[3], suspension bridge[4] and cable stayed bridge[5] (Fig. 4-8). Some famous examples are given in Table 4-7.

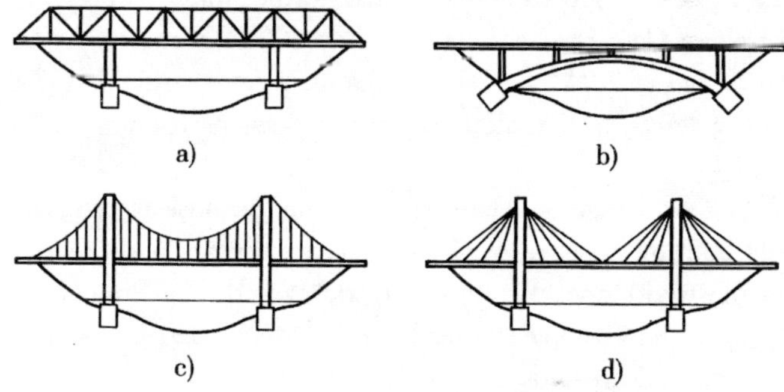

Fig. 4-8 Constructions of Bridges

a) truss girder bridge; b) arch bridge; c) suspension bridge; d) cable stayed bridge

Some Famous Construction Examples of Bridges Table 4-7

Construction	Examples	
	Foreign	Domestic
Truss girder bridge	Quebec Bridge (Canada)	Changjiang River Bridge at Nanjing
Arch bridge	Sydney Harbor Bridge (Australia)	Zhaozhou Bridge in Hebei
Suspension bridge	Golden Gate Bridge (US)	Chaoyang Bridge at Chongqing
Cable stayed bridge	Brotonne Bridge (France)	Huanghe River Bridge at Jinan

The typical truss girder bridge in China is the Changjiang River Bridge at Nanjing. It has 9 piers[6] and each stride extends 160 m[7]. The main bridge[8] is 1 570 m long. The upper grade is a highway of four lanes and the lower grade is a railway of two lanes. The grade of highway is 4 500 m long and its approach bridge[9] is made of hyperbolic arch structure[10].

The renowned Zhaozhou Bridge in Hebei Province[11] was a stone-arch bridge and was built in Sui Dynasty[12] 1 400 years ago. It is incredible that this bridge is still in use today. The Sydney Harbor Bridge[13] is not only a famous arch bridge, but also a beautiful landscape. Its main stride extends 503 m, the longest single arch steel bridge in the world.

The Golden Gate Bridge across the Bay of San Francisco[14] is a typical suspension bridge of 2 743 meters long. Its main stride extends 1 280.2 m between two pylons[15]. 70 years have passed since its opening to traffic[16] in 1937.

Cable stayed bridge is a later construction. Because of the advantages of light weight and low cost, a lot of cable stayed bridges have been built throughout the world since the end of World War II. The Brotonne Bridge in France[17] is a good example. Its main stride extends 320 m and is supported by single pylon and one-side cables[18] only.

Tunnel is a passage dug through the mountain, underground or underwater to link roads.

Between France and Italy, there is a world famous highway tunnel called the Mount Blanc Tunnel[19] dug through the highest mountain of Europe. It is 11.25 km long and 3500 m under the mountain peak. Both French and Italian engineering teams began their work from each side in 1959. They met in the tunnel 3 years later and the tunnel was finished and opened to traffic in 1965.

本节注释：[1]壮丽多姿；[2]桁架梁桥；[3]拱桥；[4]悬索桥；[5]斜张桥；[6]桥墩；[7]一跨的长度为 160 m；[8]正桥；[9]引桥；[10]双曲拱式结构；[11]河北省的赵州桥；[12]隋朝；[13]悉尼港口桥；[14]横跨圣佛朗西斯科湾的金门桥；[15]桥塔；[16]通车；[17]法国的布罗托内桥；[18]单桥塔和单面拉索；[19]勃朗峰隧道。

4.5.3 *ROAD TRANSPORTATION IN CHINA*

Before 1950s, there were only 81 000 km highway opening to traffic and only 51000 motor vehicles in use[1]. In that time, most of the highways were rugged and rough[2], i. e. intermediate or low type pavement.

Transportation and highway construction has been developing rapidly in recent years. By the end of 2005, more than 1.9 million km highway mileage including 41 000 km freeways were built in China and ranked the second place in the world (Table 4-8). Not only mileage, but also pavement quality had increased greatly.

World Top Five Countries of Freeway Mileage in 2005

Table 4-8

Rank	1	2	3	4	5
Country	United States	China	Canada	Germany	France
Mileage(km)	88 000	41 000	16 500	11 000	10 000

Advantages of freeway transportation are high operation speed (average 100 km/h for cars and 70 km/h for large and medium motor vehicles), high productivity[3] and low accident ratio (only 30% ~40% of that on common highways). In the developed countries, freeway mileage is only 0.3% ~1.7% of highway mileage, but consists of 10% ~25% of the total quantity of highway transportation. That is why China makes great effort to build freeways, annual growth of freeway mileage more than 4 000 km in recent years. In the next 30 years, freeway mileage will reach 85 000 km to connect all the large and medium cities including not only cities in the Mainland[4], but also Hong Kong, Macau, and cities in Taiwan.

本节注释: [1]汽车保有量; [2]崎岖不平; [3]生产率;[4]大陆

本章参考文献

4.1 余志生.汽车理论.北京:机械工业出版社, 1981

4.2 范立.汽车安全科学驾驶.北京:人民交通出版社.2004

4.3 关文达.轿车维修手册.北京:机械工业出版社,2000
4.4 交通部公路局.公路标准规范汇编.北京:人民交通出版社,2005
4.5 J. Y. Wong. Theory of Ground Vehicles. John Wiley Sons Inc. , 1978
4.6 Horsp Bauer. Automotive Handbook(Bosch)(4th Edition). Stuttgart: Robert Bosch GmbH, 1996
4.7 George A. Peters. Automotive Vehicle Safety. London, New York Taylor & Francis, 2002
4.8 Herbert L. Nichols, David A. Day. Moving the Earth. New York McGraw-Hill Professional, 2005
4.9 Michael Pollard. Roads and Tunnels. Belitha Press Ltd. , 1996

CHAPTER FIVE
DESIGN AND MANUFACTURE

5.1 DESIGN STUDIO

5.1.1 *DESIGN AND DESIGNER*

Design is a procedure for a designer to have a plan in mind and to express the idea by some means, such as drawing, description or model. This definition has two aspects, taking product design as an example: firstly, the designer should have a creative idea to shape a product; secondly, proper means should be taken, for example drawing and explanation, in order to allow the manufacturer understand the designer's idea.

The process of modern production is essentially different from that of handicraft production. The former is cooperative team work, whereas the latter is individual activity. That is, the craftsman runs the whole process of planning and making individually[1]. The craftsman's idea is not expressed to others and the product is made by the same person. The process of handicraft production does not have the second aspect mentioned above.

In order to increase the value of the product and to show wonderful skill, the craftsman would strive to choose precious material and finish work[2]. Such valuable products only serve for the rich but not for the common people. To our regret, for thousands of years in China's history, there had been numerous wonderful handicraft products, but they did not help people change their poverty and backwardness. It can be sure that industrialization is a broad way leading the country to be strong and prosperous. Design is an important part of modern industry and therefore a powerful support of China's development.

In modern production, design is the first step. It makes up only 10 percent of the total work in the product development and 5 percent of the total cost of the product, but has great influence on the success of the enterprise. Figure 5-1 is a famous chart "Whose shadow is the biggest?" introduced by Harvard University. It describes four factors (design, material, labor and overhead[3]) affecting product quality. Although the cost of design is a little, its influence is very critical.

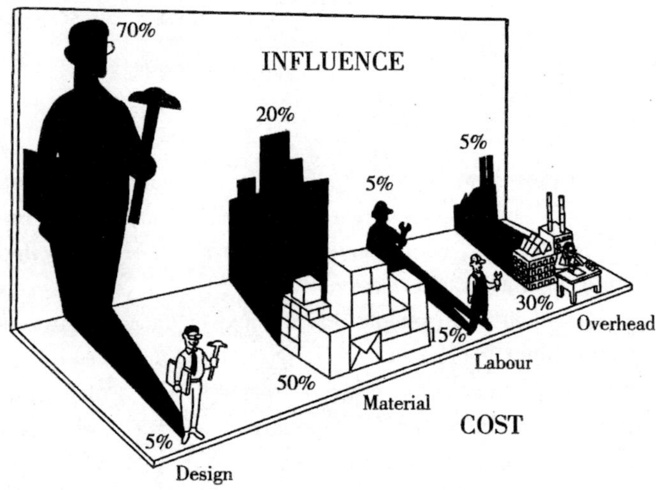

Fig. 5-1 Whose shadow is the biggest?

A designer is the executer of design. Two aspects could be concluded to show the designer's quality. A designer should be creative. To renew the old, the required quality of a good designer should be acute to observe, capable of discovering and breaking through and courageous to imagine and practice[4]. Imitation seems easy, but it may be regarded as incapable and poor[5]. Without active creation, the society would be dull and retarded. Without active creation, a product would not prevail in the serious market situation and an enterprise would fail and even go bankrupt. A designer should have comprehensive knowledge, i. e. good grasp of fundamentals and deep understanding of his/her specialty. All objects and things relate, affect and promote each other. Knowledge required for an automotive designer covers not only engineering science, but also social science such as aesthetics, management affairs and market business. It is evident that the CEO (Chief Executive Officer)[6], the chief designer and the department leaders should have comprehensive knowledge and experience. Even the current task of a young designer would involve many kinds of science and technology.

Motor vehicle is a very complicated product. Even the most experienced designer, it is impossible for one person to understand every detail in the motor vehicle and to undertake all the design processes. Therefore, the job should be assigned among different designers united in an effective working team. An excellent design means not only good quality of every designer, but also their cooperative team work.

本章注释：[1]手工匠人独自一人包揽计划与制作；[2]昂贵的材料和精工细作；[3]指行政管理；[4]为了推陈出新，一个优秀的设计师所应具备的素质是敏于观察，善于发现和突破，并且敢想敢干；[5]模仿别人似乎容易，但会被视为无能和可怜；[6]首席执行官。

5.1.2 *DESIGN PROCESS*

5.1.2.1 DEFINITION PHASE

Definition phase is the early period in the product design and development. To define an automotive product means to determine a particular type of motor vehicle and its specifications[1]. According to the requirement of a country or an enterprise, product development program[2] is released by the national administration or enterprise headquarters.

At first, feasibility analysis[3] should be carried out. According to customer investigation, market situation, technical potential, manufacturing analysis and cost accounting[4], prediction should be made to check whether the product is suitable and beneficial to the enterprise.

Then, a preliminary draft[5] should be presented by some drawings, calculations and selections of performances and technical parameters of the motor vehicle.

At last, a document of design task[6] should be issued. The document includes the type of the motor vehicle and its specifications, such as main dimensions, weight targets, performance targets and requirements for the assemblies. It should be approved by the national administration or the top leader of the enterprise and sent to the design department.

Production program and investment expenditure[7] should be considered carefully at the same time.

An important task of the early period in the product development is to analyze various influences and to make the goal and the work procedure clear. Otherwise, without careful investigation, discussion and study, blind production would lead to problems such as product incompetent, sluggish sales, overstock and manufacturing impediment[8], thus heavy loss of the company.

本节注释: [1]规格;[2]产品开发规划;[3]可行性分析;[4]用户调查、市场形势、技术潜力、制造分析、成本核算;[5]初步方案;[6]设计任务书;[7]生产纲领和投资费用;[8]产品缺乏竞争力、滞销、积压和生产停滞。

5.1.2.2 PROTOTYPE DEVELOPMENT PHASE

PACKAGE

Package[1] is to arrange the assemblies, occupants and goods at proper positions so as to make the assemblies match harmoniously, the occupants ride comfortably and the goods carried conveniently. In order to provide rational interrelation between various assemblies, it is necessary to have key dimensions controlled[2] (Fig. 5-2 and Table 5-1). They are called "hard points[3]". During this step, the key work is the sketch of package[4] to show the positions and the contours of the engine, the chassis assemblies, the driver, the occupants and the goods including their motion ranges (such as the wheel jounce/rebound[5] travels and rotation when steering). After this step, the key dimensions and basic contour of the motor vehicle[6] can be determined.

An enterprise may produce several series[19] of motor vehicles and a particular model is only a part of the general program of products[20].

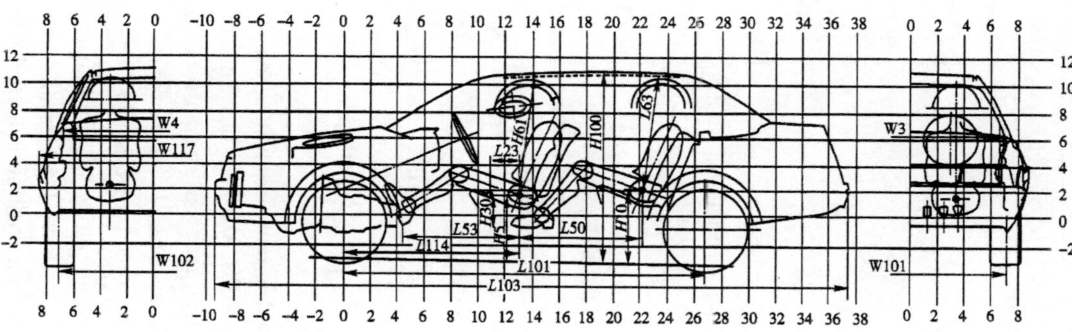

Fig. 5-2 Some Key Dimensions Necessary for Car Body Package (see Table 5-1)

Examples of Key Dimensions (mm) Table 5-1

Code *	Item	Audi A6	Santana 2000	Jetta
L103	Overall Length[7]	4886	4680	4385
L101	Wheelbase[8]	2850	2658	2471
W103	Overall width[9]	1810	1700	1695
W117	Body width	1776	1676	1682
H100	Overall height[10]	1451	1423	1424
W101	Front track[11]	1540	1414	1464
W102	Rear track	1569	1422	1446
L114	Front wheel center to *R* point	1329	1304	1297
L53	Horizontal distance from *R* point to heel point[12]	833	866	833
L50	Front seat *R* point to rear seat *R* point	940	904	735
L23	*H* point horizontal travel of front seat	193	216	223
H5	Front seat *R* point to ground	494	494	509
H10	Rear seat *R* point to ground	506	512	518
H30	Vertical distance from *R* point to heel point	267	289	228
H61	Effective head room[13] of front seat	999	977	967
H63	Effective head room of rear seat	960	967	946
W3	Shoulder room[14] of front seat	1427	1376	1365
W4	Shoulder room of rear seat	1415	1370	1364

* Defined by SAEJ 1100[15]

R point is the seating reference point[16] and *H* point is the hip point[17] of the 3D manikin[18].

Therefore many vehicle models have identical assemblies and parts. For example the light truck CA1020, the light bus CA6440 and the medium class car CA7220 are provided with the same engine series CA488. One of designers' responsibility is to cut cost, which means to use not so many blocks (called modules[21]) to construct as many types of motor vehicles as possible. They should be skillful at modular architecture[22], that is, select the suitable modules carefully, unite them together and make up a perfect product. For this reason, skillful package is a good way to increase the number of vehicle models and to make the enterprise profitable.

It is worth introducing the famous platform strategy of the firm

Volkswagen[23]. In this firm car models (nearly 4 million units annually[24]) are grouped on four platforms named A0, A, B and C/D. Motor vehicles on the same platform have a lot of identical modules and some different modules. Taking platform A as an example, it can derive various car models such as Audi A3, Golf, Bora, Seat and Skoda. [25] Every car model may choose different modules or sub-modules[26] to derive several variations. Variety of car models and variations can meet the requirement and personality of a particular customer, resulting in the flexible policy of "one to one salesmanship" [27].

Organization of a modern automotive corporation is somewhat like a pyramid[28]. At the top of the pyramid is the OEM (original equipment manufacturer) [29]. Beneath the top, there are a lot of suppliers divided into 4 tiers[30]. The first tier suppliers provide the OEM with modules, the second tier suppliers provide the first tier suppliers with sub-modules, the third tier suppliers provide the second tier suppliers with parts[31] and the fourth tier suppliers provide the third tier suppliers with raw materials. A good method called PIM (product information management) [32] is used to run the whole "pyramid". Therefore, such organization is the most economical and effective.

本节注释：[1]总布置、总体设计;[2]为了保证各个总成之间的合理相互关系，必须对一些重要尺寸加以控制。[3]硬点;[4]总布置图;[5]车轮上跳/回弹;[6]汽车的基本轮廓;[7]总长;[8]轴距;[9]总宽;[10]总高;[11]轮距;[12]踵点;[13]头部空间;[14]肩部空间;[15]美国汽车工程师协会(SAE)刊登规则和标准的期刊(Journal)第1100号中规定的代号;[16]座椅基准点；[17]胯点;[18]三维人体模型;[19]系列;[20]产品总纲领;[21]模块;[22]模块构筑法;[23]亟应推介大众汽车公司著名的平台战略;[24]每年近400万辆;[25]以A平台为例,它可衍生出多个车型如奥迪A3、高尔夫、宝莱、西雅特、斯柯达等。[26]分模块;[27]灵活的一对一营销策略;[28]金字塔;[29]原始设备制造商(此处指汽车总厂);[30]分为4个层次的许多供应商;[31]指零件;[32]产品信息管理。

STYLING

(1) Idea Sketch and Rendering

Idea sketch[1] and rendering[2] are based on the main dimensions and the basic contour of the motor vehicle given by package.

Idea sketch (Fig. 5-3) is the fast drawing to record the stylist's idea as a flash of inspiration[3]. In the early stage of styling, a great number of sketches are needed to show the creative ideas of the stylists. They should think actively and work hard. A stylist should draw at least 4 to 5 sketches within one hour and 30 to 40 sketches within one day. At the end of the step of the idea sketch, the stylist should conclude and select some good sketches for renderings.

Fig. 5-3 Idea Sketch

Idea sketch is informal whereas rendering is formal to show the elegant appearance of the motor vehicle. The word "formal" means a rendering should have correct proportion, regular perspective projection and perfect expression of texture[4]. Renderings may include exterior rendering (Fig. 5-4), interior rendering (Fig. 5-5) and partial rendering[5]. When a considerable number of renderings have been finished, they will be presented to the styling team for

Fig. 5-4 Exterior Rendering *Fig. 5-5 Interior Rendering*

discussion and for the next step of scale model[6].

本节注释: [1]构思草图;[2]彩色效果图;[3]灵感;[4]正确的比例、规范的透视投影和完美的质感表达;[5]室外效果图、室内效果图和局部效果图;[6]缩小比例模型。

(2) Scale Model

Scale model (Fig. 5-6) is the next step to express the styling idea. It is three dimensionally sensible[1] and therefore is more realistic[2] than two dimensional[3] rendering. Scale model is made of clay[4] attached on a frame work. The suitable proportion for a car scale model is 1:5, that is, one fifth of a real car. Clay is a greasy mixture and needs to be heated before it is attached on the framework. And then, the clay can be scraped and smoothed to meet the idea of the stylists.

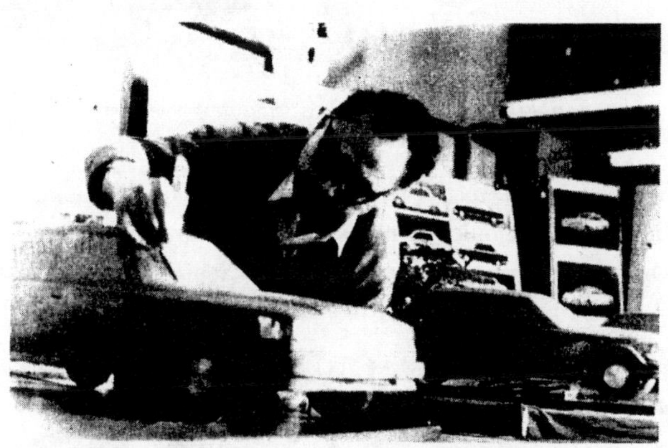

Fig. 5-6 Stylist is making a car scale model.

本节注释: [1]三维立体感觉的;[2]真实,逼真;[3]二维的;[4]造型泥,油泥。

(3) Styling Discussion and Selection[1]

As the styling step of scale model being completed, a meeting (Fig. 5-7) should be held to discuss and compare different presentations[2] made by every stylist. Every set of presentation includes one scale model and several renderings. Final conclusion should be summed up and focused on only one model, i. e. to select and determine the most suitable appearance or style of the motor vehicle. This model will play the role of the basis for the technical design.

Fig. 5-7 Styling Discussion and Selection

On the basis of the model determined by the final conclusion, aerodynamic model[3] should be made and tested in a wind tunnel[4], that is, to check whether its shape is aerodynamically reasonable. The test result will be fed back[5] to the styling department.

本节注释：[1]造型的讨论和选型；[2]方案展示；[3]空气动力试验模型；[4]风洞；[5]反馈。

(4) Tape Drawing

Tape drawing[1] (Fig. 5-8) is a full size[2] (1∶1) drawing of the whole body shape made by sticky tapes on a board which may show the contour of components and body curves. Data of the tape drawing come from enlargement of the curves on the scale model. The

Fig. 5-8 Tape Drawing

curves on the board should be checked to see whether they are satisfactory, if not, this tape can be taken off and stuck again.

Tape drawing is helpful to make the full size exterior and interior models[3].

本节注释: [1]胶带图;[2]全尺寸的(等大的);[3]全尺寸外部和内部模型。

(5) Full Size Rendering

Full size rendering[1] (Fig. 5-9) is attached to great importance in modern styling. Realistic sensation of a full size object is totally different from a scale object[2]. For example, a round corner of R10 on the one fifth scale model seems elegant, but if it is enlarged five times, the round corner of R50 on a full size model will not give the original sensation as R10. It will be dull. Therefore, final styling determination of a product[3] must come from careful rectification of the details of full size rendering and full size model instead of direct enlargement of scale rendering and scale model.

Fig. 5-9 Full Size Exterior Model(front) and Full Size Rendering(back wall)

本节注释: [1]全尺寸彩色效果图;[2]全尺寸物体与缩小比例物体的逼真感截然不同;[3]产品最终的造型定型。

(6) Full Size Exterior Model

Full size (1:1) exterior model (Fig. 5-9 and 5-10) is the top basis of styling determination[1]. The stylists would strive to make its appearance as real as they could, and then put it on a revolving platform[2] to examine its elegance carefully from various visual directions.

Fig. 5-10 Making Full Size Exterior Model

According to the data from both the scale model and the tape drawing, full size exterior model can be made. It is a sculpture on a four wheeled framework covered by clay and needs at least 1.5 tons of clay. In order to make the model look like a real car, precise dimensions, fluent curves, smooth surfaces and elegant details should be worked out. Therefore, to complete such a model needs time and labor, at least several weeks.

本节注释：[1]造型定型的首要依据；[2]旋转台。

(7) Full Size Interior Model

The aim of a full size interior model has two aspects including examination of interior styling and examination of interior dimensions[1]. Making the full size interior model should keep pace with the full size exterior model, both designs and dimensions should match each other. In this model, shape, color and texture of the upholstery[2] should give observers such a feeling that they are in a real interior of a motor vehicle (Fig. 5-11). For some luxury cars, stylists even spare much more efforts on the interior model then the exterior model.

Fig. 5-11　Full Size Interior Model

本节注释：[1] 验证室内造型和验证室内尺寸；[2]室内装潢的形状、色彩和纹理质感。

(8) Styling Approval[1]

Four items including full size exterior model, full size interior model, renderings and tape drawing should be demonstrated in the show room and ready for approval. Members of the approval committee are top leaders of the enterprise including the CEO, the chief engineer and some experts. The chief stylist has to report the whole styling program to the committee, answer questions and wait for conclusion. After the program has been approved, the conclusive document[2] should be signed by the CEO.

Motor vehicle styling is a very good way to increase sales volume and it is taken into consideration by the headquarters of the enterprise highly. For example, GM[3] has set up the largest styling center. There are 36 styling studios and 1 200 staff members in this center, which is 15 percent of the total 8 000 staff members in the research and development center of this firm. Toyota[4] also has a considerably large styling department of 450 staff members. Not only do big companies spare no expense on styling, but also small companies are willing to pay much money to hire renowned stylists. As a result, many individual design companies and studios are scrambling for styling orders[5]. Consequently, a lot of skillful designers and stylists have become well known throughout the world, such as the American designer Raymond Loewy[6] in 1940s, the Italian stylists Pininfarina and Nuccio Bertone[7] in 1950s, the Italian designers Giorgetto Giugiaro and Marcello Gandini[8] in recent years, etc. Some design companies become outstanding and can cover design processes from styling, structural design to making prototype cars[9], for example the Italian companies Pininfarina, Bertone and Ital Design[10] and the British IAD (International Automobile Design)[11]. Moreover, many young people are eager to study in the art schools famous for training stylists such as the Pasadena Art College in California[12], the Royal College of Art in London[13], etc.

本节注释：[1]造型审批;[2]首席执行官签发;[3]通用汽车公司的略写字母;[4]丰田;[5]争揽造型订单;[6]美国设计师雷蒙·娄威;[7]意大利造型师平宁·法里纳和努西奥·博通;[8]意大利设计师齐奥吉多·乔治亚罗和马歇罗·甘迪尼;[9]样车;[10]意大利设计公司;[11]英国的国际汽车设计公司;[12]加利福尼亚州的帕萨迪纳艺术学院;[13]伦敦的皇家艺术学院。

CONCEPT DESIGN AND CONCEPT CAR

In the early period of product development, an enterprise always takes concept design[1] as an effective way to study the trend of the vehicle style. Concept design is opposite to practical design[2]. Practical design is the design being carried out or having been made, whereas concept design is the design of future or distant study. It is the brief description of the overall concept of the next generation model[3] or distant motor vehicle[4]. Aiming at the shortcomings of the current product and also comparing with the similar models made by the opponent enterprises[5], the designers should work out further project of more adaptable and updated model.

A concept car is the product of concept design. Concept design may stop at the description of documents and drawings, which is called "virtual" concept car[6]. It is also possible to make a real car for research and experiment. Concept design may be a referential draft or a technical reserve[7], and may be put into the product development program of a new generation model.

本节注释：[1]概念设计；[2]现实设计；[3]下一代车型；[4]远景车型；[5]竞争企业；[6]虚拟的概念车；[7]一种参考方案或一种技术储备。

5.1.2.3 PRODUCT DEVELOPMENT PHASE

STRUCTURAL DESIGN

Structural design[1] is to determine the structure of a motor vehicle, choose or create assemblies and parts. That is, the engineer should choose suitable parts to make up an assembly and suitable assemblies to make up a motor vehicle.

A part is the basic and indivisible unit of a product[2]. Without doubt, design of parts is the root of a product design. Design steps of a part may be as follows. At first, consider the function and requirement of this part in the assembly. And then, choose suitable material and shape of the part to meet the requirement. At last, see how this part matches the other parts in the assembly.

Materials used may include metallic and non-metallic[3]. Metallic materials may further include two kinds, i. e. ferrous metal[4] and non-ferrous metal[5]. Various kinds of non-metallic materials are used in motor vehicles such as plastics, rubber, wood, glass, textures, ceramics, leather, fuel, lubricants and chemicals[6].

Among the above materials, steel is the most important and constitutes the majority[7] in a motor vehicle. Advantages of steel are high strength, stiffness and hardness[8]. For this reason, it is suitable to make parts under heavy load, high temperature and high speed.

High strength means the material is capable of withstanding heavy load without damage. High stiffness means the part deforms very little as a large force is exerted. When parts are working, some of them are stretched and tend to increase length, e. g. a string of the parking brake[9]; some are compressed and tend to decrease length, e. g. a rod under the pedal; some withstand bending moment[10] and tend to curve, e. g. a side rail of the frame[11], and some withstand torque[12] and tend to twist, e. g. a propeller shaft. Practically, load conditions of many automotive parts are more complicated than the above examples. For instance, shafts in the gearbox withstand various forces including stretch, compress, bend and twist at the same time. Moreover, not only static loads, but also complicated dynamic loads[13] would act on parts in a motor vehicle.

Usually an engineer can make sure that a part works in good condition without overload[14], i. e. its strength within the tolerant limit[15]. Besides, some of the parts need calculations of strength and stiffness; some of the parts need thermodynamic calculation[16], e. g. the engine piston; some of the parts need aerodynamic calculation[17], e. g. the engine intake and exhaust manifolds; and some of the parts need optical calculation[18], e. g. the head lamps.

To determine the shape of the part require the designer's wisdom and hard work. For example, the shape of the cylinder block is very complicated. Arrangement of cylinders and the water jacket, connections with the cylinder head and the oil sump and installation of the crankshaft, manifolds and other accessories are not easy. Even the shape of a small oil passage drilled through the iron casting[19] should be considered very carefully. Every detail should not be left out[20]. For the second example, to determine the shape of a gear is not easy either. The shape of a tooth is really an involute[21]. The design depends on the work condition of the gear, so some times it needs to be modified[22]. To determine the shape of a helical bevel gear[23] in the final drive, solution of more than 20 equations[24] step by step will be needed. For the third example, the surface of the body is very special, because it is neither a plane nor a round surface, neither a hyperbolic nor a parabolic surface[25]. It is an arbitrary curved surface created by the aesthetic idea of the stylist[26]. How to use some mathematical equations to express the body surface has much to do with a course named computational geometry[27]. Moreover, as the shape of the part is being worked out, manufacturing processes should be considered, such as the ways to fix and localize the work piece[28], to operate the cutter[29], to convey and file up the finished products[30], etc.

本节注释：[1]结构设计；[2]零件是产品基本的不可分割的单元。[3]非金属的；

[4]黑色金属;[5]有色金属;[6]塑料、橡胶、木材、玻璃、纺织品、陶瓷、皮革、燃料、润滑剂和化学制品;[7]占大多数;[8]高强度、刚度和硬度;[9]驻车制动器的钢丝绳;[10]弯矩;[11]车架的纵梁;[12]转矩;[13]不仅是静载荷,而且还有复杂的动载荷;[14]过载;[15]容许极限;[16]热力学计算;[17]空气动力学计算;[18]光学计算;[19]铁铸件;[20]遗漏;[21]渐开线;[22]指齿形修正;[23]螺旋伞齿轮;[24]方程式;[25]既不是双曲面,也不是抛物面;[26]它是造型师的审美思维创造出的一个任意的曲面。[27]名叫计算几何学的一门学科;[28]工件装夹和定位;[29]刀具;[30]成品传送和堆叠。

EXPRESSION OF DESIGNER' S IDEA

A designer should express the ideas by technical drawings[1], or we can say technical drawings are used to describe the structure of a product and are the exchangeable "engineering language" between designers and makers.

The national administration has issued more than 10 National Standards (GB) to specify the regulations of technical drawings. The engineering colleges and technical schools provide a special course to give students a good grasp of the drawing skill. Drawing regulations are based on the principle of projection[2]. By some views (elevations), sections and partial enlargements[3], the shape and the inner structure of a product can be expressed clearly. A technical drawing should take a designated proportion and write down some technical requirements for a product. The drawing of a part[4] needs to mark the dimensions in detail, whereas the drawing of an assembly[5] should indicate the relation between parts and mark the assemble dimensions[6]. To design a motor vehicle, thousands of technical drawings would be needed. Some of them are very complicated. The length of some drawing sheets can be three to five meters.

As an assembly is made up by parts, dimensions of a part and an adjacent part should fit each other. For example, if a screw of outer diameter 6 mm goes through a hole, the inner diameter of the hole must be bigger than 6 mm (assumed 6.2 mm). Practically, the diameter of the screw would not be precisely equal to 6 mm because of manufacturing error[7]. For the same reason, the diameter of the hole would not be precisely equal to 6.2 mm. Therefore, it is necessary to permit some dimensional deviations[8] as the product is finished. For example, the tolerance[9] of the outer diameter of the screw may be within the range of 5.8 to 6.0 mm and the tolerance of the inner diameter of the hole may be within the range of 6.2 to 6.4 mm. That is, it is necessary to permit the dimensional deviation of each part within the range of 0.2 mm. The result of the fit[10] of both parts is from 0.2 minimum to 0.6 mm maximum.

The above relationship between the enclosing part and the enclosed part is called the "principle of tolerance and fit" [11]. To design a product, it is important for the engineer to follow National Standard of Tolerance and Fit. Because of manufacturing error, a straight line would not be absolutely straight, it is only permissible within a considerable range of straightness[12]; a plane would not be absolutely flat, it is only permissible within a range of planeness[13]; a round part would not be absolutely round, it is only permissible within a range of roundness[14]; a smooth surface would not be absolutely smooth, it is only permissible within a range of roughness[15], etc. Therefore, the national administration has released a document called National Standard of Shape and Position Tolerance[16].

During manufacturing and assembling processes, if the permissible deviation is small, it is called high accuracy[17] and if the permissible deviation is pretty big, it is called low accuracy. It is very important for the designer to select suitable accuracy. High accuracy is not always acceptable because it leads to manufacturing difficulties. It needs precise machine tools and measuring instruments[18] and thus results in expensive cost.

For a motor vehicle designer, it is important to follow the regulations and standards issued by the national administrations. For export products, it is necessary to follow foreign standards issued by the authorities[19] such as ISO (International Standardization Organization) [20], SAE (Society of Automotive Engineers) [21], EEC (European Economic Community) [22], ECE (Economic Commission of Europe) [23], FMVSS (Federal Motor Vehicle Safety Standard) [24], JIS (Japanese Industrial Standard), ADR (Australian Design Regulation), etc.

本节注释：[1]工程图；[2]投影原理；[3]通过一些视图、剖面和局部放大；[4]零件图；[5]总成图；[6]装配尺寸；[7]制造误差；[8]尺寸偏差；[9]公差(容许值)；[10]配合；[11]上述包容零件与被包容零件之间的关系称为“公差与配合原理”。[12]直线度；[13]平面度；[14]圆度；[15]粗糙度；[16]形状与位置公差国家标准；[17]高精度；

[18]精密的机床和量具;[19]权威机构;[20]国际标准化组织;[21]美国汽车工程师协会;[22]欧洲经济共同体;[23]欧洲经济委员会;[24]美国联邦机动车安全标准。

5.1.3 *ADVANCED DESIGN BASED ON HIGH TECHNOLOGY*

5.1.3.1 DESIGN REVOLUTION BY COMPUTER

If all the design processes mentioned above are carried out manually, engineers would spend a lot of labor and time. Computer has many advantages such as high speed, large storage, accurate computation. By the use of computer, engineering design has changed dramatically. Not only product quality can be improved, but also design period can be shortened greatly. CAD (Computer Aided Design) [1] has become the main feature of up-to-date design. It is advisable for readers to compare the following design steps with those mentioned in the above paragraphs.

INFORMATION TECHNOLOGY (IT) [2]

To obtain correct information promptly is the key to lead a company to successful policy decision[3], especially in the diverse and changeable world that we are living in. For instance, Ford Motor Company takes information technology as a strategic asset[4] and carries out "five rights" [5], i. e. in the right time and the right location give the right information of the right format to the right user.

Ford has built up a worldwide information system for communication, including hardware and software network, access of database, tools for development and support of business processes[6]. The system provides enough security because it is protected by internal internet (called "intranet") [7].

Ford also has proceeded to link its 7 design centers in the United States, England, Germany, Japan, Australia and Italy as a whole (called the Global Studio[8]) through high bandwidth telephone lines[9]. Engineers around the world can exchange the required information and discuss the same sketch or digitized photograph visually in the same time through their computer terminals[10] or television conference. A lot more specific problems can be handled in real time through such higher communication technique than a mere phone call can do and certainly reducing the requirement for extensive travels of engineers between continents[11]. Team work formed by specialists across different geographic locations can be called "Virtual Co-location" [12].

本节注释：[1]计算机辅助设计；[2]信息技术；[3]决策；[4]把信息技术看作战略资产；[5]五个正确；[6]信息技术包括软硬件网络、数据的存取、开发工具和业务过程的支持。[7]内联网；[8]全球设计室；[9]宽频电话线；[10]计算机终端；[11]工程师们就不需要频繁地洲际旅行；[12]跨越不同地理位置的专家们组成的团队工作可称为"虚拟同地"。

REVOLUTION OF DESIGN PROCESSES

Just a few years ago, if you went to the stylist's studio, you would see a number of recognized things such as paper, drawing board, brushes[1], color tubes[2], clay and sculpture tools. They were not quite different from those in Leonado Da Vinci's[3] studio 500 years ago. Today, in an advanced styling studio, stylists would not draw pictures on paper or canvas[4], but on the computer screen. They would not use clay to make real car models, but build up digital model in the computer. Computer based software such as ALIAS or CDRS can aid the creative and visual process of developing styling concepts more realistic than the above traditional tools. We can call the process Computer Aided Styling (CAS)[5].

New styling process has changed into the following steps. First, the package sketch of a motor vehicle can be transferred to the stylist's computer through internal network (intranet). Then, the stylist can use lines and color to cover the given sketch so that the renderings can meet the dimensional requirements of the motor vehicle easily. At last, with the help of the transforming and processing packages of the computer software, the 2D rendering can be changed into a 3D digitized model. Moreover, the stylist can continue his work to check and modify the shape of the 3D model on the computer screen until he or she is satisfied.

The above steps have covered the whole process of the design from package to scale model. The pith and marrow[6] of the computer software is the principle of computational geometry, i. e. to express the body curved surfaces of the motor vehicle through a set of mathematical equations. We can call such a model digitized model or mathematical model[7]. Comparing to the scale model made by manual labor (can be called physical model[8]) in paragraph 5.1.2.2, mathematical model is smoother and more accurate, therefore is with higher quality.

The next step is to make full size (1:1) model. A small rendering in the computer can be enlarged and projected[9] to a large screen to become full size rendering easily. The stylist can continue to modify and mend the detail of the full size rendering with the aid of computer. But most of the top leaders are not willing to check the styling work merely on the large screen, or we can say they are not adapted to do that. For this reason, a real full size model is still needed. The model can be cut by a five axis NC milling machine[10] (Fig. 5-12). Actually, the realistic sensation of such a model is much better than that on the screen. Besides, the stylists also have chances to check the model and take further step to modify it. Because the digital data of the surface has been given, to operate the NC milling machine and to complete the work of the model only need several days, which is much faster than handmade.

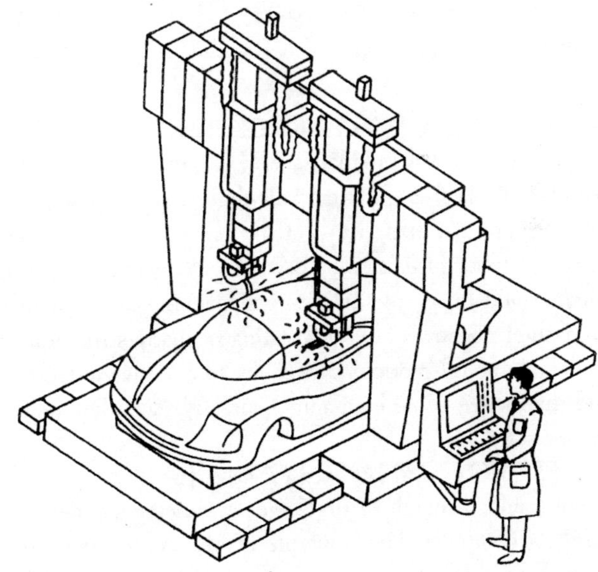

Fig. 5-12 The five axis NC milling machine is making a full size model.

For CAD of components and parts, a great deal of software have been used, for examples, UG used by the General Motors, I-DEAS used by Ford, CATIA used by Chrysler, etc. The functions of the software include design of solid parts, 2D and 3D technical drawing and development of curved surfaces. Designers can handle the software to draw the component in mind conveniently. Because the computer has stored rich data of various parts, it is quite easy to construct an assembly by making up the data of parts.

After the designer uses a computer to shape a part, it seems necessary to link the computer with the plotter[11] to print a sheet of technical drawing of this part, then to hand it over to the manufacturing department. Have you ever thought if the data of this part in the designer's computer can be conveyed to the manufacturer's computer directly, it is possible to exchange graphics without sheets of paper? The idea of non-paper office and non-paper studio is not just a dream, it has come true.

本节注释：[1]指绘画的毛笔；[2]颜料软管；[3]达·芬奇；[4]画布；[5]计算机辅助造型；[6]精髓；[7]数字化模型或数学模型；[8]物理模型；[9]投影；[10]五轴数控铣床；[11]绘图机。

5.1.3.2 COMPUTER AIDED ENGINEERING (CAE) [1]

After the structure of a product is worked out, engineers should examine its performances (Table 5-2) through calculations. CAE is exactly the method to analyze the structural rationality[2] of the product. The disadvantage of traditional manual labor is that it is very difficult or even impossible to deal with complicated and huge calculations. For example, the automotive body is a complicated shell construction[3] consisting of many structural members. The traditional method should reduce[4] the body to a rather rough mechanical model[5] and then solve some equations manually. Accuracy and reliability of its solutions are very low.

FINITE ELEMENT METHOD (FEM) [6]

Application and research of finite element method is developing rapidly since the birth of computer. The principle of FEM is to divide the structure into many small units and to be solved thousands of equations. Taking a bus body skeleton as an example, we can divide it into about 300 unit structural members (or bar elements[7]). On the basis of mechanical principle, each

CAE Tools Table 5-2

Item	Content	Tools
Structural Analysis	Strength, Stiffness, Vibration, Elasticity and Plasticity[4], Heat Transfer	NASTRAN, ANSYS, MARC, BEASY
Vibration, Noise	Motor vehicle and Components	NASTRAN, SYSTAN
Analysis of Mechanism Dynamics[5]	Motor vehicle Braking Stability and Handling stability, Dynamics of Mechanisms	ADAMS, DADS
Analysis of Fluids	Motor vehicle Aerodynamics, Engine Internal Flows and Combustion	NAGARE, FLUENT, KIVA
Motor vehicle collision	Motor vehicle Frontal, Lateral and Rear Collisions, Occupant and Pedestrian Collision	DYNA3D, PAM-STAMP MADYMO
Analysis of Forming	Forming Analysis of Sheet Metals, Forming Analysis of Plastic Parts	PAM-STAMP STRIM-100

end of a bar has 6 degrees of freedom[8]. Both ends have 12 degrees of freedom and need 12 equations. If restrained deformation[9] is considered, a bar element needs 14 equations. Therefore, to be solved a bus body skeleton having 300 bar elements needs to be solved 4200 (300 × 14) equations. Evidently, it is nearly impossible to cope with such a huge equation group by hand calculation, but it can be easily done by computer. In actual practice of today's body design, equations required to solve are much more than 4200. In order to have a better analysis of a modern car body, a mechanical model with more than a hundred thousand meshes[10] should be constructed and several hundred thousand (even more than one million) equations are needed to solve.

两节注释：[1]计算机辅助分析;[2]结构合理性;[3]薄壳结构;[4]简化;[5]较粗略的力学模型;[6]有限元法;[7]简单梁单元;[8]自由度;[9]约束变形;[10]网格。

OTHER CAE TOOLS

Besides the CAE tool of analyzing structural strength and stiffness, there are other tools including NVH (Noise, Vibration and Harshness) [1], CFD (Computational Fluid Dynamics) [2], analysis of multi-body dynamics[3], analysis of motor vehicle collision, etc. The tools offer perfect accuracy and reliability and are suitable to aid the processes of making decisions and examining product structure. Some examples are given in Table 5-2.

本节注释：[1]振动、噪声、平顺性；[2]计算流体动力学；[3]多体动力学；[4]弹性和塑性；[5]机构动力学分析。

5.1.3.3 OPTIMUM DESIGN[1]

Optimum technique is to look for the best one from all the possible ways. Besides it is necessary for a product to meet the prerequisites for some performances, it is hopeful to look for the smallest volume, weight and the lowest cost, that is, to look for an optimum solution.

Take the following simple problem as an example (as shown in Fig. 5-13a). Four little squares at the corners of a squire steel panel with each side 60 cm long need to be cut off, and then four sides may be folded up to make a container by welding them together. In order to obtain the biggest volume of the container, how long is the side x of the little square?

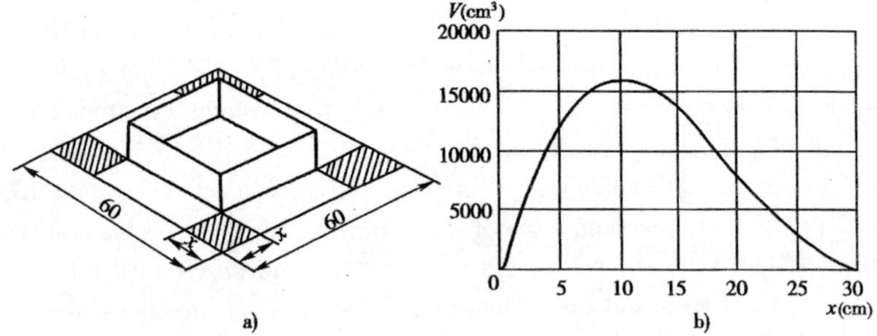

Fig. 5-13 Looking for the Maximum Volume of the Square Container

To solve this problem, it is necessary to give a formula of the relation between the volume V and the variable[2] x.

$$V = x(60 - 2x)^2$$

We can use a visualized curve (Fig. 5-13b) to show this relation. The horizontal coordinate is x and the vertical is V. The curve expresses that V relates the change of x. We can easily see when x is 10 cm, V will be the biggest. If we use differential method[3], it is very easy to find out the maximum volume.

Indeed, the practical problems do not seem always as simple as the above example. Influential factors are complicated, not only one x, but also possible several variables. An optimum result comes from comparisons of solutions one by one, and therefore it is inevitable to make intensive calculations. Development of computer technique provides strong tools to deal with complicated problems and intensive calculations which would not be solved by manual labor.

The process of optimum design can be divided into the following steps.

(1) Understand the design problem. For example, use a square steel panel to make a container and obtain the biggest volume.

(2) Build up mathematical model or target function[4]. For example, determine the functional relation[5] of the volume V with the length x and give a formula to show the relation.

(3) Calculate, compare and evaluate. For example, assume $x = 5$ and obtain $V = 12500$, compare this result with others if it is the biggest. If not, make another calculation and comparison until the biggest is found out.

Figure 5-14 shows the process of optimum design.

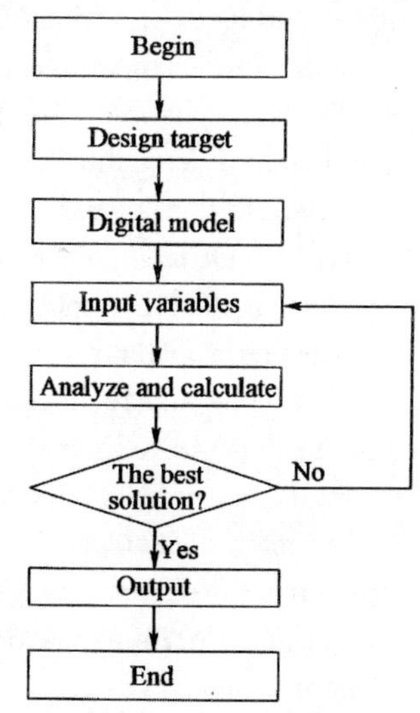

Fig. 5-14 Process of Optimum Design

本节注释：[1]优化设计；[2]变量；[3]微分方法；[4]目标函数；[5]函数关系。

5.1.3.4 INTELLIGENT DESIGN

Intelligent design or artificial intelligence (AI) [1] is to imitate human's thinking process by computer. For example, IBM (International Business Machines Corporation) began to compile a program of playing chess in 1960s. After that, some expert systems (ES) [2] were developed. Based on the experiences of the experts, the system can come up with a conclusion by reasoning [3], for example, the application of computer to diagnosis of sickness in 1970s. Data base[4] and reasoning program are the two main supports of the artificial intelligent system which is quite different from the traditional computer program supported by calculation method and input data.

The research and development (R&D) process of modern products consists of many loops including investigation, plan, design, manufacturing, marketing, maintenance, repair, obsolescence, and reuse. It needs to draw on the experiences of various experts and to make comprehensive analysis. The traditional design which relies on hand labor is quite difficult to avoid many disadvantages including lack of data and experiences, imperfect plan, slow reaction, low quality and accuracy of product, waste of time and labor. It is incredible that a product of high technology such as the Boeing 747 jetliner [5] which has more than 6 million parts can be developed by such an out of date method. It is only possible to rely on new computer technology.

Although a motor vehicle is not as complicated as a jetliner, various kinds of science and technology involved in motor vehicle design is not inferior to those in jetliner design. Certainly, without modernized design tools, there would not be excellent design.

The main advantage of intelligent design is to enrich the ideas of the inexperienced designers, that is, to remind and instruct them to carry out every design step. As a new design method, KBE is a good example of intelligent design.

KBE (Knowledge Based Engineering)[6] has two main supports. The first one is the functional software of CAD, CAE and CAM. The second one is the combination of a reasoning program with a data base which has stored a lot of experts' experiences and design regulations. The special software compiled by KBE principle serves a designer as an advisory committee formed by experts which can tell a designer what is the reasonable way, how to choose main parameters and how to shape the structure, and even tell him/her every detail in the design process until the satisfactory solution is obtained. Relying on KBE, the designer feels confident of doing difficult jobs which he or she is not familiar with. With the help of KBE, a young designer will go through the design process smoothly without negligence and serious mistakes and will come to the correct solutions quickly without wandering on the wrong way and reciprocal mending[7].

This does not mean "Relying on KBE, a fool can be a good designer". In fact any of the intelligent design software is just an assistant tool. The designer's creative idea is of the first importance and the advanced design tool is its strong support. Undoubtedly, with the development of advanced design tools, the quality of the designers should improve correspondently. The combination of both designer's quality and advanced design tool is a broad way leading to wonderful design and perfect products.

本节注释: [1]智能设计或人工智能;[2]专家系统;[3]推理;[4]数据库;[5]波音 747 喷气式客机;[6]基于知识的工程;[7]反复修改。

5.2 AUTOMOTIVE PROVING GROUND[1]

5.2.1 *MOTOR VEHICLE TEST- AN IMPORTANT STAGE OF R&D*

Scientific experiment and theoretical study[2] are two main ways for the development of science and technology. Theory is based on experiment and experiment is conducted by theory.

A theory can be acceptable only after it has been examined by practice. In other words, all kinds of theories and calculations used in engineering design including computer software and simulation methods should be based on scientific experiments. Many kinds of modern theories and calculations used in motor vehicle design are reliable and valuable, those methods have been examined by practice and therefore can be used as the support tools in the design process of the automotive products.

Modern scientific experiment is an independent course created by summing up or sublimating[3] a great deal of ordinary practice. It has been well developed and provided with perfect equipments and accurate measuring instruments. An automotive proving ground can cover most kinds of operation conditions in the practical use of various motor vehicles. For example, the life evaluation of a new type of motor vehicle is not necessary to wait for the final conclusion during its whole life process of ordinary operation after many years, it could be examined by a strengthened test method[4] on the proving ground within a considerable short period. Test results measured by accurate instruments under standard test procedures and criteria may precisely reflect the practical operation condition of the motor vehicle during certain time span. Actually, scientific experiment is not directly equal to ordinary practice, but it should be in imitation of ordinary practice. We can say scientific experiment is the sublimation[5] of ordinary practice, and it is at a higher level than ordinary practice.

After the design of a new motor vehicle has been completed, the enterprise would make some prototypes[6] ready for performance tests. The task of automotive experiment is to make a comprehensive analysis which is by means of carrying out a series of tests to measure the performance targets of the motor vehicle according to the standard test criteria. Based on the evaluation report given by the test department, the design department would focus on the problems discovered by tests, taking mending measures to improve the product structure. Then, the design program can be given to the manufacturing department for production arrangement. In a word, design quality of a new type of motor vehicle should be guaranteed[7] by experiments.

本节注释：[1]汽车试验场;[2]科学实验与理论研究;[3]归纳与提炼;[4]强化的试验方法;[5]升华;[6]样车;[7]把关,保证。

5.2.2 *PROVING GROUND AND TYPICAL TESTS*

There are many tests to measure the performance targets of a motor vehicle. According to the structure of the motor vehicle, tests can be classified into vehicle test, component test and part test. According to the test facilities, they can be classified into road test (outdoor) and rig test (indoor) [1]. According to paragraph 4.2 chapter 4, they can be classified into various performance tests.

Because motor vehicle tests hold an important position in the R&D process of the motor vehicle, many automotive enterprises spare no expense to build their own proving grounds, for example, the Milford Proving Ground of General Motors[2], the Proving Ground of Japanese Research Institute[3], the English MIRA (Motor Industry Research Association) [4], the Hainan Proving Ground in south China, etc.

本节注释: [1]道路试验(室外)和台架试验(室内);[2]通用汽车公司的密尔福德汽车试验场;[3]日本汽车研究所汽车试验场;[4]英国迈拉(汽车工业研究协会)。

5.2.2.1 ROAD TEST

HIGH SPEED RUNWAY

High speed runway[1] is a ring road[2], normally circular at both ends and straight at its central part, but some of the runways are elliptic. Most of the runways are 4 to 8 km long and have 3 lanes (Fig. 5-15). Design speed of the runway is more than 200 km/h. It can provide long term continuous driving to examine the high speed performance and reliability of the motor vehicle, its components and parts.

Fig. 5-15 High Speed Runway

STRAIGHT DASH

It is a straight runway for high speed dash[3] (to develop the maximum speed). It is 2.5 to 4 km long and can be used to examine traction performance, braking performance, fuel economy, etc. In order to save construction investment, many proving grounds widen the central part of the ring runway and combine both functions together.

ROADS FOR RELIABILITY AND DURABILITY TEST

During its whole life process, a motor vehicle may work on various road conditions. Therefore, roads of different pavement should be built on the proving ground to imitate the actual road conditions. Besides asphalt and concrete roads, other kinds of roads are needed, such as sandy, muddy, rocky, etc. The motor vehicle will make strengthened test on different road pavements so that the report of life evaluation can be obtained after a rather short period. Figure 5-16 shows a road of the so-called "washboard[4] pavement" and figure 5-17 shows a cobble[5] road. They can be used to examine the vibration of suspensions or shock absorbers.

Fig. 5-16 Washboard Road Pavement

BODY TWIST[6]

This kind of road pavement is made of trapezoid bumps arranged left and right alternatively[7] (Fig. 5-18) and can imitate the crucial twisting situation of body, frame, front axle, rear axle, transmission system, etc.

以上四节注释: [1]高速跑道;[2]环形路;[3]冲刺;[4]搓衣板;[5]鹅卵石;[6]车身扭曲路面;[7]左右交错排列的梯形凸块。

Fig. 5-17 Cobble Road

Fig. 5-18 Body Twist

SLOPES

On the proving ground there should be some slopes of different gradients[1] to examine the hill climbing performance of the motor vehicle. Other tests such as braking effectiveness and working condition of clutch can be examined on the slopes too.

FACILITY FOR HANDLING STABILITY TEST

The most common facility is a circular field of cement concrete pavement with a diameter of 100 m. The test vehicle should make S-shape or 8-shape driving on the field to measure its deviation from the given direction[2]. Water can be added to the field to make the pavement more slippery.

Slippery pavement is used to examine the operation performance or braking performance of a motor vehicle under low adhesive condition. Surface polish[3], water, ice or snow can be used to lower the adhesive coefficient[4] of the pavement.

Lateral wind Installation[5] can examine the aerodynamic stability of a motor vehicle. Figure 5-19 shows such installation made by Toyota. There are 15 big fans of diameter 2.7 m arranged in a line[6] beside the test road to develop strong wind perpendicular to the direction of the road. Lateral wind blowing onto the body makes the vehicle tend to deviate from its driving direction.

Fig. 5-19 Lateral Wind Installation

两节注释：[1]不同坡度的斜坡；[2]偏离给定的方向；[3]打磨；[4]附着系数；[5]横向风装置；[6]排成一行。

POOL TEST

There are two kinds of pools on the proving ground, i.e. shallow pool

(200 mm deep) and deep pool (1 to 2 m deep). The motor vehicle should go through the pool to examine the influence of water on its components such as electric equipment, brakes, engine exhaust pipe, etc.

FACILITY FOR COLLISION TEST

Figure 5-20 shows a facility for vehicle-barrier collision test[1]. It includes a fixed barrier[2] 1, four high speed cameras[3] 3 on the left, right, top and bottom of the car, illumination lights 2 and ditch[4] 4 for installation of bottom camera. The above items are installed indoors. During the collision test, the test car 8 driven by the motor 11 and the winch[5] 10 through a wire cable 9 goes down the slope 7 and gradually accelerates. Then the speed of the car should be adjusted to a given constant speed. Being separated from the cable hook by the separating device 5, the car crashes to the barrier lastly.

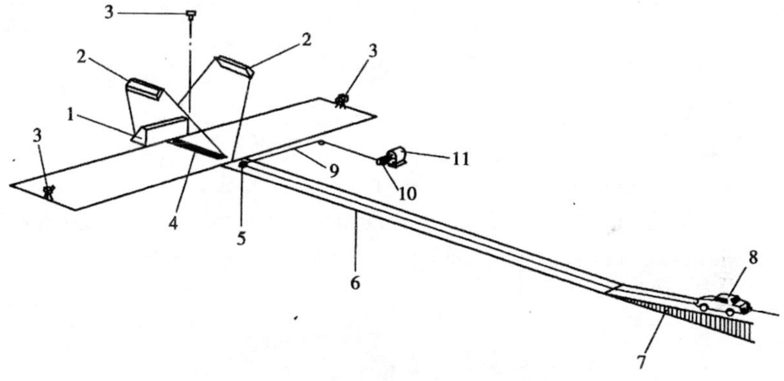

Fig. 5-20 Vehicle-Barrier Collision Test

1-barrier;2-lights;3-high speed cameras;4-ditch;5-separating device;6-runway;7-slope;8-test car;9-wire cable;10-winch;11-motor

Besides the above facility for head-on collision test, there are also facilities for lateral collision test[6], rear collision test, rollover test[7], etc.

Dummies[8] (Fig. 5-21) are installed in the test car to imitate the motion of the occupants during the collision test.

两节注释：[1]汽车－屏壁碰撞试验;[2]固定的屏壁;[3]高速摄影机;[4]地沟;

[5]绞盘;[6]侧面碰撞试验;[7]翻车试验;[8]假人模型。

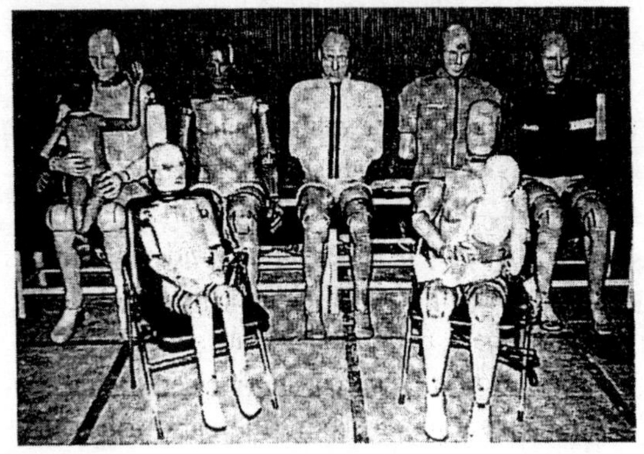

Fig. 5-21 Dummies

5.2.2.2 RIG TEST

ROLLER

Roller[1] is an indoor test facility possible to make the motor vehicle run at a fixed location. Figure 5-22 shows the traditional structure of a roller. The drive wheels of the test motor vehicle 3 are placed on a roller 5 and can

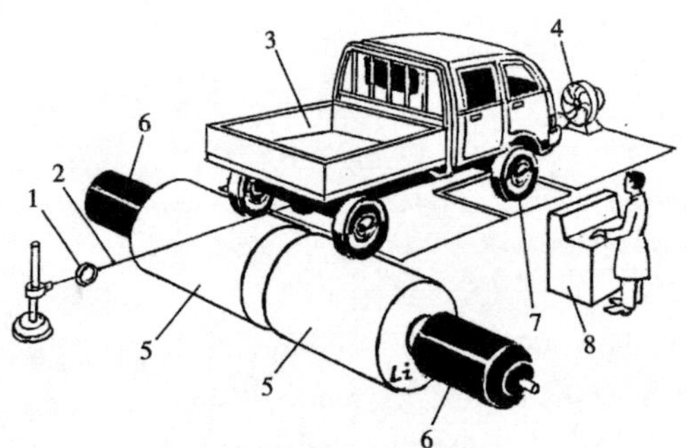

Fig. 5-22 Roller Test

1-dial scale;2-wire cable;3-test motor vehicle;4-fan (for cooling the engine radiator);5-roller;6-dynamometer;7-platform scale;8-control desk

rotate at different speeds. Having the same axis with the roller, the dynamometer[2] 6 provides some resistant forces to the drive wheels of the motor vehicle. At the same time, it will measure the work done by the motor vehicle[3]. Because the traction force acted on the drive wheels by the roller tends to push the motor vehicle forward, a cable 2 is needed to balance this force and keep the motor vehicle standing at the location. The reading on the dial scale[4] 1 is the magnitude of the traction force. Readings of the platform scales[5] 7 under the front wheels of the motor vehicle may be different as it runs at different speed.

本节注释: [1]转鼓;[2]测功器;[3]汽车所做的功;[4]测力表;[5]台秤。

HYDRAULIC SERVO VIBRATION TEST[1]

The test rig is an indoor test facility controlled by computer to imitate the forces caused by uneven road surfaces acting on four wheels of the motor vehicle. The test can be used for the study of vibration and life evaluation of the whole vehicle, its components and parts, which is a good way suitable for strengthened tests.

During the test, four road wheels are placed on four hydraulic actuators[2] controlled by computer. According to a special computer program, the actuators reconstruct[3] the uneven road condition, push the wheels of the motor vehicle up and down as if they are bumping on a real road (Fig. 5-23). Moreover, the vibration amplitude[4] can be enlarged easily for strengthened test.

In order to represent the real road condition, it is necessary to make a measuring apparatus rolling on typical roads to collect enough data, so called the "road pattern[5]", which can be processed and compiled to become a special computer program.

本节注释: [1]液力伺服振动试验;[2]执行器,激振头;[3]重现;[4]振幅;[5]路谱。

WIND TUNNEL

Wind tunnel[1] is the facility to examine the aerodynamic performance of the motor vehicle. It can be used to measure six components (drag, side

Fig. 5-23 Hydraulic Servo Vibration Test

force, lift, pitching moment, yawing moment and rolling moment) [2], to measure pressure distribution, and to display flow pattern[3]. During the styling process, a special scale model should be made for a wind tunnel test to improve the body shape and its aerodynamic performance. It is impossible to measure six components at the same time by a road test. Therefore, the wind tunnel test has become an effective method for the study of aerodynamic performance of a motor vehicle.

According to the dimension, wind tunnel can be classified into two kinds, i. e. scale model wind tunnel and full size wind tunnel[4]. According to the manner of the air flow, wind tunnel can be classified into two kinds, i. e. open circuit wind tunnel and closed circuit wind tunnel[5].

Figure 5-24 shows an open circuit wind tunnel. The tunnel consists of three sections, i. e. the contraction[6] 2, the working section[7] 3 and the diffuser[8] 5. Under the action of the fan 7, air enters the tunnel through the honeycomb[9] 1, accelerates in the contraction 2, blows to the car /or car model 4 in the working section 3 and flows out through the diffuser 5. To install the car, a fixture[10] connected by the six component balance[11] 9 is needed. Through the instruments in the working room 10, six components acting on the car can be measured.

Besides the measurement of forces, the wind tunnel can also measure pressure distribution on the body surface of the car[12] and display the flow pattern by the help of smoke, tuft[13], oil film[14], etc.

It is quite easy to know that air flowing out from the open circuit wind tunnel still has speed and kinetic energy. In other words, a considerable amount of energy wastes away. In order to save energy, a closed circuit to conduct the air flow from the diffuser back to the contraction is needed. That is the basic principle and basic structure of the closed circuit wind tunnel.

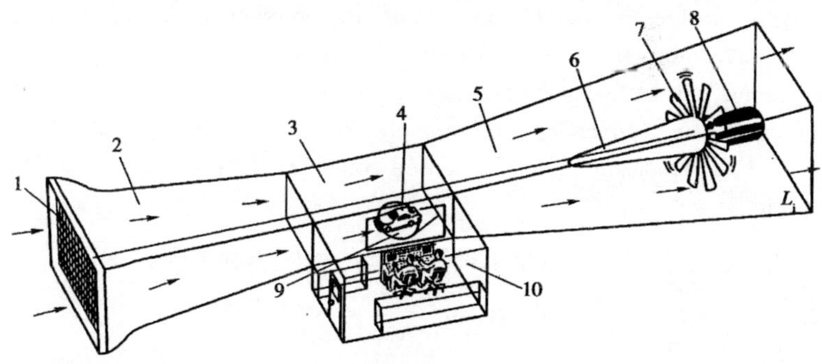

Fig. 5-24 Open Circuit Wind Tunnel

1-honeycomb; 2-contraction; 3-working section; 5-car; 5-diffuser; 6-fairing[15] 7-fan; 8-motor; 9-fixture and six component balance; 10-working room

本节注释：[1]风洞；[2]六分力(阻力、侧向力、升力、俯仰力矩、横摆力矩和侧倾力矩)；[3]流谱；[4]缩小比例模型风洞和全尺寸风洞；[5]直流式风洞和回流式风洞；[6]收缩段；[7]工作段或测量段；[8]扩散段；[9]蜂窝栅；[10]夹具；[11]六分力天平；[12]汽车车身表面的压力分布；[13]丝带簇；[14]油膜；[15]导流罩。

ENGINE PERFORMANCE TEST

The basic feature of an engine test rig is to connect the engine with a dynamometer. The dynamometer loads the engine and measures the torque and speed output by the engine. If electric dynamometer[1] is used, it is essentially a generator[2] to change the mechanical energy to electric energy which should be consumed by some electric equipments.

By means of the engine test rig, a number of engine performances can be measured such as the engine characteristics, emission analysis[3], comparison of different accessories, etc.

本节注释: [1]电力测功器;[2]它实质上是一台发电机;[3]废气排放分析。

TRANSMISSION PERFORMANCE TEST

The main feature of a transmission performance test rig[1] is to connect the input end of the test component to an electric motor and its output end to the dynamometer. The electric motor puts the component into action and the dynamometer absorbs the energy output by the component. Various components can be installed between the motor and the dynamometer to examine their performances, for example the torque and efficiency characteristics measurement of a torque converter[2], the gearbox performance test, etc.

本节注释: [1]传动系试验台;[2]液力变矩器转矩和效率特性的测定。

5.2.2.3 INSTRUMENTATION

SENSOR

Sensor[1] is used to transmit the information at the measured point. Most of the measuring instruments are electronic instruments. Therefore, the structural principle of the sensor is to change the non-electric parameters such as displacement, velocity, acceleration, force, and temperature into electric parameters such as resistance, current, voltage, capacitance and inductance [2]. For example, we normally use a sliding resistor[3] to measure displacement. As the slider of the resistor[4] changes its position together with the displacement of the object, the magnitude of resistance changes too, then the displacement information would be changed into resistance information.

本节注释: [1]传感器;[2]把非电量参数(例如位移、速度、加速度、力、温度等)转换为电量参数(例如电阻、电流、电压、电容、电感等);[3]滑线电阻;[4]电阻的滑动触头。

STRAIN GAUGE

The shape of a strain gauge[1] is like a thin chip with a grid-shape resistant wire on[2]. It can be stuck on the measured point of a sample[3], stretching or compressing together with the sample.

According to the principle of common physics, when a resistant wire is stretched, its resistance increases and when it is compressed, its resistance decreases. For this reason, the information of the sample deformation can be changed into the information of the resistance change.

Besides the use of measurement of strain and stress[4], strain gauges are also widely used on some kinds of sensors.

本节注释: [1]电阻应变片;[2]在其上面贴有栅状电阻丝的薄片;[3]试样;[4]应变与应力。

THE FIFTH WHEEL

The fifth wheel[1] is a measuring apparatus like a bicycle wheel (Fig. 5-25) and it is attached to a motor vehicle for the measurement of its traction performance, braking performance, etc. The circumference[2] of the wheel represents the driving distance of the motor vehicle and can be recorded. Combining with the timer[3], the apparatus can derive velocity and acceleration easily.

Fig. 5-25 The Fifth Wheel Attached to a Car

The old type fifth wheel uses a mechanical device to make a pen draw lines on a paper tape. The new type uses sensors, analyzing instrument, microprocessor[4] and electronic displayed screen[5] and therefore it is more accurate and convenient.

本节注释：[1]第五轮仪；[2]圆周；[3]计时器；[4]微处理机；[5]电子显示屏。

OTHER MEASURING INSTRUMENTS

There are a lot of measuring instruments used in motor vehicle tests. It is difficult to describe them all in this book. So only some of them are introduced as follows.

A fuel flowmeter[1] is installed in serial connection[2] with the piping of the fuel supply system to measure the engine fuel consumption. As a chamber of given volume (for example 1 mL) in the flowmeter is full, an impulse will be sent out, then the digital display screen will move ahead one unit.

The function of an electric charge amplifier[3] is to enlarge the weak signal of a sensor to a proper level, so that it can be measured and recorded.

A tape recorder[4] is a kind of widely used instrument and it can record the test data by the change of the magnetic property of the tape. The test data can be replayed by the tape recorder easily. The only problem is that the recorded data should be changed into visualized results by a special processing instrument and a display instrument.

A noise meter or sound meter[5] is used to measure the magnitude of noise or sound (dB[6]) according to its pressure level[7]. It can also be used to analyze the sound frequencies[8].

A four-wheel aligner[9] is used to measure and adjust the alignment parameters, i.e. caster, kingpin inclination, camber, toe-in and tracking (see Paragraph 3.3.10 in Chapter Three).

A three dimensional measuring apparatus is shown in figure 5-26. It is a precise apparatus controlled by computer to measure positions and shapes. As the probe tip[10] contacts a given point of the measured object, the coordinates x, y, z of the tip can be recorded and displayed on the screen of the computer. The whole shape of the object can be measured by the method of scanning[11]. The apparatus is used to measure and inspect the curved surfaces such as motor vehicle body and stamp dies[12].

Fig. 5-26 Three Dimensional Measuring Apparatus

A straining meter[13] directly connects with a number of strain gauges to measure the magnitude of strain and stress of the test sample. With the help of a bridge[14] and an amplifier, the resistance of the strain gauge can be change into visualized reading.

During the test process, some of the equipments are also needed such as power supply adjustment[15], voltage stabilizer[16], remote sending and receiving instruments[17].

本节注释：[1]流量计；[2]串联；[3]电荷放大器；[4]磁带记录仪；[5]噪声测量仪或声音测量仪；[6]分贝；[7]压强级、声压级；[8]声频；[9]四轮定位仪；[10]测量头的尖端；[11]扫描；[12]冲模；[13]应变仪；[14]电桥；[15]供电调节；[16]稳压器；[17]远距离发送和接收仪器。

5.3 WORKSHOP

5.3.1 *MANUFACTURING METHODS*

5.3.1.1 CASTING

Casting[1] is a method to obtain products by pouring molten metal into a hollow mold. During the manufacturing of automotive products, the parts requiring to make blanks[2] with casting iron is 10 percent of the total weight of a motor vehicle, for example cylinder block, case of gearbox, rear axle housing, brake drum, and brackets.

Sand molds[3] are used to make castings. The raw material of sand molds is mainly sand, and there are other mixtures including binder[4] and water. The material of sand molds should have enough binding strength to hold the required shape and to resist the flush of the high temperature liquid without collapse[5].

In order to make a hollow shape identical to the casting, it is required to make a wooden model. Because the liquid metal may contract after cooling up, the dimension of the wooden model should be a bit larger than that of the casting. Moreover, the machined surface[6] should be thickened. A hollow casting needs a sand core and its wooden core box[7].

To obtain a good casting, a flask (sand molding box) [8] is needed. A wooden model should be placed into the box to shape the hollow. It is required to consider how to take the wooden model out, i. e. to separate the upper box[9] and the lower box[10], and how to run the molten metal, i. e. to arrange the runner[11] and the riser[12].

Metal is molten in the furnace[13], conveyed by a hand shank[14] and then poured to the sand molding box. The proper pouring temperature of the liquid iron is 1250 to 1350 degrees centigrade and it is higher in the furnace. After a cooling period, sand can be removed thoroughly from the casting at 450 degrees centigrade.

Steel and iron are main contents of iron element. Their difference lies in the carbon content. Carbon content less than 0.02 percent is industrial pure iron[15], from 0.02 to 2.06 percent is steel and from 2.06 to 6.67 percent is pig iron[16]. With the increase of carbon content, the percentage of tri-iron carbide[17] (Fe_3C) becomes greater and it makes the material more brittle and less plastic. That is to say, toughness and plasticity[18] of steel are much better than those of pig iron.

Cast iron used in products is always gray pig iron[19]. Because of a greater content of carbon than steel, strength of gray iron is smaller than steel. In order to improve its mechanical property, an agent is added into the furnace to spheroidize[20] the slice carbon in the iron, thus a new kind of cast iron called ductalloy[21] can be made. Another kind of high strength cast iron is malleable cast iron[22]. It is made by resolution[23] of the tri-iron carbide into graphite flocks[24].

Mechanical property of cast steel is better than cast iron, but its disadvantages are high melting point, low flowing property and large contraction and therefore it needs higher technology. Besides, heat treatment[25] is required for cast steel products.

There are quite a lot of parts of aluminum castings in a car such as cylinder head, cylinder block, cases[26], etc. Some of the aluminum parts such as piston and wheel hub are made of pressure casting (die casting)[27], a method of forcing the molten metal into the hollow mold under pressure.

本节注释: [1]铸造,铸件;[2]毛坯;[3]砂型;[4]粘合剂,粘结剂;[5]具有足够的结合强度以保持所需的形状并抵御高温液体的冲刷而不致崩塌;[6]机械加工表面;[7]砂芯和木制芯盒;[8]砂箱;[9]上砂箱;[10]下砂箱;[11] 浇口;[12]冒口;[13]炉子;[14]手转动的铁水包;[15]工业纯铁;[16]生铁;[17]碳化三铁;[18]韧性和塑性;[19]灰口铁;[20]球化处理;[21]球墨铸铁;[22]可锻铸铁;[23]分解;[24]石墨絮状物;[25]热处理;[26]箱体;[27]压力铸造(压铸),压铸件。

5.3.1.2 FORGING

Forging[1] is widely used in automotive manufacturing which includes free forging and die forging[2].

Free forging is a manufacturing method to shape a metal piece placed on an anvil[3] through hammering[4] or pressing. The blacksmith's work is an example of free forging. The metal piece should be heated in fire, put onto the anvil and a hand hammer is used to beat it until its shape is satisfactory. In modern workshop, hand hammers have been replaced by pneumatic hammers or presses[5]. The blanks of gear or shaft of a motor vehicle can be made by free forging.

Die forging is a manufacturing method to shape a metal piece placed into a die through hammering or pressing. It is somewhat like a dough[6] changed into a cake in a die under pressure. Comparing with free forging, die forging can make more complicated and more accurate products such as engine connecting rod, crankshaft, front axle beam, steering knuckle, etc.

本节注释: [1]锻造,锻件;[2]自由锻和模锻;[3]铁砧;[4]锤打;[5]汽锤或压床;

[6]生面团。

5.3.1.3 STAMPING

Stamping[1] is a manufacturing method to shape a metal sheet in a die[2] through shearing[3] or pressing. Pans, pots and lunch boxes used in daily life are made by stamping.

For example, to make a lunch box, we should cut a rectangular metal sheet with four circular corners. This step is called punch shearing or blanking[4]. After that, we can place the sheet between the upper die (the draw punch[5]) and the lower die (the cavity block[6]) and operate the upper die by pressing it into the lower die. This step is called drawing or stretching[7]. During the drawing step, the plane metal sheet is changed into a box, its four sides bend upward and materials on four corners accumulate together thus folds[8] can be seen.

A great number of parts of a motor vehicle are made by stamping, such as the engine oil sump, the brake base plate, the side rail and the cross member of the frame, most of the body panels, etc. Normally, manufacturing steps of those parts include blanking, punching[9], bending, drawing, flanging[10] and edge shearing[11].

Press and die are the two important items in stamping. Usually a set of dies is divided into two blocks. The upper die is connected with the movable slide[12] whereas the lower die is immovable and is fixed on the base of the press. First, the work piece[13] is placed between the upper die and the lower die. And then, as the upper die goes down and presses against the lower die, the stamping operation is finished. Stamping is a manufacturing method of high productivity. It is capable of not only making more than 100 products within one minute, but also complicated products of high accuracy.

本节注释:[1]冷冲压,冲压件;[2]模具;[3]剪裁;[4]冲裁或落料;[5]凸模;[6]凹模;[7]拉深或拉延;[8]皱纹;[9]冲孔;[10]翻边;[11]剪边,修边;[12]滑块;[13]工件。

5.3.1.4 WELDING

Welding[1] is a manufacturing method to heat two pieces of metal partially[2] and to connect them together.

We often see a worker carrying a shield (with colored glass) [3] on the one hand and an electrode holder (pliers)[4] on the other hand makes an electric arc[5] flash at the contact point of the electrode (welding rod)[6] with the steel work pieces, which causes high temperature to melt them together. A cabinet (welding transformer)[7] serves the system as power supply and connects the holder through a cable. This kind of welding is called manual arc welding[8], but it is not widely used in motor vehicle manufacturing.

Another welding method we often see in the repair workshop is oxy-acetylene welding[9]. A blowpipe (torch)[10] mixes oxygen and acetylene together and lights them, which causes high temperature to melt the filler rod[11] and the work pieces together. The blowpipe is supplied by an oxygen cylinder[12] and an acetylene generator[13] through an oxygen hose[14] and a gas hose. Either a welding nozzle[15] or a cutting nozzle[16] can be fitted on the blowpipe, and the latter is used to cut metal pieces. Disadvantage of this kind of welding is a large heating zone destroying the metallurgic structure of the metal[17]. Therefore, it is not popular in motor vehicle manufacturing either.

Spot welding[18] is a method widely used in automotive body manufacturing. It is suitable for connection of thin steel panels. During the welding process, two copper electrodes press the steel panels hard together[19] and make a strong electric current flow through the contact point of a circular area with a diameter of 5 to 6 mm to melt the panels together. Spot welding is not continuous connection but multi-spot connection[20]. Distance between every two spots is 40 to 80 mm. To complete the welding operations of a whole car body needs more than one thousand welding spots. Strength of a spot is high enough to withstand a stretching force up to 5 kN. Even if the panel is torn off[21] the spot could not be separated.

本节注释: [1]焊接,焊接件;[2]使两块金属部分加热;[3]有色玻璃面罩;[4]电极夹持器(焊钳);[5]电弧;[6]电极(焊条);[7]供电柜(焊接变压器);[8]手工电弧焊;[9]氧-乙炔焊(气焊);[10]喷焊枪;[11]气焊条;[12]氧气钢瓶;[13]乙炔发生器;[14]软管;[15]气焊喷嘴;[16]气割喷嘴;[17]较大的受热区破坏了金属的金相结构;[18]点焊;[19]两个铜电极把钢板紧压在一起;[20]多点连接;[21]被撕裂。

5.3.1.5 METAL CUTTING

Metal cutting[1] is a manufacturing method of using a cutter to peel a metal work piece layer by layer[2] and to obtain a product of the required shape, dimension and surface roughness. It can be classified into two kinds, i. e. bench work[3] and machine work. Bench work is the manufacturing method of using hand tools to cut the work piece. It is convenient, flexible and suitable for repairing work and assembling work. Machine work is carried out by machine tools including lathe, shaper, planer, milling machine, grinding machine and drilling machine[4].

As shown in figure 5-27, different manufacturing methods have different cutting motions, different machine tools and different cutters. In this figure, *v* is called the main motion[5] having high cutting speed and consuming the most of energy whereas *s* is called the feeding motion[6], i. e. the auxiliary motion sending the metal work piece to the cutter continuously.

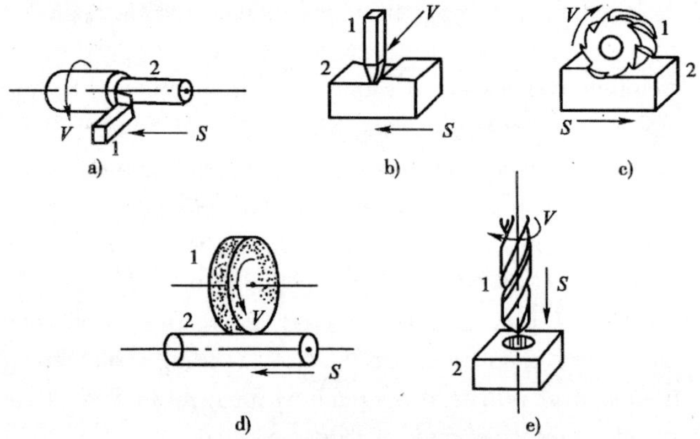

Fig. 5-27 Cutting Motions

a) turning; b) shaping; c) milling; d) grinding; e) drilling[7]

1-cutter; 2-work piece

v-*main motion*; s-*feeding motion*

Undoubtedly, hardness of the cutter material should be higher than that of the work piece, for example carbon tool steel, alloy tool steel, high speed steel and hard metal alloy[8]. Carbon tool steel is made of high carbon steel[9] containing 0.7 to 1.3 percent of carbon. Alloy tool steel is made of carbon tool steel added a small amount of chrome, tungsten, manganese, etc[10]. High speed steel contains quite a lot of tungsten and chrome to form metal carbides[11] in alloy steel. Hard metal alloy is a kind of non-iron alloy[12] made by powder metallurgy[13] on the basis of tungsten carbide and titanium carbide with cobalt as binder[14].

本节注释: [1]金属切削;[2]用刀具把金属工件逐层剥离;[3]钳工;[4]机床包括车床、牛头刨床、龙门刨床、铣床、磨床和钻床;[5]主运动;[6]进给运动;[7]由 a 至 e:车削、刨削、铣削、磨削、钻削;[8]例如碳素工具钢、合金工具钢、高速钢、硬质合金等;[9]高碳钢;[10]铬、钨、锰等;[11]金属碳化物;[12]非铁合金;[13]粉末冶金;[14]在碳化钨和碳化钛的基体上以钴为黏结剂。

TURNING

Turning is a manufacturing method to cut a work piece with a cutter (bite[1]) on the lathe. The main motion of the work piece is rotary and the feeding motion of the bite is linear. A lathe is suitable for cutting round surfaces such as outer and inner columns or cones. It is used to cut the end surface too. If the feeding speed is large enough, screw threads[2] can be cut. A lot of automotive parts such as shafts, gear blanks are made on the lathe.

本节注释: [1]车刀,刨刀;[2]螺纹。

SHAPING

Shaping is a manufacturing method to cut a work piece with a bite on the shaper. The main motion of the bite is linear and the feeding motion of the work piece is also linear but vertical to the main motion. Shaper is suitable for cutting horizontal, vertical and inclined planes and also grooves and slots. Many automotive parts such as surfaces of cylinder head, cylinder block and cases are made on the shaper.

MILLING

Milling is a manufacturing method to cut a work piece with a fraise[1] on the milling machine. The main motion of the fraise is rotary and the feeding motion of the work piece is linear. Milling machine is suitable for cutting planes, curved surfaces and even complicated contour such as the teeth of a helical gear[2]. Compared to shaping, the productivity of milling is higher and the cutting quality is better and more accurate. Almost all the work done by shaping can be replaced by milling. It is widely used in automotive manufacturing. For example, the curved surface of the stamp die is made by milling.

Numerical controlled (NC)[3] milling machine is a kind of advanced manufacturing equipment. Being controlled by the computer, the fraise can move along a very complicated trajectory[4].

本节注释: [1]铣刀,绞刀;[2]如斜齿轮的齿那样复杂的形状;[3]数控;[4]非常复杂的轨迹。

DRILLING AND BORING

Drilling and boring[1] are manufacturing methods to make holes with cutters. The main motion of the cutter is rotation around its axis and the feeding motion is linear motion along the axis. A twist drill (bit) which we are quite familiar with has helical grooves[2]. Its main cutting edges are on both sides of the tip and its secondary cutting edges[3] are the edges of helical grooves. The diameter of a drilled hole is equal to that of the drill. Boring is suitable for enlarging a big hole which had been cast on the work piece. As a typical example, a cylinder block casting has some cylinder holes required to be bored.

Fraising[4] is a manufacturing method to cut fine[5] holes. A fraise has more helical cutting edges than those of a drill[6]. Cutting speed of the fraise is low and cutting deepness is small.

本节注释: [1]钻削和镗削;[2]我们较熟悉的麻花钻头具有螺旋槽。[3]副切削刃;[4]铰孔;[5]精细的;[6]绞刀比钻头具有较多的螺旋切削刃。

GRINDING

Grinding[1] is a manufacturing method to smooth a work piece with a sand wheel[2]. The main motion of the sand wheel is rotation around its axis and the feeding motion of the work piece is linear motion. Grinding is a kind of fine machining, i. e. it can make very precise and very smooth products.

Grinding can also cut very hard surfaces such as automotive products after heat treatment.

Polishing[3] is a manufacturing method of fine grinding. It can make mirror surface[4] with the help of a soft wheel with polishing paste on[5]. Polishing can not increase accuracy. It is only used in decorative parts as a ready process before electroplating[6].

本节注释: [1]磨削;[2]砂轮;[3]抛光;[4]镜面;[5]涂抛光膏的软轮;[6]它仅作为电镀前的预备工序用于装饰零件。

GEAR CUTTING

There are many kinds of gears and their manufacturing methods are different from each other and rather complicated. We can use the following easy example to explain the manufacturing principle.

A pair of gears can match each other harmoniously. If one of them was a cutter, the other would be cut. That is to say, the cutter of a gear-work piece is somewhat like another gear matching it.

FIXING AND LOCALIZING[1]

A work piece should be fixed tightly on the machine tool to avoid slipping and trembling[2]. Besides, the work piece should keep correct position with the cutter to ensure accurate cutting. Therefore, besides machine tools, cutters and work pieces, fixtures[3] are also needed.

A fixture can not only fix the work piece tightly, but also provide correct localization. For example, the chuck (head stock) of the lathe[4] is a typical fixture not only to hold the work piece tightly, but also to ensure the axis of the work piece overlapping together[5] with the main axis of the lathe.

本节注释: [1]安装与定位;[2]串动与颤动;[3]夹具;[4]车床的卡盘;[5]重叠在一起。

5.3.1.6 HEAT TREATMENT

Heat treatment is a manufacturing method to change the metallurgic structure of a product by reheating, temperature preserving and cooling processes.

Heat treatment includes annealing, normalizing, hardening (quenching) and tempering[1]. Annealing is a method to reheat the steel work piece, to preserve its temperature for a certain time and then to cool it slowly together with the furnace. It can result in small and uniform structure in the work piece to reduce its hardness for easier cutting. Normalizing is a method to heat the steel work piece, to take it out from the furnace and to cool it in the air. It is suitable for fine treatment of low carbon steel[2]. Hardening is a method to heat the steel work piece, to preserve its temperature and then to cool it in water or oil. It can increase hardness of the steel product. Tempering is a successive process[3] of hardening by the way of reheating the steel work piece and then cooling it after preserving its temperature. It can make the structure stable and reduce brittleness[4].

Some of the automotive parts require both a tough core and a hard surface. To meet such requirements, the heat treatment methods including high frequency hardening[5], carburizing (cementing)[6] and cyanide hardening (cyanide carburizing)[7] are used.

本节注释：[1]退火、正火、淬火和回火；[2]低碳钢的细化处理；[3]后续工序；[4]脆性；[5]高频淬火；[6]渗碳；[7]氰化。

5.3.1.7 ASSEMBLING

Assembling[1] is a method to connect parts together into a whole component or to connect components together into a whole machine with screws, bolts, nuts[2], etc.

No matter assembling a component with parts or a whole motor vehicle with components, the requirements of fitting relations given on the drawings[3] should be met. For example, to install the gearbox on to the clutch housing, it is necessary to make the axis of the input shaft of the gearbox center[4] with the axis of the crankshaft of the engine. Method of centering is not adjusted by the worker during assembling process but is determined by structural requirements designed by the engineer. To bore the localized hole of the clutch housing, it is necessary to fix it onto the cylinder block before boring and use the same manufacturing datum[5] with the block. Moreover, an outer localized circular surface should be made on the front end cap of the gearbox[6] so as to fit the localized hole on the clutch housing.

The most attractive place in an automotive enterprise for a visitor worth going is the overall assembling line of the motor vehicle[7]. A motor vehicle can be produced from this assembling line in every interval of a few minutes. Take the assembling line of the truck Jiefang CA 1092 as an example. It is a chain conveyer[8] of 165 m long. Components moving together with the chain conveyer are assembled one by one gradually to form a whole motor vehicle. Assembling steps are as follows.

a) Place the frame (upside down) on to the chain conveyer.

b) Install the rear axle (including left and right leaf springs and wheel hubs) and the front axle (including left and right leaf springs, steering knuckles and wheel hubs) onto the frame.

c) Turn over the frame and install the steering system, the braking reservoir and piping, the fuel tank and piping, the cluster of wirings[9], wheels, etc.

d) Install the engine (including clutch, gearbox and hand brake) and connect it with the propeller shafts.

e) Install the cab and the front end panels.

After that, the truck can be driven to the test rigs to examine its performances and to adjust beams of the headlamps[10]. The last assembling step (cargo carrying platform installation) is not carried out on the assembling line. The truck needs to go to the platform workshop to finish the last step.

The overall assembling line of the car in FAW-VW[11] can produce a car in every interval of 1.5 minutes. That is 40 cars per hour, 640 cars per day (16 working hours, 2 shifts[12] per day) and 160 thousand cars per year (250 working days per year). Evidently, to meet the requirement of 160 thousand cars, the number of every kind of parts and components should not be less than 160 thousands. If all the parts are produced in the same enterprise, it would be a huge production system leading to a lot of problems such as supply difficulty, management difficulty, etc. Actually, most of the components and parts are produced by different levels of suppliers (see Paragraph 5.1.2.2. in this Chapter), and then they are gathered and transported to the overall assembling line in the OEM.

A car can be produced in every interval of 1.5 minutes. It does not mean that all the parts and components can be assembled onto a car within 1.5 minutes. It is impossible! The overall assembling line of the car in FAW-VW is 880 m long and has 153 working positions[13]. The whole assembling process of a car begins at the starting point of the chain conveyer and terminates at its end. It needs 153 × 1.5 = 229.5 minutes to pass through the whole assembling line. That is to say, the whole assembling time of a car is 229.5 minutes, not 1.5 minutes.

本节注释：[1]装配；[2]螺钉、螺栓、螺母；[3]图纸上所给定的配合关系；[4]对中心；[5]制造基准或工艺基准；[6]变速器的前端盖；[7]汽车总装配线；[8]传送链；[9]电线束；[10]前照灯的灯光；[11]一汽－大众汽车公司；[12]轮班；[13]工位。

5.3.2 *ECONOMICAL SCALE*

What is economical scale[1]? The explanation is as follows.

Assuming a part needs to drill 10 holes, if one worker with one drilling machine can drill one hole within 3 minutes, to produce one part needs 30 minutes. That is, he can produce 16 parts per day (8 hours). According to paragraph 5.3.1.7, 640 parts per day are required. Therefore 40 workers and 20 drilling machines are needed (2 shifts per day).

Table 5-3 is the comparison of small scale production[2] (1000 parts annually) with large scale production[3] (160 thousand parts annually). The table is based on the assumption of annual salary per worker[4] 10 thousand yuan and price per drilling machine 2500 yuan which is planned to retrieve[5] in 5 years (500 yuan per year). We can see figures in column G (total cost per product) of small and large scale are not the same. The latter is less than the former. We can understand from this simple example that large scale production has lower cost per product, better quality and more competitive potential than small scale production.

Moreover, large scale production is possible to use specialized machine tools[6] to increase productivity and to reduce cost. For example, we can use a specialized drilling machine equipped with 10 drills to cut 10 holes simultaneously (require 3 minutes). That is, productivity will increase to 10 times. To reach the number of 160 thousand products per year, we only need 2 specialized drilling machines and 4 workers. Assuming the price of a specialized drilling machine 10 thousand yuan and 2 year retrieval (5000 yuan per year), we can obtain the total cost per product only 0.31 yuan through the calculation method given in table 5-3.

Comparison of annual cost (salary and retrieval) of small scale with large scale Table 5-3

A	*B*	*C*	*D*	*E*	*F* = *D* + *E*	*G* = *F*/*A*
Annual production (Unit)	Number of workers (Person)	Drilling machines needed (Unit)	Annual salary (Yuan)	Annual retrieval (Yuan)	Total cost (Yuan)	Total cost per product (Yuan)
1 000	1	1	10 000	500	10 500	10.50
160 000	40	20	400 000	10 000	410 000	2.56

Economical Scale of Passenger Car Production Table 5-4

Annual production (×1000 units)	100	200	300	400	>400
Investment(%) Cost per unit(%)	100 100	140 92	180 89	240 87	No profit

We say large scale production has many advantages, but it does not mean production scale can expand without limit. Each production equipment has its life limit. For example, the life of a stamp die is to make 200 thousand stampings. If production scale is more than 200 thousand units, another stamp die should be provided. Overexpansion of the production scale[7] would result in renewal of much more production equipments and therefore is not profitable. Besides, an overbuilt enterprise would lead to many problems such as difficulties of management, supply, transport, etc. For this reason, study should be taken to find out the most economical production scale.

After investigating the production scale of passenger cars, an English research institute pointed out: "For a car factory of production scale with 100 thousand units per year, if its production scale increases to 200 thousand units per year, investment would increases by 40 percent and the cost per unit would reduce by 8 percent; If the production scale increases to 300 thousand units per year, another 40 percent of investment would be needed and the cost per unit would reduce another 3 percent; If the production scale increases to 400 units per year, investment would add another 60 percent and the cost per unit would reduce another 2 percent; If production scale is more than 400 units per year, it may not be profitable."

The conclusion can be described clearly in table 5-4 which may be said like this: "The economical scale of passenger car production is 300 thousand units per year."

本节注释：[1]经济规模；[2]小批量生产；[3]大批量生产；[4]每个工人的年工资；[5]收回（这个设备的投资）；[6]专用机床；[7]生产规模过度膨胀。

5.3.3 *ADVANCED PRODUCTION PROCESS*

5.3.3.1 COMPUTER AIDED MANUFACTURING

Computer aided manufacturing (CAM)[1] is to control the production equipments and to carry out production management by the use of computers. Numerical controlled (NC) manufacturing is a typical kind of CAM. Before NC manufacturing, the shape of the automotive part should be changed into digital model and then a special computer program can be compiled on the basis of the digital model. During the process of NC manufacturing, the production equipment is controlled by the computer program. The following is an example of stamp die manufacturing.

We have mentioned before that the shape of a body part can be expressed by an accurate and smooth digital model which serves as the basis of stamp die design. That is, the digital curved surfaces of the upper die (the draw punch) and the lower die (the cavity block) are worked out on the basis of the digital model of the body part and then the computer program of NC manufacturing is compiled on the basis of the curved surfaces of the upper and lower dies.

Because metal cutting process should be carried out layer by layer[2], the computer program of NC manufacturing is not simple. It needs to select the cutting tool (fraise), to determine the speed of the main shaft and the feeding speed of the NC milling machine, to plan the trajectory of the fraise in every cutting step[3], etc. Comparing to the traditional tracer control method (profile milling) [4], CAM of the stamp die has many advantages such as high accuracy and short production period.

Before profile milling, a wooden model of the same curved surface profile as the die should be ready with the help of a set of templates[5]. After that, the wooden model is installed on the profile milling machine and a tracer device can imitate the wooden profile to control the trajectory of the fraise[6]. Evidently, all the work needs a lot of labor and time. Moreover, the handmade wooden model and templates are less accurate and lead to reciprocal mending.

Computers used on the flow production line and automatic production line[7] make all the working position cooperate effectively and precisely. It will benefit the implementation of lean production and "just in time (JIT)[8]".

Integration of CAD and CAM[9] is a main feature of advanced production. Because computers at both the design department and the manufacturing department link together and share the same data base[10], integration of CAD and CAM results in high accuracy, high quality and high productivity. Application of computer to production helps to bring about automatic production and flexible manufacturing[11]. NC equipments and robots[12] controlled by computer not only replace almost all the manual work and heavy labor, but also lead to quick tempo, uniform rate and accurate action[13] which are impossible to be done by manual labor..

Manufacturing flexibility[14] is to make different products on the same equipment. That is to say, the equipment can change its operation manner flexibly to meet the manufacturing requirements of the product. For example, a drilling machine is capable of replacing drills of different diameters and changing different drilling directions to meet different cutting operations of holes.

The specialized machine tool mentioned before for drilling 10 holes has the advantages of high productivity, but its disadvantage is that it is only capable of matching the special shape of one single product. Once the product is changed into another shape or replaced by a next generation product, such specialized drilling machine would not be adaptable and useful.

If the design of a motor vehicle is changed or renewed by a next generation, it would result in giving up[15] many specialized machine tools, specialized fixtures and specialized production lines though they are not worn out. At the same time, huge investment is needed to buy a lot of new specialized equipments to meet the production requirements of a new motor vehicle. For this reason, the flexible manufacturing system (FMS)[16] adaptable to both the old and the new products is a good way to save investment and to reduce production cost.

There are three main components to form a flexible manufacturing system, i. e. NC machine tools, robots and computer controls. It would be quite easy to change the operation manner of the NC machine tools and robots by changing the computer instructions[17]. FMS is not only adaptable to continuous change of product generations, but also capable of making a variety of products of different specifications in small batches under the program of large scale production[18]. FMS has shown its clear superiority[19] and has been widely used in enterprises.

When you walk into a modern automotive factory, the most attractive place is the overall body welding line[20] (Fig. 5-28) formed by many spot welding robots. They move their calipers[21] to designated points and finish the work perfectly. It is quite easy to change the welding point and the operation manner of a spot welding robot by changing the computer instructions. Therefore, several kinds of bodies can be welded on the same production line. The work of a welding robot can replace 3 to 4 workers. Including depreciation charge[22], a welding robot costs 5 US dollars per hour whereas the salary of a common worker in the automotive enterprise of America is 15 dollars per hour. That is, the cost of a robot is 1/9 to 1/12 of the cost of workers.

本节注释：[1]计算机辅助制造；[2]金属切削过程应是逐层进行；[3]计划每一步骤的刀具轨迹；[4]仿形法(仿形铣)；[5]样板；[6]跟踪机构可模拟木制的形面操纵铣刀的轨迹；[7]流水生产线和自动生产线；[8]有利于实施精益生产和准时制；[9]CAD

Fig. 5-28 Overall Body Welding Line of the Car Vocane[23]

和 CAM 一体化;[10]共用同一数据库;[11]柔性制造;[12]机器人;[13]快节拍、均匀速率和精确动作;[14]制造柔性化;[15]废弃;[16]柔性制造系统;[17]计算机指令;[18]在大批量生产的纲领下有可能制造小批量、多品种、不同规格的产品;[19]明显的优越性;[20]车身总装焊接生产线;[21]焊钳;[22]折旧费;[23]富康轿车。

5.3.3.2 VIRTUAL REALITY

Virtual reality (VR)[1] is to feel a virtual event through visual, audible and tactile senses[2].with the help of computer. Technique of virtual reality is widely used in research and development process of modern products including design, test and trial-manufacturing[3].

To design an automatic production line needs very careful consideration. It would be beneficial if we use VR to imitate and to analyze the action and cooperation of equipments and then choose the optimum solution.

An advanced technique called virtual proving ground (VPG)[4] has been used in motor vehicle design. Before a motor vehicle is made, from the computer screen we can see a virtual motor vehicle driving on different virtual roads to examine its performances. That is, performance prediction and evaluation[5] can be obtained and many difficult problems can be solved much earlier before a real motor vehicle is made and tested.

The technique of VR is especially suitable for such projects as motor vehicle collision, weapon test[6], etc. In order to test a new car, if we can use virtual collisions to replace real collisions, it is evident that it would save much money and shorten the design and development period. If we are planning to launch a rocket explorer[7] to the Mars[8], it is unable to carry out real launching test and only VR is the most suitable method for us to choose.

本节注释: [1]虚拟现实;[2]视觉、听觉和触觉;[3]试制;[4]虚拟汽车试验场;[5]性能的预测和评价;[6]武器试验;[7]火箭探测器;[8]火星。

5.3.3.3 CONCURRENT ENGINEERING

Concurrent engineering or simultaneous engineering[1] means that the steps of the product development process are not carried out serially[2] (one by one) but parallelly[3]. The development process of a motor vehicle includes planning, styling, engineering design, prototyping, testing and production preparation. If the steps are arranged serially, that is, the next begins after the former ends, assuming every step needs 1 year, then we need 6 years to go through the whole process. In order to shorten the development process, the steps following should begin as early as possible. Figure 5-29 is the comparison of serial arrangement with parallel arrangement. We can see the advantage of the latter is a much shorter development period which leads to faster market reaction. Therefore, an enterprise can be active and take a more advantageous position in the serious market situation.

With the support of advanced development tools, the former step can provide requisites for the next step to move up[4]. For example, the styling department can provide a digital model of the body surface earlier and makes the steps of structural design, engineering analysis and stamp die manufacturing move up.

本节注释: [1]并行工程或同时同步工程;[2]串联,先后次序;[3]并联,同时并举;[4]提前。

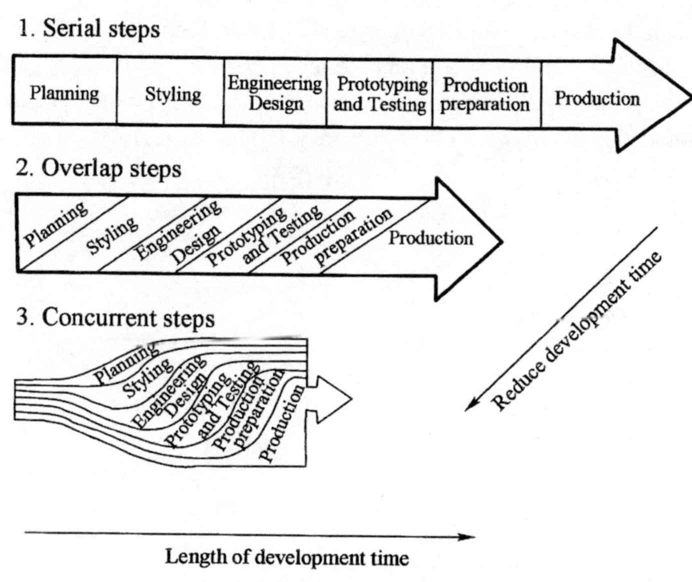

Fig. 5-29 Diagram of Concurrent Engineering

本章参考文献

5.1 柳冠中,王明旨. 设计的文化. 北京:展示设计协会编印,1987

5.2 刘惟信. 汽车设计. 北京:清华大学出版社,2000

5.3 李卓森. 现代汽车造型. 北京:人民交通出版社,2005

5.4 邱毓强. 汽车拖拉机试验学. 北京:机械工业出版社,1981

5.5 王宝玺. 汽车拖拉机制造工艺学. 北京:机械工业出版社,1981

5.6 乌尔里希·赛费特,彼得·瓦尔泽 著. 严机 等译. 汽车技术未来展望. 北京:人民交通出版社,1987

5.7 斋藤明彦. 丰田汽车的开发体制与特征. 北京:国际汽车技术研讨会论文,1996

5.8 斋藤明彦.计算机辅助开发与高度信息化.北京:国际汽车技术研讨会论文,1996
5.9 Robert Dockstader. Ford Product Development Technologies for the World.北京:国际汽车技术研讨会论文,1996
5.10 P. N. Blumberg. Information Technology: Enabling Product Development around the World.北京:国际汽车技术研讨会论文,1996

CHAPTER SIX
THE FUTURE

6.1 AUTO SHOWS

Auto show is a good way to promote the sales of the products, to demonstrate the development trend of design and to build up the corporate image as well as a good place of advertisements and business activities.

6.1.1 *SITUATION OF AUTO SHOWS*

6.1.1.1 WORLD FAMOUS AUTO SHOWS

The motor car was demonstrated first in the 1898 Paris International Exhibition. It might be a grand exhibition which attracted more than 140 000 viewers. Compared with the telephone invented by Alessandro Bell which was the center of attraction, the motor car seemed to be neglected in that Exhibition. Such awkward situation changed eleven years later when the 1900 Paris Exhibition was held. The exhibition space of automotive products was expanded to two big showrooms and almost all the new types of the European motor vehicles were shown. After that, automotive products became an indispensable part in various kinds of exhibitions. For example, in the 1915 San-Francisco Exhibition, the most eye-catching place to go was Ford's demonstration of a whole flow production line of Model Ts. Shortly later, with the rapid development of the automotive industry, motor shows began to appear independently as a kind of famous exhibitions in the world.

The targets to determine a high level motor show are scale of exhibitors, level of exhibits, quantity of automotive products and concept cars, exhibition space, level of supporting facilities, service quality of sponsor, participation of news media, number of viewers and level of professional technology. The

Frankfurt Auto Show, the Paris International Motor Show, the Geneva Auto Show, the North American Auto Show and the Tokyo Motor Show are recognized as the top five motor shows.

Frankfurt Auto Show, the largest auto show of the world, was founded in 1897. With plentiful and all-sided exhibits the Frankfurt Auto Show is regarded as the "Olympic-Games" of the worldwide automotive industry. Its predecessor[1] is Berlin Auto Show, and has moved to Frankfurt after the 35th.

Paris International Motor Show began in 1898, and its predecessor was International Motor Salon. Since 1976 it has been held every other year, alternating with the Frankfurt Auto Show. Paris International Motor Show is the second largest auto show of the world. Creative and concept cars are the highlights of the Show.

The beginning of the North American International Auto Show, previously called the Detroit Auto Show, dates back to 1907. It is one of the earliest auto shows of the world. In 1989, it became the North American International Auto Show (NAIAS). NAIAS features a huge number of concept and production debuts[2].

Since its first show in 1905, the Geneva Auto Show has more than 100 years of history. Its location in Switzerland represents neutral ground for automakers from around the world to show off new models and concepts. As "vane of the international automotive fashion", it also features limousines[3] and modifications[4] with high performance.

Tokyo Motor Show was born in 1954, and then it was called All Japan Motor Show. On the show a plenty of domestically produced small cars are demonstrated. Release of new products[5], unconventional concepts and electronic technology are also the highlights of Tokyo Motor Show.

本节注释：[1]前身；[2]初次亮相；[3]高级轿车；[4]改装车；[5]新产品发布。

6.1.1.2 *CURRENT SITUATION OF AUTO SHOWS IN CHINA*

The first Shanghai International Exhibition of Automotive Industry (Auto Shanghai) was held in July 1985. It attracted 328 OEMs and suppliers from 22 countries and regions, covering an exhibition space of 15 000 square meters. 1985 was the first year when Shanghai Automotive Industry Corporation (Group) set up the joint venture[1] with Volkswagen Germany. The first local-made[2] VW Santana was introduced to the public on this exhibition. Therefore, the success of this exhibition can be regarded as a milestone of the Shanghai automotive industry and also the industrial modernization of China. Hence Shanghai Auto has been held every two years.

The first Beijing International Exhibition of Automotive Industry (Auto China), previously called Beijing International Exhibition of Automobile and Technical Equipment, was held in June 1990 by Chinese Corporation of Automotive Industry and Chinese Council for Promotion of International Trade. With an area of 20 000 square meters, the exhibition attracted 372 exhibitors (among them 72 foreign exhibitors) from 17 countries/regions and 100 000 visitors.

After rapid development for over 20 years, Beijing and Shanghai auto shows have become the top level automotive exhibitions in the world. However, owing to their short history they are not as famous as the world's top-class auto shows in the cultural aspect, and need time to sum up experiences and to develop their own style.

本节注释:[1]合资企业;[2]国产的。

6.1.2 *CORPORATE IMAGE*

Corporate image[1], also called corporate public image, is the whole viewpoint and general impression given by the public or consumers on corporation, corporation behavior and corporation events. It can be transferred into basic conviction and comprehensive comments.

6.1.2.1 CORPORATE IMAGE POSITIONING[2]

With the coming of the new century, the market competition is getting increasingly fierce. The competition of products and brands has been changed into competition of corporate image, followed by the increasingly diversified series of competitive means including advertisement and price wars. By convincing the public, the corporate image will lead their decisions and comments on the products to a great extent. Therefore, as the most important invisible capital[3] among the corporation resources, corporate image has become a crucial factor in the market competition. Good image promotes the corporation to win customers' trust, to attract talents, to obtain cooperation and aid, to solve problems and troubles and to push forward spiritual cultivation[4].

The public is the commentator of the corporate image. The comments given by the public on corporate image is based on certain standards. Corporate image is the result of the corporation's long-term effort and pursuit. The recognition of the corporate image is comprehensive, not partial. It is the final impression of the public's rational choice and thought. Therefore, the corporation should analyze some related factors, highlight its own advantages and determine its own image positioning.

两节注释: [1]企业形象;[2]企业形象定位;[3]无形资产;[4]精神文明。

6.1.2.2 CORPORATE VISION[1]

Combined with self-image positioning, the corporation should integrate many resources to build up corporate image successfully.

Corporate image can be classified into many kinds or types according to different standards. Although they have different names, they are all based on some carriers[2]. As corporate image is the general opinion and impression of the social public on the corporation's activities, the carriers of corporate image building can be no doubt concluded in three aspects, i. e. corporation, corporation behavior[3], and achievements of corporate events[4].

The first carrier, the corporation, is the principal part of image-building. It is the carrier of the surface image of the corporation which can leave the public the "first impression" most directly and quickly. In order to inform the public the industry features, business features, and corporation advantages from the "first image", the corporation needs to design an external sense which includes the appearance of the factory, office places, office facility, advertisements and publicity[5], exhibition and demonstration and even employees' dressing, attitude and behavior.

The second carrier of the corporate image is corporation behavior which includes production behavior, management behavior, business behavior, sales behavior and public relation behavior. The corporation behavior brings forth the employee image, management image, business image, marketing image and social image in the corporation. It is restricted totally and directly by the corporate culture. The corporate value, corporate objective, corporation democracy, corporate system and corporate constitution[6] of the corporate culture will be fully exercised in the corporate behaviors, which also shows fully that corporate culture is the soul and backbone of the corporate image.

The third carrier of the corporate image is the corporate event achievements. Corporation events are the contradiction entity[7] of the actual labor and social labor, the result of which is to provide commodity or service of usable value to the society, including the after-sale service which is especially important in the automotive industry. The commodity and service must be chosen and used by customers through circulating links[8]. During the process of use, the customers will make their evaluations on the commodity or service offered by the corporation so that the product image and after-sale service image are pictured.

本节注释: [1]企业形象表现;[2]载体;[3]企业行为;[4]企业活动成果;[5]宣传;[6]章程;[7]矛盾的统一体;[8]流通环节。

6.1.3 *AUTOMOBILE PRODUCT MARKETING*

6.1.3.1 AUTOMOBILE PRODUCT STRATEGY[1]

MODERN PRODUCT MARKETING ABOUT PRODUCT CONCEPT

The GB/T 9000 series standard defines the term “product” as “the result of the activity or the process” or “the activity or the process itself”. The concept given by this definition may be visible (such as material object), invisible (such as service, software), or the combination of both. For example, it can be a product manufacturing process controlled by computer.

Marketing[2] is a process to meet the customer's needs. The customer's needs may be material and/or mental. Mental needs of the car buyers may be identity, status, wealth and honor. In addition, the car buyers also want the manufacturer or the dealer to provide high-quality after-sale service including abundant spare parts, convenient service shops and "three-guaranteed service[3]". Evidently, modern product marketing is an overall concept containing three layers, i. e. the substantial product, the form product and the expanded product[4]. The substantial product is the core content of the customer's requirements. It is the basic effect or benefit of customers. The substantial product of a car is to meet the customer's requirements for transportation and spiritual pleasure. The form product is an existent form based on the substantial product. It consists of the structure form, the quality level, the special features, style, trademark, and the package. The expanded product is the additional service or benefits gained by the customers, such as a credit, free delivery, adjustment, service and warranty. The modern marketing has already formed the concept of "system sale", which not only provides the form product (i. e. the visible products mentioned above), but also includes the expanded product.

本节注释: [1]汽车产品战略;[2]营销;[3]三包服务;[4]实质产品、形式产品和扩增产品。

AUTOMOTIVE PRODUCT PROMOTION STRATEGY[1]

The market situation is always changeable, especially when it is weak and competition is crucial. Promotion method is important for the enterprise to maintain its long-term and stable development and to pass through the difficult time. Promotion ability is an important part of the marketing ability of an enterprise.

Promotion refers to the transmission of the product information and the way of purchase from the marketing department of the enterprise to customers through a certain way. It is a series of activities to stimulate the customer's interest, to strengthen their desire, even to create their needs.

The essence of promotion is disseminating and exchanging information, and its purpose is to enhance sales and expand the market share of the corporation. There are mainly two ways for communication. The first one is unidirectional communication[2], which means either communication from "seller-to-buyer" such as advertisements, exhibitions, instruction booklets and publicity reports, or communication from "buyer-to-seller" such as user' s prospectus and customer's feedbacks. The second way is bilateral communication[3], for example, visiting sales or spot-negotiated sale. The modern marketing system groups the above items into four categories, i. e. advertisement, personnel promotion, business promotion and public relations (PR) [4]. The combination of these four is defined as promotion combination[5]. The strategy of the promotion combination can be described as how to match and utilize these four components during the operating period of a corporation. Furthermore, for the marketing of automobile, there is another important promotion method which is sales technique service[6] (including after-sale service). It can be said that, in the modern automotive market, if you do not set up the sales technique service, especially after-sale service, no market can be maintained. If the service you provide can not meet the requirements of the customers, you will eventually lose your market. This is especially significant and meaningful for the sales of automotive products.

In brief, the overall function of the promotion is buying the market. But when enterprise makes decision on promotion combination, it should match various kinds of promotions pointedly and consider the relations between the effect and the cost of the promotion.

本节注释:[1]汽车产品促销战略;[2]单向沟通;[3]双向沟通;[4]公关;[5]促销组合;[6]销售技术服务。

AUTOMOBILE BRAND STRATEGY[1]

Brand

Brand is also called the trade mark. It is the name created by the seller for a product. It is usually consists of such factors as words, symbol, shape and color and is composed of the meanings of brand name, sign and trademark.

Brand is one of the most important resources of the enterprise for its sustainable development. In the growing process of the automobile market, the brand concept is receiving more and more attention. But, many executives don't have a clear concept about the brand concept. They often attach importance to a good company image and the promotion of the products, not the value and the function of the brand. As far as an enterprise is concerned, the enterprise image is of the first importance, the brand image is the second, and the product image is the third. A brand must exist in the enterprise, and depends on the visible product[2]. But, the brand can also be independent of the enterprise which it represents and the product which it depends on. The business enterprise can be annexed, united or reorganized, even bankrupt, and also the product can be changed or renewed, but the value of the brand is eternal and increases continuously. Changing into a famous brand, the same product will increase its value many times. For example, the Lamborghini supercar, no matter before or after its enterprise was purchased by VW, the core value of the brand image has not changed with the acquisition of the enterprise. Therefore, to develop, foster and manage a brand is the base of the enterprise image and the expression of the product personalization[3]. The brand means the market positioning and the quality, the performance, the technology, the equipment and the service. This is especially true to a car having strong personality in the automotive products. It finally embodies the management idea of the enterprise. The brand image comes from the consumer's approval. It is a "Positive plus Positive" value chain[4]. This kind of value chain is worked by the "word of mouth[5]" and "use effect[6]". If the channel of the consumer's communication is not established, the enterprise cannot obtain the consumer's trust, and the brand value is equal to zero.

Brand Name and Brand Mark

Brand name[7] refers to the content in the brand which can be expressed in language. Brand mark[8] refers to the specific symbol which can be distinguished but not expressed in language. It is composed by shape, color, and art lettering[9].

The automotive companies rack their brains[10] trying to find a nice brand name for their products so as to attract the customers and even to make known and remembered to everybody. The good examples of brand names are as follows.

(1) To use the names of famous persons: Lincoln (the 16th President of the United States), Cadillac (the founder of the city Detroit), Pontiac (a chief of an Indian tribe[11]) and Mercedes (an auspicious name of a beautiful

girl);

(2) To use the names of goddesses/gods, especially in Greek mythology[12]: Dyna (goddess of the Moon, a Toyota light truck), Fury (goddess of avenge, a Plymouth car), Apollo (god of the Sun, a Buick car) and Aeolus (god of wind, Chinese SAW[13] brand name);

(3) To use the names of famous places: Eldorado (gold nation, a Cadillac car), Granada (Spanish city, a Ford car) and Fairlane (Henry Ford's manor, a Ford car);

(4) To use the names of lovely animals: Mustang (a Ford sportcar), Firebird (a Pontiac sportcar), Panda (a Fiat supermini) and Chaika (Seagull, a Soviet luxury car);

(5) To use digits: Porsche 911, BMW 760, Mazda 929 and Oldsmobile 98;

(6) Other good names: Century (a Buick car), Tornado (a Cadillac car), Intrepid (a Dodge car), Crown (a Toyota car) and Sonata (a Hyundai car).

Figure 6-1 shows the brand marks of the top ten famous enterprise groups (see the color pages).

The scale and complexity of automotive industry especially the car market has greatly changed since the end of 20th century. It has become an important strategy for many world automotive manufacturers to consolidate or promote their competitive advantages by strengthening the brand operation. Under the mother brand of a product series, there are different cars competing in different segmented markets.

本节注释: [1]汽车品牌战略;[2]有形产品;[3]产品个性化;[4]"正加正"的价值链;[5]口碑传播;[6]使用效果;[7]品牌名称;[8]品牌标志;[9]美术字;[10]绞尽脑汁;[11]印第安酋长;[12]希腊神话;[13]中国二汽。

6.1.3.2 AUTOMOBILE PRODUCT MIX[1]

Product is the physical condition of marketing. The goal of the marketing activities of an enterprise is to seize the market. The enterprise must enhance the development of the product and the decision-making of the launch of the product to meet the needs of the target market.

The product Mix (also called product assortment[2]) includes all the products marketed. It refers to the combination or matches of all product lines[3] and product items[4] provided to the market by enterprise.

The product mix contains some concepts below:

PRODUCT LINE AND PRODUCT ITEM

Product line is a sub-division in product mix. It refers to a group of closely linked products. Regarding automotive products, it means vehicle series.

Product item is the smallest unit of products which can be distinguished by certain product attributes. It is the smallest unit of the constitution of product mix and product line.

PRINCIPLE OF PRODUCT MIX DECISION MAKING

The automotive product mix decision-making has great significance to the marketing decision-making of an enterprise. To increase the breadth (vehicle series) of the product mix and expand the business scope may reduce the risk of a singular model. To increase the length (many varieties) of the product mix may make the product line plentiful, increasing more change factors of each product, and it is advantageous to subdivide the market and enhance the market share and the customer satisfaction. When the competition is fierce in the market, increasing the variety of the product is the commonly used method to enhance the ability of competition. At present in the automotive market of our country, each kind of vehicle model has big room for development except the medium trucks which have already become mature. And the space for development of the vehicle series of passenger cars and heavy trucks is also very big. So the automotive enterprise must improve their product lines and make a good decision-making of the product items to seek more space for the development.

本节注释:[1] 汽车产品组合;[2]品种搭配;[3]产品线;[4]产品项目。

6.1.4 *AUTO SHOW STRATEGY*

6.1.4.1 OVERVIEW OF STRATEGIC MANAGEMENT

The strategic management is a process of decision and execution based on adequate information. It consists of three correlative tasks, i. e. strategy-making, strategy-implementing and strategy-evaluating and controlling[1]. These three phases including seven links and their relations are shown in Fig. 6-2.

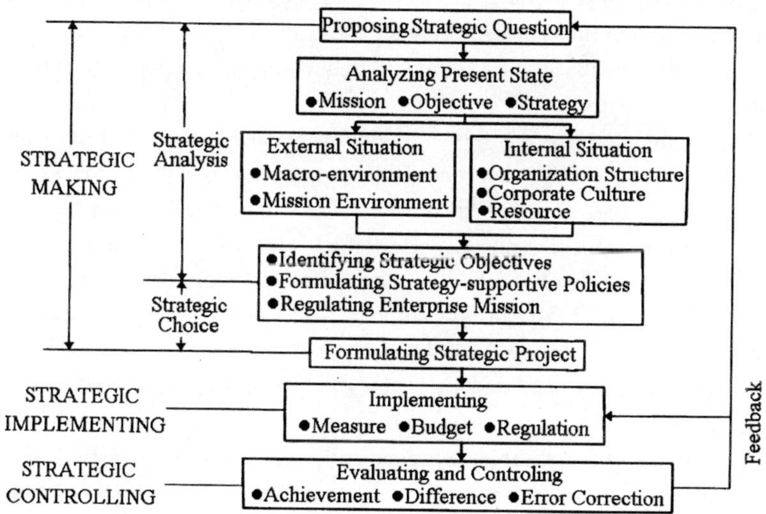

Fig. 6-2 Three Phases of Strategic Management Including Seven Links and Their Relations

Understanding the present condition of an enterprise is the start of strategy-making. The manager should propose the strategic question[2] at first. The strategic question could be the problem which the enterprise really faces (a negative question), and could also be the challenge that the enterprise has to conquer by developing its internal resource or making use of the external opportunities (a positive question). On the basis of the strategic question, the enterprise should analyze its current mission, objective and the current strategy, and then make an audit[3] of the external and internal circumstances to find out opportunities and threats from the external environment and the strength and weakness of its internal resource. The external environment of the enterprise includes macro-environment, such as politics, economy, law, technology, population, nature, society and culture. The internal environment consists of organizational structure, corporate culture, management ability, production capacity, marketing ability, financial resource and human resource. Based on the above analysis, the enterprise defines its mission, strategic policy and the strategic objectives again.

After the strategic analysis, the enterprise could shape and determine a suitable strategic policy, then enter the strategy-implementing process. By implementing, the enterprise should pay attention to the harmony and adaptation between the strategies of different levels. The strategies could be divided into three levels: overall strategy, business-unit strategy and functional strategy[4]. The overall strategy is at the highest level, business-unit strategy is the strategy of a business unit, a division or a subsidiary company, and functional strategy is the strategy of each main functional department. Each of these three levels has particular key point, so the enterprise should handle them systematically and make them match each other. The auto show strategy belongs to the functional strategy, and the enterprise should pay attention to its relation with strategies of other levels.

During the strategy-evaluating phase, the enterprise should analyze and supervise the process and effects of strategy-making and strategy-implementing to ensure the effective execution and to obtain the anticipated results. The enterprise establishes achievement criterion to evaluate the actual accomplishment and then compares the actual achievement with the expected target. In this way, problems in the process of strategy-making or strategy-implementing could be found, and relevant error-correcting activities could be taken. All these steps should not be carried out after the process of strategy-implementing, but in pace with it.

From the above description, it is evident that strategic management is a process of reciprocation and continuous development. In the strategy-making and strategy-implementing process, relevant information should be transferred back to the strategy-evaluating and strategy-controlling system to handle the whole operating activity effectively, to adjust the original strategy accordingly or even to make a new strategic plan again. Through this dynamic process of strategic management, the strategic decision-maker can control the internal logic among the activities of strategy-making, strategy-implementing, strategy-evaluating and controlling actively rather than follow the changes of the internal or external environment passively.

本节注释：[1]战略制定、战略实施以及战略评估与控制；[2]战略问题；[3]审计；[4]总体战略、业务单元战略和职能战略。

6.1.4.2 STRATEGIC MANAGEMENT OF AUTO SHOW

The auto show strategy could be regarded as a kind of strategy made by a functional department of the automotive enterprise, i.e. an important component of the marketing strategy. As the strategy of a functional department, it is necessary to consider how to achieve the overall goal of the enterprise, how to coordinate it with other strategies of the enterprise, how to demonstrate and elaborate the functional objectives, and how to determine the strategic key points and steps of the functional department.

MAKING AUTO SHOW STRATEGY

For making auto show strategy, environment-audit is also an essential work. Under the framework of the higher level strategy mentioned above, it is necessary to analyze the condition of the enterprise, including its products, and to consider the influence of the external environment, such as market and competition, sufficiently. Only based on these studies, the strategic objectives can be defined and the suitable strategic policy can be chosen.

The targets of the auto show strategy can be qualitative, quantitative or a combination of both. They should express the anticipated achievements which the enterprise wants to obtain through the show and related activities. They can be divided into marketing target, profit target[1] and social target.

IMPLEMENTING AUTO SHOW STRATEGY

The implementing process of the auto show strategy includes the following steps: action plan, budget, executing regulation and execution.

For formulating the action plan, the enterprise should work out a combined program of different media and communication forms at first. As mentioned above, combination of exhibition and meetings have become an important trend of the exhibition industry. Therefore the action plan should be a systematic project centering at the show and including demonstration, advertisement and some activities such as new product launch, news release and direct reception.

With an instructing action plan, the enterprise drafts a budget accordingly. As a strategic component of functional department, the show budget should take the overall financial budget of the enterprise and the budget of the relevant functional departments as preconditions.

According to the action plan and the budget, the enterprise should work out detailed implementing regulations as the rule for execution. During the implementation of the show strategy, the practical forms of these regulations are the plan of demonstration and the schemes of the related meetings and events.

The strategy should follow the implementing regulations strictly, accompanied by the strategy-control process. Effective strategy-control requires not only analyzing whether the strategy has been executed according to the original plan but also finding out whether anticipant results have been obtained. As mentioned, control should be carried out not only after but also in pace with the process of strategic implementation.

CONTROLLING AUTO SHOW STRATEGY

The process of strategic control contains three essential elements: evaluation criterion, evaluating achievements and result feedback. In practice, controlling the auto show strategy contains two aspects: evaluation of the implementary performance and strategy modification.

During its implementing process the show strategy is represented by a series of demonstrations, related meetings and events, therefore the performance analysis of the strategic implementation can be treated identically as analyzing effects of the demonstrations and activities mentioned above. At the beginning of the process, the enterprise should set up the criterion. Generally speaking, the relevant strategic targets can be regarded as the evaluating criterion. In practice, the enterprise should embody these targets into quantitative or qualitative indexes which are easy to measure, and then choose suitable means to collect data for evaluation.

By evaluation of the working performance, the enterprise should compare the actual effect not only with the criterion but also with that of the rivals. Performance of the rivals and the average data of the whole industry can be obtained from open information, such as quarterly or annual report of the guild. The enterprise could also add related contents in the self-organized investigation to gain the required information.

If warps[2] have been checked out, the enterprise must find out the reason and take proper measures which include revising the strategic target or modifying the strategic plan and process of the strategy execution.

Evaluation and supervision of auto show strategy requires a unification of openness, overall consideration, stability and flexibility. The enterprise should not work blindly but consider the change and influence of external environment. Moreover, for evaluation and supervision of the show strategy we should not only take the partial strategic target and plan as a criterion, but also take the mission and general target of the enterprise and the functional department into account. In addition, the strategic evaluation and supervision are supposed to ensure the stability of strategy-implementation and should also have appropriate flexibility to adapt to the necessary strategic reform.

本节注释: [1]盈利目标;[2]偏差。

6.2 MOTOR RACING

Motor racing is a contest of speed between motor vehicles under particular regulations. The world famous motor racings on four wheeled vehicles include Formula one racing, La Mans 24 hours racing, rally racing, Indianapolis 500 racing and drag racing[1].

Motor racing is not only a kind of sports, but also has tremendous social effect. Several weeks before the beginning of a motor racing, newspapers, advertisements, broadcasts and TV programs do their best to attract people's attention. Not only the race teams and the organizers are active in good preparations, but also the businessmen plan to earn money by every possible means[2]. Thousands of fans long for the skillful performances of their respectful drivers. Even a long time after the race they would not forget the exciting moments.

Not only motor racing, but also breaking the world land speed record is significant in promotion and development of science and technology of the society because they are harsh examinations of engineering potential between racing cars and all sorts of cutting-edge technologies are used to develop their top performances.

本节注释：[1]一级方程式汽车竞赛、勒芒 24 小时汽车竞赛、汽车拉力赛、印第安纳波里斯 500 汽车竞赛和汽车冲刺赛；[2]千方百计赚钱。

6.2.1 *WORLD LAND SPEED RECORDS*

6.2.1.1 THE LIST OF WORLD LAND SPEED RECORDS

The land speed record is defined as the fastest speed achieved by a vehicle on flat ground. It is standardized as the speed over a certain distance[1], averaged by two runs in opposite directions[2]. Table 6-1 only includes the absolute speed records for four wheeled vehicles on ground. The current record holder is the Thrust SSC, breaking the sound barrier[3].

本节注释：[1]固定的距离；[2]正反方向两次行驶的平均；[3]突破音障(超声速)；[4]场地。

6.2.1.2 SOME FAMOUS RECORD BREAKERS

The internal combustion engine has dominated the power in motor vehicles and has played a big role in increasing vehicle speed. There are so many engineers and inventors working hard on the innovations of the automotive structures as well as so many courageous drivers breaking records one after another. Some of them have given their lives for such a glorious cause and have written touching chapters in the history[1].

In 1924 Ernest Eldridge drove a Fiat racing car with a six cylinder airship engine of 21.7 liters (Fig. 6-3) on a tree lined road at Arpajon, near Paris, setting a new world land speed record of 234.97 km/h.

Many new records were rewritten from 1920s to 1930s by two distinguished British drivers named Malcolm Campbell and Henry Segrave. Campbell broke land and water speed records 9 times and was conferred a knight[2] for his contributions (Fig. 6-4).

In 1926, Segrave installed a V12, 4L supercharged engine combined by

World Land Speed Records Table 6-1

Year	Driver	Car	Venue * [4]	Speed (km/h)
1898	G. Chasseloup-Laubat	Jeantaud	Acheres(F)	63.15
1898	C. Janatzy	La Jamais Contente	Acheres(F)	105.88
1902	L. Serpolet	Serpolet Steamer	Nice(F)	120.79
1905	A. Macdonald	Napier	Daytona(A)	168.42
1909	V. Hemery	Darracq	Brooklands(B)	176.46
1911	R. Burmen	Benz	Daytona(A)	197.87
1914	L. Homstead	Benz	Brooklands(B)	199.72
1919	R. Palma	Packard	Daytona(A)	207.58
1922	K. Guinness	Sunbeam	Brooklands(B)	215.24
1924	E. Eldridge	Fiat	Arpajon(F)	234.97
1924	M. Campbell	Bluebird	Pendine(B)	235.22
1925	M. Campbell	Bluebird	Pendine(B)	242.62
1926	H. Segrave	Sunbeam	Southport(B)	245.14
1927	H. Segrave	Sunbeam	Daytona(A)	327.96
1928	M. Campbell	Bluebird	Daytona(A)	333.04
1928	R. Keech	White Triplex	Daytona(A)	334.01
1929	H. Segrave	Golden Arrow	Daytona(A)	372.46
1931	M. Campbell	Bluebird	Daytona(A)	396.03
1933	M. Campbell	Bluebird	Daytona(A)	438.47
1935	M. Campbell	Bluebird	Bonnaville(A)	484.61
1938	G. Eyston	Thunderbolt	Bonnaville(A)	575.35
1939	J. Cobb	Railton	Bonnaville(A)	594.96
1947	J. Cobb	Railton	Bonnaville(A)	634.39
1964	D. Campbell	Bluebird	Eyre(Aus)	648.71
1965	C. Breedlove	Spirit of America	Bonnaville(A)	966.55
1970	G. Gabelich	Blue Flame	Bonnaville(A)	1 001.64
1983	R. Nobel	Thrust 2	Black Rock(A)	1 019.43
1997	A. Green	Thrust SSC	Black Rock(A)	1 227.73
* (A)-USA; (Aus)-Australia; (B)-GB; (F)-France.				

two six-cylinder Grand Prix[3] engine blocks in a racing car named "Sunbeam

Fig. 6-3 1924 World land speed record Breaker, Fiat Racing Car

Fig. 6-4 Malcolm Campbell(Front Row, Standing) and His "Bluebird" on Pendine Sands in July 1925

Tiger". He pushed the record up to 245.14 km/h, only a bit more than Campbell's record in 1925.

In 1927, a Welsh[4] driver Parry Thomas took the speed to 275.22 km/h by putting an aero engine of 27L in a racing car. But Campbell built a new "bluebird" went beyond him at 281.43 km/h. Thomas did not admit his failure and went back to the runway in Pendine Sands. When he was traveling at nearly 274 km/h, the driving chain of his car broke, smashed through the windshield and decapitated[5] him, after which the car turned over and burst into flames.

The final winner in 1927 was Segrave. He had Sunbeam Company build a new car for him in which he sat between two engines. Each was a 12 cylinder engine of 22.4 liters. The combined power was 1 000 hp (735.3 kW). The front engine had one radiator and the rear had two. In spite of the 7.14 m long car made of aluminum panels, its total mass was more than three tons. The car set a new record of 327.96 km/h at Daytona Beach in Florida[6] (Fig. 6-5). At the end of his run, the brakes of his car failed and he had to drive into the sea to stop.

Fig. 6-5 Henry Segrave and His Racing car "Sunbeam" on Daytona Beach in 1927

In 1928 an American driver Ray Keech established the land speed record of 334.01 km/h in the car "White Triplex" with three big engines (each 27 liters, total 81 liters). The car was difficult to handle because of its large size and poor brakes. Keech was lucky to survive his dangerous record run.

In 1929 Segrave had a new car designed by Captain Jack Irving, 8.4 m long and with a 12 cylinder 930 hp (638.8 kW) engine. The racing car was named "Golden Arrow" (Fig. 6-6). At Daytona he achieved 372.46 km/h. Thousands of people went to watch the race as Segrave captured the record again. In the same year he was knighted by King George V[7], but was killed one year later in a boat when setting a water speed record.

The Bonnaville Salt Flats in Utah[8], U. S. —a huge and dry desert

Fig. 6-6 Segrave's Racing Car "Golden Arrow", 1929 World record Breaker

plain[9] is a perfect place for record breaking. In 1935 Campbell's attempt at higher speed in his last "Blue Bird" was full of danger. The windshield was coated by oil and exhaust gases filled the cockpit, so it was difficult for him to see and to breathe. And also a tire caught fire. But Campbell completed his runs and set a new record of 484.61 km/h. After that, he broke world water speed records twice in 1937 and 1938.

In 1938 George Eyston drove a racing car named "Thunderbolt" and pushed the world record to 575.35 km/h (Fig. 6-7). In 1939, shortly before

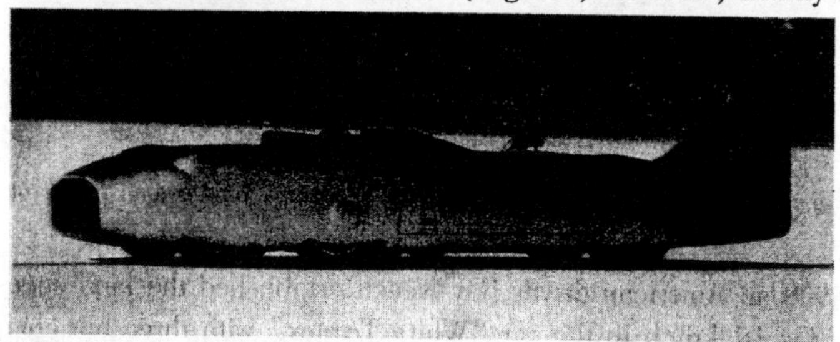

Fig. 6-7 Racing car "Thunderbolt", 1938 World Record Breaker

World War II, John Cobb set a new record of 594.96 km/h in his racing car "Railton". After the war in 1947, he went back to Bonnaville and set the record of 634.39 km/h. The record lasted till 1964, though he was killed in 1952, when trying to break water speed record.

Malcolm Campbell's son Donald was a record-breaker too. In 1964, on the bed of the dried up Lake Eyre in Australia, Donald achieved 648.71 km/h. His car was powered by aircraft turbine engine[10] and named "Blue

Bird", the same as his father's car had been (Fig. 6-8). In fact, this speed had already been exceeded by Craig Breedlove, an American, in his "Spirit of America". But it was not recognized a world record because his car was a three-wheeler (classified as a motorcycle), and because it was jet-propelled and not driven through the wheels.

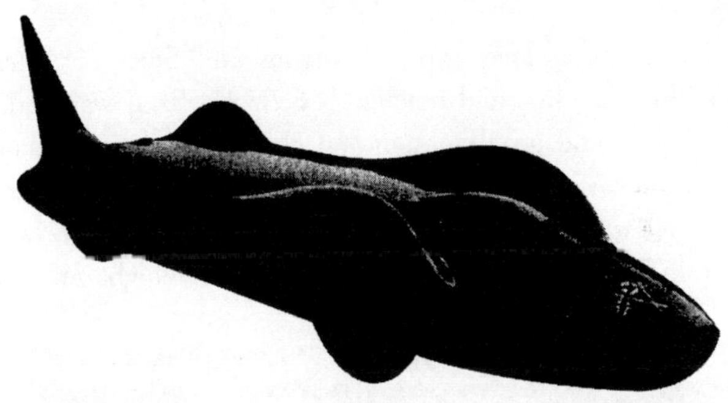

Fig. 6-8 Donald Campbell's "Bluebird" set up a new world record in 1964.

本节注释：[1]写下了动人的历史篇章；[2]授予爵士；[3]汽车大奖赛（注意：采用法语读音）；[4]威尔士；[5]斩首；[6]佛罗里达州；[7]英王乔治五世（注意写法和读法）；[8]犹他州；[9]沙漠平原；[10]航空燃气轮机。

6.2.1.3 JET-PROPELLED RACING CAR

As mentioned in Chapter 4, a conventional motor vehicle is driven by wheel-road interaction. The traction force reacted by the road is nearly impossible to increase beyond the limit of the adhesive force. Therefore, the speed of a conventional vehicle driven by wheels cannot increase unlimitedly. Many experts admit that Donald Campbell's record of 648.71 km/h might be very close to the maximum speed limit of this kind of motor vehicles.

Evidently, in order to push the land speed record up to a higher level, it is necessary to replace the wheel-driven structure with jet-propelled structure which is able to provide the car with powerful propulsion, just like jet plane and rocket. The gun-powder[1] rocket car "Opel Rak 2" mentioned in Paragraph 2.2.11, Chapter Two might be the earliest example of the jet-propelled structure.

In November 1964, the rules governing world land speed record were amended: "Any vehicle is eligible provided it has a driver and it depends on the ground for support". In the rules, jet-propelled vehicles are acceptable but magnetic-levitating, air-cushion vehicles and unmanned vehicles[2] are not.

In 1965 Craig Breedlove drove his racing car "Spirit of America Sonic 1" at Bonnaville Salt Flats and reached 966.55 km/h. It was equipped with a jet-fighter[3] engine and an aluminum and glass fiber[4] body, somewhat like a jet-fighter without wings (Fig. 6-9). Actually, it was much faster than Donald Campbell was. By this time Campbell shifted to pursue world water speed record. In 1967 he died when his racing boat caught fire and exploded[5].

Fig. 6-9 Craig Breedlove's Jet Racing car on Bonnaville Salt Flats

Gary Gabelich, an American who had been trained as an astronaut[6], went after Breedlove's record in a racing car "Blue Flame" with a rocket engine like those used in spacecrafts. Fueled by liquefied natural gas and hydrogen peroxide[7], the engine was installed in a record car, 11.65 m long with a tail fin ending 2.48 m above the ground. It was a four-wheeler, although the two front wheels were so close set that they looked like one. Gabelich took the record to 1 001.64 km/h in 1970 (Fig. 6-10). Parachutes[8] were used to provide effective braking after the end of his successful run.

13 years later, on Black Rock Desert in Nevada[9], U. S. A. Blue Flame's record was broken by a jet car "Thrust 2" (Fig. 6-11). Driver

Fig. 6-10 Gary Gabelich's rocket car "Blue Flame" was dashing on Bonnaville Salt Flats.

Richard Noble went 1 019.43 km/h which was very close to the sound speed. People began to talk about the possibility of breaking sound speed. From aviation principle, it is necessary to provide extra powerful propulsion to break through the sound barrier. To develop such a car required a great deal of money which might terrify somebody who is eager to have a try[10].

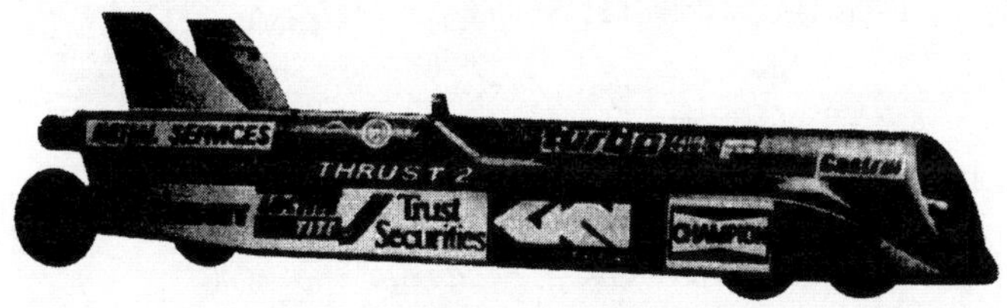

Fig. 6-11 Richard Nobel's "Thrust 2"

Time flew quickly. Although Nobel was getting old, his ambition was not fading. Finally he was successful to form a strong line-up of 260 companies as sponsors[11] to provide financial, technical and material supports. A research and development project of enormous cost (expense never divulged[12]) was worked out and put into action. Nobel's engineers took six years to go through the process of design and manufacture. The car was equipped with two Rolls-Royce jet engines of total output 80 thousand kW. It was 16.5

meters long and weighed 10 tons. Nobel and his engineers believed that the car would break the sound speed and they gave it the name "Thrust SSC". Here SSC meant Super-sonic[13] Car. On October 13, 1997 and also on Black Rock, Andy Green, a royal air force[15] officer drove the car and broke the sound barrier at 1 227.73 km/h, the highest world land speed record up to now (Fig. 6-12).

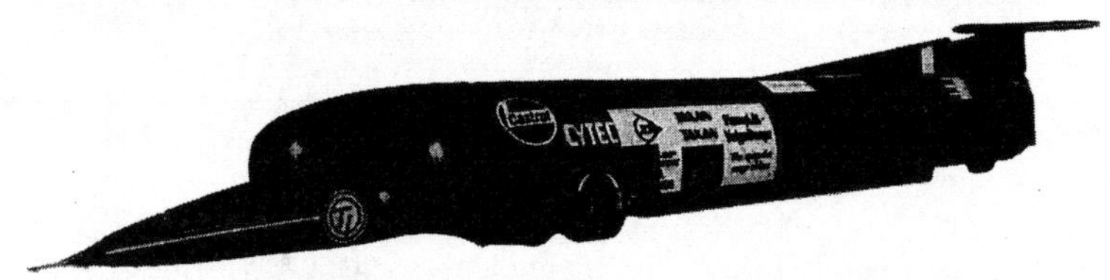

Fig. 6-12 World Land Speed Record Holder "Thrust SSC"

本节注释：[1]火药；[2]磁悬浮车辆、气垫车辆和无人驾驶车辆；[3]喷气歼击机；[4]玻璃纤维；[5]爆炸；[6]宇航员；[7]液化天然气和过氧化氢；[8]降落伞；[9]内华达州；[10]使跃跃欲试者生畏；[11]赞助者；[12]从未透露；[13]超声速；[15]皇家空军。

6.2.2 *WORLD FAMOUS RACINGS*

6.2.2.1 LE MANS 24 HOURS

The Le Mans 24 hours is the world's famous sports car endurance race[1] held on a circuit in the town Le Mans near Paris. The first race was held in 1923, and has been run annually in June except 1936 and the period from 1940 to 1948 (interrupted by World War II). It is organized by the Automobile Club de L'Ouest (A. C. O).

The race is run on a semi-permanent track, which in its current configuration, is 13.65 km long, utilizing mostly country roads that remain open to the public for the majority of the year. Usually, around 50 cars race simultaneously in a number of different categories and classes, from dedicated prototypes to street cars[2], the final winner being the car that has covered the greatest distance in 24 hours of continuous racing.

Within one day a racing car could run 5 000 km at an average speed about 200 km/h. Engines roar and cars run in such a risky way that no driver dares to distract his attention[3] even for a short moment. The race is a tough test of cars and drivers. Therefore, every racing car needs to shift[4] drivers. In recent years, each car has a team of three drivers. Before 1970 only two drivers per car were allowed.

The most successful brand in the history of the 24 hour race is Porsche, with 16 overall victories (including seven in a row[5], from 1981 to 1987), followed by Ferrari with nine (including six in a row, from 1960 to 1965). The early years were dominated by Bentley and Alfa Romeo, with four consecutive wins[6] from 1927 to 1930 and from 1931 to 1934 respectively. The 1950s were dominated by Jaguar with their C-type and D-type cars. The turn of the century saw a new power arrive in the Audi V8 powered R8 (wins in 2000, 2001, 2002, 2004 and 2005) and Bentley Speed 8 (2003).

In late 1960s Ford's "new weapon" brought to the champion was the GT 40, so called it because it was just 40 inches (1 016 mm) high (Fig. 6-13). A skillful driver named Bruce McLaren became well known for Ford's four consecutive wins from 1966 to 1969. Since then, He formed the McLaren Racing Team[7] and won the Can-Am[8] series in a row from 1967 to 1969. Unfortunately, he was killed in 1970, when testing his new racing car M8D, before he could receive the Segrave Trophy awarded to him for his achievements as both a wonderful driver and designer.

Fig. 6-13 Ford GT 40, the Four Consecutive Winner from 1966 to 1969

All the victories were captured by European or American cars with the only exception of the Japanese Mazda, which won the 59th race in 1991 with its rotary-engine 787B prototype. But the regulation was revised in later months to refuse rotary engine. So the championship returned to an European Peugeot in 1992. However, the victory was a good chance to show the powerful potential of the rotary engine.

Many accidents had happened in Le Mans. The most miserable one happened on June 11, 1955. When an Austin deviated to the side of the runway, a Mercedes-Benz 300SLR crashed into its rear and caught fire, jumping to the crowded spectators on the terrace[9]. 83 people including the driver were killed. To everybody's surprise, the race continued just a few moments after the accident. Some people criticized that the organizers and business sponsors only cared about their money and fame, not the sacrifices[10].

本节注释: [1]耐力赛;[2]此处指一般轿车;[3]分散注意力;[4]换班;[5]连排;[6]四连冠;[7]迈凯伦赛车队;[8]加拿大-美国;[9]看台上密集的观众;[10]牺牲。

6.2.2.2 INDIANAPOLIS 500

The Indianapolis 500 Mile Racing, usually shortened to Indianapolis 500 or Indy 500, is an American motor racing held annually over the Memorial Day weekend at the Indianapolis Motor Speedway in Indiana[1] since 1911. Cars should run 200 laps on a circuit of 2.5 miles long and the total distance equals to 500 miles.

The Indianapolis Motor Speedway was founded by Carl Fisher in 1906, and the Indianapolis Motor Speedway complex[2] was built in 1909. It was a rectangular shape with four round corners, 4 000 m long and 15 m wide, consisting of two 1 000 m and two 200 m straight tracks and four 400 m round tracks with maximum lateral slope of 38°. Nowadays, cars may run at an average speed from 240 to 260 km/h, but at the end of the 1 000 km track can be more than 300 km/h. Therefore, it takes about one minute to finish a lap and about three hours to go through the whole racing. There are more than 350 thousand seats on the terraces around the speedway.

The structure of the Indy 500 racing car is very interesting. Its appearance is quite similar to Formula 1 racing car, but its engine is smaller (2.65 L) and uses methanol. Because of a short speedway, the Indy car should make left turns frequently, i. e. about four turns per minute. The car body tends to lean to the right side caused by the centrifugal force, loading more to the right wheels and suspensions than the left ones. It is necessary for the designers to make the right wheels and suspensions stiffer than the left ones. That is, the left and right of the car are not symmetrical. Besides, as the car enters the round corner at the end of the 1 000 m track to lower its speed, the right front wheel withstands the maximum load, resulting in temperature increase and tire wear. What can the designers do for such special problems?

Although American native drivers and manufacturers gained their dominance of the race in early years, foreigners also took part in the race. For example, the Italian Fiat and French Peugeot won victories in 1910s. After that, many foreign drivers started choosing the United States as their primary base for their motor racing activities. Brazilian, Italian and Colombian were able to obtain good outings in 1980s. An English driver Nigel Mansell, the winner of Formula 1 championship in 1992, shocked the racing world by moving to Indianapolis 500 in 1993. Foreign drivers became a fixture of Indianapolis in the years to follow.

The cars begin the racing, traditionally 11 rows of 3, i. e. 33 cars. This started in 1919 with the AAA mandate of one car for every 400 feet of track, leaving 33 starters to the race.

Various awards would be given to the winners. A long-standing tradition of the Indianapolis 500 is for the winner to drink a bottle of milk immediately after the race. This practice first began in 1936 after winner Louis Meyer asked for a glass of buttermilk, his favorite drink, and afterward it became ritual[3] as milk companies became sponsors of the race and they would like to hand a bottle of milk to the winner to promote their product. The winner has been awarded one of the pace cars[4], or a replica, almost every year since 1936. In 1941, there were only six copies of the special Chrysler Newport Phaeton, and no production models created, so the winners did not receive it. After 1946, an oil painting and a trip to Italy were substituted as the award. A bass-relief sculpture[5] of the winner's face, along with his name, average speed, and date of victory is added to the Borg-Warner Trophy. A smaller replica of this trophy has been officially presented to the winner after the race since 1988. However prior to that, for decades, winners usually had a replica made for them.

Many people promote and share information about the Indy 500 and its memorabilia[6] collecting. The National Indy 500 Collectors Club is an independent active organization that has been dedicated to supporting such activities. Based in Indianapolis, it provided a platform available for experienced membership to discuss and advise on Indy 500 memorabilia trading and Indy 500 questions in general.

The Indianapolis Motor Speedway Hall of Fame Museum, located five miles northwest of downtown Indianapolis on the grounds of the famous Indianapolis Motor Speedway, is as one of the most highly recognized museums in the world devoted to motor racing. In 1987, the museum and Speedway grounds were honored with the designation of National Historic Landmark. Approximately 75 vehicles are on display at all times. The Hall of Fame Museum also displays the equipment and methods used for timing and scoring[7] the Indianapolis 500 from the first racing to the 21st century. A viewer-activated[8] computer presentation that explains the progress through the years is provided to the visitors.

本节注释：[1]印第安纳州；[2]综合场地设施；[3]仪式；[4]在赛车前面的引导车；[5]椴木浮雕；[6]大事记；[7]计时和计分；[8]观众操作的。

6.2.2.3 WORLD RALLY CHAMPIONSHIP (WRC)[1]

World Rally Car is a term used to describe the racing cars built to the specification set by the FIA[2] (Federation Internationale De L'Automobile) and used to compete in the outright class of the World Rally Championship.

Racing cars look ordinary but may be rebuilt. Technical regulations mandate that World Rally Cars must be built upon a production car with a minimum of 2 500 units, to which a number of modifications may be added, including engine up to 2.0 liters, a turbocharger[3], four wheel drive, sequential gearbox and aerodynamic empennages. The cars are further modified for greater torque, greater rigidity and other chassis strengthening measures.

The rally is divided into three legs[4], and typically has between 15 and 25 special stages[5]. The stages are linked by public roads - called road sections. Each day contains about 400 km of driving - a third of which are the competitive special stages. Stages vary in length from 5 to 60 km, with the cars' time being recorded after each stage to the tenth of a second. The special stages are the competitive sections of the rally - where the drivers and co-driver (navigator[6]) drive as fast as possible to achieve the quickest time.

Stages may consist of asphalt roads, gravel and dirt roads[7] of varying consistency[8], and even frozen snow-covered roads on some rallies held in northern Europe. The Hong Kong-Beijing Rally divided by 21 special stages is well known in China. The Safari Rally in Kenya, East Africa[9] is considered the most difficult because the conditions are terrible.

Cars start at one or two minute intervals, racing against the clock[10]. Their time is monitored and entered into the FIA computer. Unless they run into trouble, rivals rarely see each other during a stage. At the end of an event, the driver who has taken the least amount of time to complete all the stages is the winner.

After each group of stages is completed, the cars can visit a designated service park[11] where repairs may be carried out by the teams under strict supervision during a 20-minute time period. At the end of each day the crews are allowed a longer 46-minute period to work on the cars before they are locked away in the guarded "parc ferme"[12], until the following morning's restart.

Results achieved during each of the 16 rallies count towards the two FIA world championships - one for the drivers and one for the manufacturers. Drivers get 10 points for coming first, eight points for second place, six points for third, five points for fourth, four for fifth, three for sixth, two for seventh and one for eighth. A manufacturer can add up all the points from two nominated cars.

本节注释: [1]世界汽车拉力赛;[2]国际汽车联合会;[3]涡轮增压器;[4]赛段;[5]路段;[6]领航员;[7]天然路(土、泥泞等);[8]黏稠度;[9]东非洲的肯尼亚萨法里拉力赛;[10]和时钟赛跑(指一辆车单独赶路);[11]保修场地;[12]有看守的禁入区。

6.2.2.4 DRAG RACING

Drag racing is a form of auto racing in which cars or motorcycles attempt to complete a fairly short, straight and level course in the shortest amount of time, starting from a died stop. Drag racing originated in the United States. Drivers raced cars at the road intersection[1] as the traffic light turned green. Now it is still the most popular sport for people to watch. While usually thought of as an American and Canadian pastime, drag racing is also very popular in many countries including Brazil, Australia, New Zealand, Japan, England, Mexico, Greece, Malta, South Africa, the Caribbean, most European and Scandinavian countries[2]. There are over 325 drag strips operating world-wide.

Drag racing involves usually two cars racing each other over a set distance to see which crosses the finish line first. The most common distance is one quarter of a mile, i. e. 440 yards or 402 meters. It takes only several seconds for the cars to cover such a short distance, which extends well beyond the finish line to allow cars to slow down and return to the pit area[3]. One of the perfect facilities for drag racing is the Indianapolis Speedway (Fig. 6-14). But the sport has taken off so much in recent times that areas with no drag racing facilities have converted urban roads into drag strips.

Fig. 6-14 A "Top Fuel" Dragster Ready to Start on Indianapolis Speedway

Races of this nature really test a vehicle in terms of acceleration and top speed, and it also tests the driver with regard to skill and concentration. It is important for the driver to be fast reactive to start and accurate to control the engine throttle[4] and to shift gears. In addition to this, the fact that the driver has no time to recover from a mistake makes this a very demanding racing. Time is usually taken to an accuracy of one thousandth of a second, so you know that the competition results are very close.

Various kinds of racing cars are classified into different divisions by the criteria including engine capacity, number of cylinders, whether a turbocharger or a supercharger[5] is installed and whether nitrous oxide[6] is used. The drag racing fraternity has increased tremendously in recent years with more and more people converting their everyday street cars into powerful machines of speed. Modifications to a car can be anything from just changing the cams and exhaust to a full on power conversion such as adding on a turbo with nitrous oxide, bigger engine capacity or components, body customization by replacing standard body panels with aftermarket lightweight products. For many, drag racing and modification is just a hobby but for some, it has turned from love of cars into a business. Drag racing is a very expensive sport which requires a lot of time and money.

Figure 6-14 shows the most famous drag racing car called the "Top Fuel"[7] with a long, thin body, small front wheels and a powerful engine at the rear. The driver is like sitting on top of the rear wheels. As the engine is working, flame and smoke shot behind the car can be seen. All drivers have to wear fire-proof clothes and breathing masks to protect them from fire and fumes. Thousands of spectators enjoy such an exciting event that is called "4S", i. e. "sights, sounds, smells and speeds" to arouse everybody's emotion.

本节注释: [1]交叉路口;[2]斯堪的纳维亚半岛上的国家(有时泛指北欧5国);[3]检修区;[4]操控发动机节气门开度;[5]涡轮增压器或一般增压器;[6]氧化亚氮;[7]耗油王。

6.2.2.5 FORMULA ONE RACING

Formula One, abbreviated to F1, also known as Grand Prix racing[1], is the highest class of single-seat open-wheel[2] formula auto racing. The "formula" in the name is a set of rules which all participants and cars must meet. Some examples of the rules are given as follows.

In 2006 engine were reduced to normally-aspirated[3] V8s with a volume of 2.4liters. Only round shape cylinders are acceptable. Fuel tank capacity should be 220 liters.

In order to develop a perfect car under serious restrictions of the rules, manufacturers are very keen on all sorts of up-to-date structures including high strength aluminum engine made by vacuum casting[4], electronic multi-point injection, dual over-head camshafts (DOHC) [5],multi-valves, semi-automatic gearbox, active suspension, aluminum alloy wheel and low profile tire[6]. As everyone knows, high engine output, power-volume ratio possible up to 230 kilowatts per liter, comes from high speed. The maximum speed of a current F1 engine can be 20 000 rpm by the measure of shortened stroke[7]. The engine running at such a speed, i. e. 4 times of a conventional car engine speed, needs high level dynamic balance. Moreover, it is beneficial to develop more heat efficiency for the engine by the increase of compression ratio as much as possible. Fuel of high anti-knock property (102 RON) should be used to meet the high compression ratio. To arrange the engine behind the driver's seat and in front of the rear axle leads to the best weight distribution, low front end of wedge style[8] and small yawing moment of inertia[9]. Aerodynamic spoilers of variable attack angle[10] results in more adhesive force and more traction. A synthetic body of CFRP (carbon fiber reinforced plastics)[11] leads to light weight and safety. Total mass of such a well-equipped F1 car is not more than 600 kg.

If all the above items are taken into account, high cost seems inevitable. The research expense of a kind of F1 engine developed by Porsche is \$ 24 millions. Cars of the Renault Racing Team equipped with new F1 engines costs \$ 170 millions. One liter ELF gasoline, a famous French brand, costs \$ 240 and a full filling of 220 liters costs \$ 52 800. Besides, a F1 car may consume at least 15 sets of dry or wet weather tires for the races within a year. Roughly estimated, the average cost of one F1 car is not less than 20 million US dollars.

The F1 season[12] consists of a series of races[13], known as Grand Prix, held in most cases on purpose-built circuits, and in a few cases on closed city streets. Although there were many Grand Prix races held before World War II, they were not formalized until 1947. Formula one was first run in 1950. In the early years there were only 5 to 9 races held annually and 16 races in 1980s. Now the annual number of F1 races is 18 held in different countries from spring to autumn. Europe is Formula One's traditional center and remains its leading market; however, Grand Prix have been held all over the world and with new races in Bahrain[14], China, Malaysia and Turkey since 1999, its scope is continually expanding.

A Formula One Grand Prix event spans an entire weekend, beginning with two free practices on Friday, and one free practice on Saturday. After these practice sessions, a qualifying session[15] is held.

From the 2006 season, a knockout qualifying system[16] is introduced. The position of a car in the starting grid of the race[17] is in the order of its driving time on the timed lap[18] of the qualifying runs. In the first phase of qualifying, the slowest 6 cars were knocked out from 22 cars. These cars will make up the starting grid in the last six positions. In the second phase, also the next slowest 6 cars were knocked out. They will make up the grid in positions from eleven to sixteen. For the final period, the ten remaining cars are reset for their ranking in the order of their time.

The race begins with a warm-up formation lap, after which the cars assemble on the starting grid in the order they are qualified. A light system above the track then signals the start of the race. Races are a little over 305 kilometers long and are limited to two hours (Fig. 6-15). Throughout the race, drivers may make one or more pit stops in order to refuel and change tires.

Points are given to the top eight drivers who have finished all the required laps during one race. The winner receives 10 points, the second 8 points and the third 6 points. From the fourth to the eighth receive 5-4-3-2-1 points respectively. Two annual championships are awarded to the driver and the team who have accumulated the most points at the end of the season[19]. If any drivers and/or teams have the exact amount of points[20] and are both

Fig. 6-15 2006 Shanghai Formula One Racing

competing for the driver and/or team championships, the driver and/or team who has won more Grand Prix races during the course of the season is declared the winner.

Drivers from McLaren, Williams, Renault (formerly Benetton) and Ferrari, dubbed the "Big Four", have won every World Championship since 1984. Many records were broken in the first few years of the 21st century by German Michael Schumacher and a resurgent Ferrari. In 2001, Schumacher set the new record for the most Grand Prix ever won; the earlier record holder was Alain Prost, with 51 wins[21] to his name. In 2002, Schumacher also set a new record by winning the championship earlier in the season than any previous driver by winning the French Grand Prix in July that year. In 2003, Schumacher won his sixth championship title, beating the earlier record-holder, Juan Manuel Fangio with five championships (Table 6-2). His record in 2006 stood at 7 championships[22] (Fig. 6-16). In 2005 Fernando Alonso became the youngest ever World Driver's Champion.

From 1950 to the end of 1995, there have been 581 F1 races held and 24 drivers died, average 24 races one death. Some people criticized that over power and thus over speed are very dangerous. For example, cars equipped with turbochargers in the late 1980s were powerful enough to develop up to

1 000 hp (735.3 kW) and easier to over speed. If a car crashes to a hard

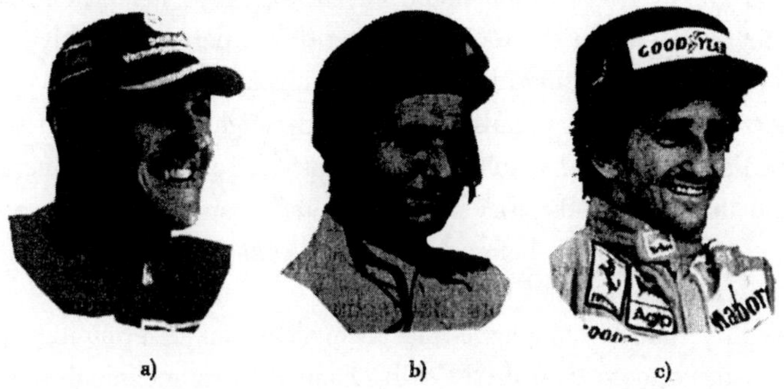

a) b) c)

Fig. 6-16 Top Winners of Formula One
a) Michael Schumacher; b) Juan Fangio; c) Alain Prost

Famous Formula One Winners (1950-2006) Table 6-2

Winner	Number of Championships	Year of Championship
Michael Schumacher(G)	7	1994, 1995, 2000, 2001, 2001, 2003, 2004
Juan Fangio(Ag)	5	1951, 1954, 1955, 1956, 1957
Alain Prost(F)	4	1985, 1986, 1989, 1993
John Braham(Aus)	3	1959, 1960, 1966
John Steward(B)	3	1969, 1971, 1973
Niki Lauda(Au)	3	1975, 1977, 1984
Nelson Piquet(Br)	3	1981, 1983, 1987
Ayrton Senna(Br)	3	1988, 1990, 1991
(G)-Germany; (Ag)-Argentina; (F)-France; (Aus)-Australia; (B)-GB; (Au)-Austria; (Br)-Brazil.		

wall at 300 km/h, deceleration would increase greatly, much more than 100 times of the acceleration of gravity[23]. Even if any part of the driver's body does not crash into anything, he could not withstand such a high deceleration. The internal organs[24] of his body might be squeezed seriously out of inertia themselves, resulting in traumas[25]. To reduce engine power output and thus speed, the FIA limited fuel tank capacity in 1984 and boost[26] pressures in 1988 before banning turbocharged engines in 1989. Engine volume also reduced from 3.5 to 3.0 liters in 1995 and 2.4 liters in 2006. The FIA, due to complaints that technology was determining the outcome of races more than driver skill, banned many technical aids in 1994. However, many observers felt that the ban on driver aids was a ban in name[27] only as the FIA did not have the technology or the methods to eliminate these features from competition.

As the world's most expensive sport, its economic impact is significant, and its financial and social battles are widely observed. Its high profit and popularity makes it an obvious merchandising environment[28] which leads to very high investments from sponsors. According to the statistic figures, sponsorship of a F1 season would not be less than one billion US dollars. The biggest sponsor must be the Marlboro cigarette producer Phillips-Morris Company, up to $ 170 millions. The other famous companies are not willing to fall behind. ELF, Shell, Goodyear, Michelin and Kent are also generous with their money and play the important roles in all sorts of business activities especially advertisements. However, in recent years, extremely high budgets[29] for the race teams have resulted in heavy burdens and several teams have gone bankrupt.

本节注释：[1]大奖赛；[2]敞开的转向盘(开式车身)；[3]普通自然吸气式；[4]真空铸造；[5]双顶置凸轮轴；[6]低断面轮胎；[7]缩短活塞行程；[8]楔形；[9]横摆惯性矩；[10]攻角、迎角；[11]碳纤维增强塑料；[12]赛季；[13]分站比赛；[14]巴林；[15]考核时段；[16]出局的考核制度；[17]在比赛的起跑格线上的排位；[18]计时圈的行驶时间；[19]在赛季结束时，两个年度冠军奖授予累计得分最多的车手和车队；[20]得分数恰好相等；[21]在51次分站比赛中得胜；[22]指舒马赫在2006年退役而止步于7冠；[23]大大超过重力加速度的100倍；[24]内脏；[25]创伤；[26]增压器；[27]有名无实；[28]商业环境；[29]预算。

6.3 FUTURE OF AUTOMOTIVE TECHNOLOGY

6.3.1 *THREE MAIN TASKS FOR FUTURE AUTOMOTIVE TECHNOLOGY*

6.3.1.1 SAFETY

Safety is a top priority for future automotive technology. All people have a common feeling that safety is the first from their experiences in daily life. Safety is an important issue concerning the risk of life and property[1].

Human has had good grasp of advanced science and technology, but has not yet made a realistically safe vehicle. The fact that the figure of fatalities and injuries in automotive accidents is too high to put down shows a crucial social problem to be solved urgently. Therefore, many countries have been sparing no effort and expense[2] in the struggle against traffic accidents.

Unfortunately, in the practical traffic conditions of high speed and heavy density, if added by bad weather and slippery road, accidents seem inevitable. Even on a dry and good road surface, stop distance of a car while emergent braking at initial speed of 80 km/h[3] will be no less than 50 m. In spite of insisting on warning the drivers of carefully keeping space with other vehicles, serious accidents still occur. For example, accidents of dozens or even more than one hundred motor vehicles bumping into one after another can be heard quite often. From the principle of mechanics, when two vehicles crash into each other, injury and damage will be inversely proportional to their masses[4]. If difference between their masses is too great, e. g. between motorcycle and heavy truck or between motor vehicle and railway train, injury and damage of the smaller one would be very serious. From this paragraph we can see that traffic safety problems are very complicated and difficult to deal with.

Solutions for traffic safety may focus on three aspects including road user[5], vehicle and environment.

本节注释：[1]生命财产攸关的问题；[2]不惜人力和财力；[3]一辆轿车在初速为80 km/h 时的紧急制动距离；[4]与它们的质量成反比；[5]道路使用者。

SOLUTIONS FOR ROAD USER

Solutions for road users are to regularize their behaviors[1], for example, training the drivers, teaching and warning the road users, as well as carrying out law and regulations to constrain their behaviors. Because of different social status, age, physique, profession and cultural background[2], quality and ability are also different from person to person. Being affected by external factors, road users behave in complicated and diversified manner. That is to say, it is impossible to expect every road user to behave consciously without making any mistake under complicated and emergent circumstances[3]. Many experts believe that to use some engineering construction to constrain the road user's behavior would be more effective than merely training and warning, for example, to set up a fence[5] to prevent the pedestrians[6] from crossing the traffic as well as to build a grade-separated junction[7] to conduct the traffic flow and to separate the pedestrians from the motor vehicles.

本节注释：[1]规范他们的行为；[2]社会地位、年龄、体质、职业、文化水平；[3]不可能指望每个道路使用者在复杂和紧急的情况下都会表现得有理智而没有差错；[5]拦栅；[6]行人；[7]立体交叉。

SOLUTIONS FOR MOTOR VEHICLE

Solutions for motor vehicle include active safety and passive safety. Active safety is to strengthen the ability of the motor vehicle to avoid accident, for example, to improve the driver's visibility[1] and operation conditions, to improve illumination[2] and to increase tire performance, braking and steering performances. Passive safety is to lighten the accident outcome, for example, to improve the structure of bumper and body shell as well as to popularize protection equipments such as seat belt, air bag, safety glass and energy absorbing steering column.

Some of the advanced applications for safety are introduced as follows.

Anti-lock Braking System (ABS)

As the brake is applied, the road wheels may slow down gradually until stop rolling or lock[3]. This does not mean the vehicle would stand still promptly. It would continue to move forward because of its inertia. When the road wheels are not rolling but slipping, adhesion of the vehicle with the ground[4] becomes worse, which increases braking distance and even results in dangerous situation of losing control (Fig. 6-17). Therefore, it is necessary

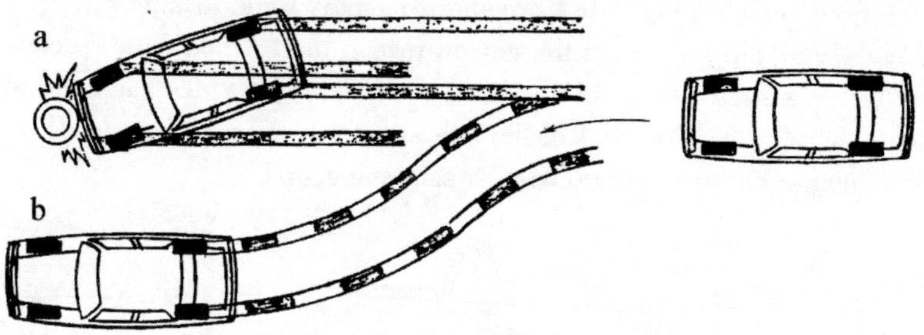

Fig. 6-17 Function of ABS While Braking

As the front wheels are locked, the car loses control and slip along trajectory "a". Being equipped with ABS, the car steers effectively and moves along trajectory "b".

to take measure to prevent the wheels from lock. Research work has proved that the best braking effect happens when slippage[5] of the wheel equals 0.15 to 0.20. That is, the wheel is nearly locked and slips a little. In the ABS, the electronic device can calculate the slippage through the comparison of the speed of the vehicle with the linear speed at the circumference of the wheel[6]. It can also control the pressure in the braking piping to prevent the wheel from locking and thus develop the best braking effect.

两节注释:[1]视野性;[2]照明;[3]抱死;[4]汽车与地面的附着性能;[5]滑移率;[6]车轮圆周的线速度。

Acceleration Skid Response (ASR)[1]

As the driver's right foot presses the accelerator very hard to increase the engine output, the traction force might increase greatly and reach the limit of the adhesive force[2]. This is especially true on the slippery road surface. For this reason, the drive wheels begin to skid and will not exert forces to the ground. Traction may be interrupted and the motor vehicle may lose control. For example, if the driver wants to change a new lane to overtake another vehicle and presses the accelerator very hard, the drive ·

wheels would begin to skid and the car would not change the lane but crash to the front vehicle (Fig. 6-18). Another example, while making a turn[3], the car would slip away from the curved road if the traction force reaches the limit of the adhesive force. In the ASR, the electronic device can keep the traction force within the limit of the adhesive force through the control of the engine output and make the operation safe and sound.

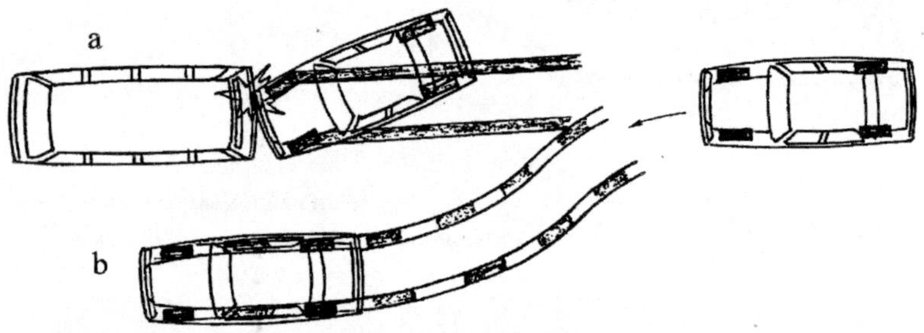

Fig. 6-18 Function of ASR While Overtaking

Changing another lane and overtaking the front vehicle, if the wheels skid, the car would slip along trajectory "a"; being equipped with ASR, the car would move along trajectory "b"

本节注释：[1]加速滑转反应装置；[2]驱动力会大大增加而达到附着力的极限；[3]转弯。

Electronic Stability Program (ESP)

Electronic stability program[1] is an advanced system developed by Mercedes-Benz. It integrates all the functions of ETS (electronic traction system)[2], ABS, ASR and provides very good handling stability for road safety. It is a four channel[3] braking system and capable of adjusting the brake force of each wheel independently. Oversteer and understeer[4] can be corrected by ESP promptly. Figure 6-19a) shows a car making a left turn. Because of the centrifugal force on the curved road, the elastic tires would deviate[3] from their theoretical directions given by the driver. This phenomenon is called yaw[5]. As shown in Fig. 6-19a), if the rear wheels deviate more than the front wheels, the yaw sensor[6] in the car would signal "oversteer" and the electronic device would brake the right front wheel to correct the oversteer. As shown in Fig. 6-19b), if the front wheels deviate more than the rear wheels, the yaw sensor would signal "understeer" and the electronic device would brake the left rear wheel to correct the understeer. Even on a slippery road surface, ESP can ensure stable steering of the car at high speed without any dangerous deviation.

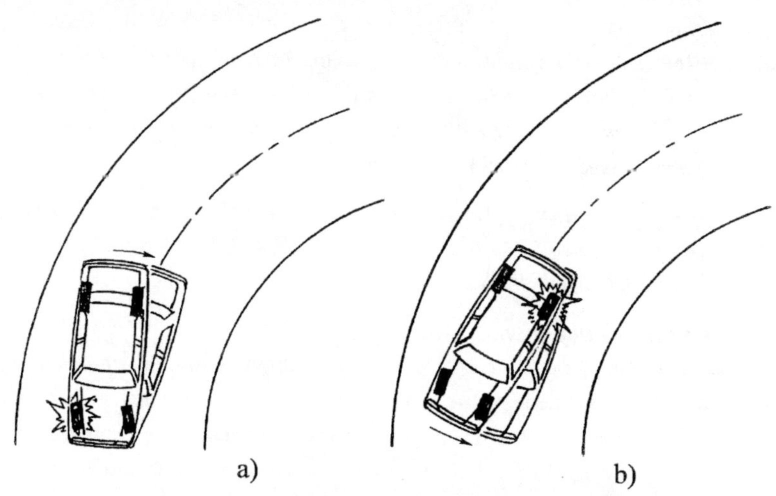

Fig. 6-19 Electronic Stability Program (ESP)
a) brake the right front wheel to correct oversteer;
b) brake the left rear wheel to correct understeer

本节注释：[1]电控稳定性程序；[2]驱动力电控系统；[3]四通道；[4]过度转向和不足转向；[5]汽车横摆；[6]横摆传感器。

Speed Sensitive Steering (SSS)[1]

Many motor vehicles are equipped with power steering system[2] which needs much less force acting on the rim[3] of the steering wheel and solves the conflict of steering force with steering sensitivity[4]. In an ordinary mechanical steering system[5], both steering force and steering sensitivity may not be gained at the same time[6]. That is to say, the increase of the steering transmission ratio[7] gains light steering force but reduces steering sensitivity whereas the decrease of the steering transmission ratio gains steering sensitivity but increases steering force. However, the power steering system can gain both.

An outstanding shortcoming of the power steering system is the decrease of its reverse property. This makes the driver feel no road sense, i. e. very small reaction from the road to the rim of the steering wheel. The driver would not feel safe and confident while driving at high speed[8]. Aiming at the shortcoming, SSS can make the power steering assistance in reverse proportion with the vehicle speed[9], i. e. larger steering assistance at low speed and more road sense at high speed.

本节注释：[1]速度感应式转向；[2]动力转向系统；[3]转向盘的周缘；[4]转向灵敏度；[5]普通机械式转向系统；[6]不可兼得；[7]转向传动比；[8]在高速行车时会觉得不安全且心中无数；[9]转向助力与车速成反比。

Electronic Brake-Force Distribution (EBD)[1]

The maximum brake force of every road wheel is limited by the adhesive force which is determined by the road adhesion and the normal load on the wheel[2]. If the payload of a motor vehicle has changed, e. g. from unloaded to full loaded, the load distribution proportion between front and rear wheels[3] would not be the same as before. Unfortunately, in the old type vehicles, brake force distribution is fixed by a factor (called synchro-adhesive coefficient[4]) given by the designer. Evidently, it is necessary to use a set of electronic device to adjust the brake force distribution between front and rear wheels to meet the requirement of different payload conditions. That is why EBD is widely used today.

本节注释：[1]电控制动力分配装置；[2]在车轮上的垂直载荷；[3]前后轮的载荷分配比例；[4]同步附着系数。

Cruise Control System (CCS)[1]

Cruise control system is a set of automatic driving device which can keep safety space between vehicles. When driving for a long time on the highway, the driver may feel rather boring[2] and difficult to concentrate attention. At this time the driver may hand over the job to[3] the CCS. The system has a laser detector[4] to measure the speed difference and the space between cars. The information detected can be conveyed to the computer processor[5] to control the car. Visual and audible signals[6] are given to remind the driver.

本节注释：[1]巡航控制系统；[2]颇感乏味；[3]把工作移交给；[4]激光探测器；[5]计算机处理器；[6]视觉和听觉信号。

Seat Belt

Seat belt[1] is the most effective equipment to reduce the number of casualties[2] greatly in collision accidents. Its advantages have been proved by a great deal of practical experiences.

Figure 6-20 shows the structure of a common three anchorage type seat belt. It consists of a shoulder belt 3 slanting across the occupant's chest[3], a lap belt 5 across the occupant's hip[4], three anchorages[5] (the outer one 7 and the inner one 8 on the floor, the upper one 1 at the top of the B

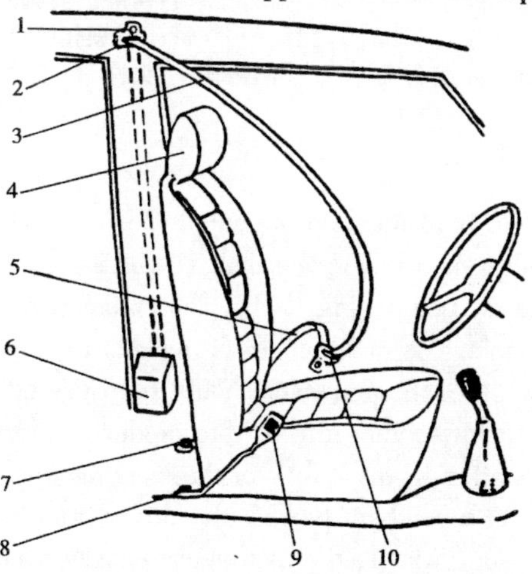

Fig. 6-20 Three Anchorage Type Safety Seat Belt and Head Restraint

1-upper anchorage; 2-guiding plate; 3-shoulder belt; 4-head restraint[13]; 5-lap belt; 6-retractor; 7-outer anchorage on floor; 8-inner anchorage on floor; 9-buckle socket; 10-buckle plug

pillar[6]), a retractor 6 at the bottom of the B pillar to wind the end of the belt webbing[7] and a buckle (buckle socket[8] 9 on the inner side of the occupant's hip and the buckle plug[9] 10 on the belt webbing). Putting the buckle plug into the buckle socket can have the occupant restrained[10] and pushing the red button on the buckle socket can free the restraint.

In normal condition, the belt is just attached on the occupant's body without any restraint of action. As the occupant bends forward[11], the webbing would be pulled from the retractor 6 through the guiding plate[12] 2 and as the occupant returns to original sitting posture, the retractor would wind up the excess webbing to have it attached to the body. However, at the situation of emergency, i. e. deceleration of the vehicle too sharp or inclination of the motor vehicle too serious, the retractor would grab the webbing tightly to fix the occupant on the seat effectively.

本节注释:[1]座椅安全带;[2]受害者;[3]斜挎乘员前胸的肩带;[4]绕过乘员胯部的腰带;[5]固定点(锚点);[6]B 立柱;[7]织带;[8]锁扣的插座;[9]锁扣的插板;[10]对乘员约束;[11]向前弯腰;[12]导向板;[13]头枕、头部后仰的限制装置(在追尾撞车时)。

Air Bag

Air bag system is also called the supplementary restraint system (SRS)[1]. It consists of collision sensors[2] 1 and 2, microprocessor[3] 3, gas generator[4] 5 and air bag 6 (Fig. 6-21). The collision sensors detect the severity of the impact. The microprocessor accepts the signals from the sensors and determines whether the generator should be triggered[5]. The gas generator is filled with sodium nitride[6] to produce nitrogen through burning. The air bag is installed in the hub[7] of the steering wheel and may be inflated within 0.05 seconds to prevent the driver from hitting the objects in front, i. e. the steering wheel, the instrument panel or the windshield. Some of the cars are provided with two air bags, one in the hub of the steering wheel and another in the right of the instrument panel. Some of them even have air bags for side collisions.

本节注释:[1]辅助约束系统;[2]碰撞传感器;[3]微处理器;[4]气体发生器;[5]触发;[6]氮化钠;[7]毂。

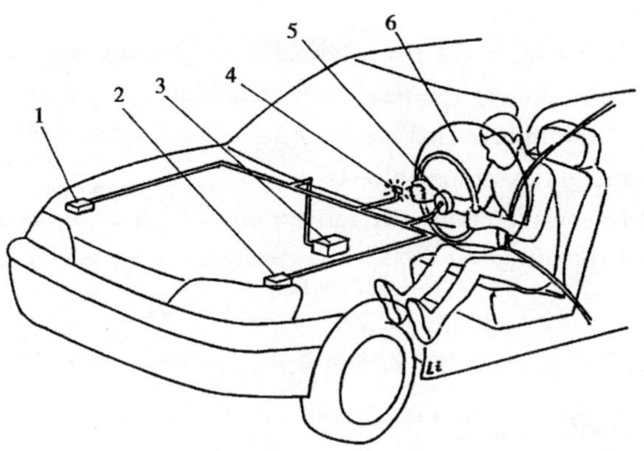

Fig. 6-21 Structure of Air Bag System
1-right front sensor;2-left front sensor;3-microprocessor;4-indicator light;5-gas generator;6-air bag

Safety Glass

There are two kinds of safety glasses, i. e. toughened glass[1] and laminated glass[2]. Toughened glass is cooled rapidly at high temperature to be prestressed and strengthened[3]. Being broken, toughened glass is split into many pieces without sharp edges, which would not result in serious scratch[4]. Laminated glass consists of three layers. Its intermediate layer[5] has high toughness[6] and serves as a sticker[7] to connect the other two layers. Being cracked, the layers of the laminated glass are stuck together without any separated piece to prevent the road users from injury. In the laminated glass for motor vehicle, thickness of the intermediate layer doubles. It is called high penetration resistant (HPR) safety glass[8] and is widely used to make windshields of the motor vehicles.

本节注释：[1]钢化玻璃；[2]夹层玻璃；[3]使具有预应力和提高强度；[4]刮伤、划伤；[5]中间层；[6]韧性；[7]黏合层；[8]高抗穿透性安全玻璃。

Safety Cage

To design the body shell, it is important to strengthen the passenger compartment and to weaken the front end and the rear end[1]. As collisions happen, the front end or the rear end collapses and absorbs most part of the collision energy to protect the passenger compartment from deformation and the occupants from injury. This structure is called "safety cage" [2] and should be examined by collision test.

For safety consideration, the interior should not have sharp edges and corners[3] and should be covered by soft materials, for example polyurethane foam[4].

本节注释: [1]车头和车尾;[2]安全构架;[3]棱角;[4]聚氨酯泡沫塑料。

Experimental Safety Vehicle (ESV)[1]

ESV is an experimental vehicle combined with a lot of safety measures. The task of the ESV is to have comprehensive analysis and evaluation of the overall result of the measures and their mutual effect. More than dozens of safety items are installed in the vehicle such as improvement of visibility and illumination, electronic controlled steering, braking and suspension systems, high performance tires, EA (energy absorbing) bumpers[2], safety cage, seat belts, air bags, and HPR safety glasses. Even in the collision at the initial speed of 80 km/h, ESV is capable of protection of the occupants from injury.

本节注释: [1]试验安全汽车;[2]吸能保险杠。

SOLUTIONS FOR ENVIRONMENT

Solutions for traffic environment are to improve road conditions and road furniture[1] and to carry out effective traffic management. However, a particular measure only focuses on a key point, i. e. the most dangerous point where many accidents have happened or a road segment[2] of heavy and complicated traffic. Because of the shortage of money, constructions are not possible to be carried out everywhere.

The main feature of the traffic situation in China is so-called "mixed traffic[3]". That is, pedestrians, non-motor vehicles and motor vehicles are mixed together. The effective measure is so-called "channelized management[4]" to separate them from each other, i. e. to provide pedestrians with a side walk[5], non-motor vehicles with a slow lane[6] and the motor vehicles with a carriage way[7].

No matter what measure may be taken, it is impossible to come up with a perfect solution without any other problems. For example, to widen a road could reduce accidents (positive effect) because of more vehicle-to-vehicle space and could also increase accidents (negative effect) out of higher vehicle speed. Another example, the driver's careless mind and adventurous behavior (negative) would arise from good traffic environment and perfect car structure (positive) and lead to disaster. Therefore, a measure must not be one-sided[8]. A good measure only comes from careful investigation, research and analysis by summing up all the influences of road user-vehicle-environment.

本节注释：[1]道路设施(注意原文词汇较特殊，是指交通标志、路灯等)；[2]路段；[3]混合交通；[4]渠化管理；[5]人行道；[6]慢车道；[7]行车道；[8]片面的。

6.3.1.2 SAVING ENERGY

REDUCING VEHICLE WEIGHT

Vehicle weight reduction is the most effective way to save energy. As the motor vehicle is moving, work should be done to overcome some resistance. Except air resistance, the others, i. e. rolling, gradient and acceleration resistances[1], are proportional to the weight of the motor vehicle. If the weight of the vehicle can be reduced, the above three items are also cut down to a considerable proportion. Most of the experts believe that the effective method of light weight is to replace the steel and iron materials consisting of 70% of the weight of the vehicle by other light materials, especially plastics and aluminum.

Forty years ago the use of plastics per car was only about 10 kg but now it is more than 100kg. The growth of the total production value of the world plastic industries (7% to 9% per year) is more than the growth of the total production value of the world economy (4% to 5 per year). Because the automotive industry plays an important role among the consumers of plastics, we can expect that the tendency of using plastics and compound materials to motor vehicles will be speed up.

In recent years, more and more automotive parts are made of aluminum.

Besides the engine cylinder block, cases and housings in the chassis and wheels mentioned in the above chapters, it is also widely used in body manufacturing. A remarkable example is the all-aluminum body of the German car Audi A8. Its body carcass[2] is made of 100 extruded[3] bars of aluminum alloy, which is 2/3 less than the number of the structural members of a traditional steel body. In order to avoid welding problems, the bars are connected by aluminum joints made by pressure casting[4]. The all-aluminum body cuts down 40% weight compared with the steel body and its manufacturing investment cuts down 33%. Because the weight of a body makes up more than half the total weight of a car, the use of more and more aluminum to car body affects the light weight policy tremendously.

For the weight of the body has greatly reduced, the suspensions and the tires which support the body can be smaller. At the same time a smaller engine also a smaller transmission system can be used. Such chain reaction[5] of light weight is of great benefit to saving energy.

本节注释：[1]滚动、坡道和加速阻力；[2]骨架；[3]挤压成型；[4]压铸；[5]连锁反应。

IMPROVING ENGINE FUEL ECONOMY

Based on emission improvement, many new structures mentioned in the above chapters can be used such as to increase engine efficiency, to improve combustion, to select a higher air-fuel ratio and to use electronic fuel injection.

REDUCING TIRE ROLLING RESISTANCE

The tubeless radial tire[1] is an important tendency of tire development. As described in chapter three, cord string direction[2] of a radial tire is perpendicular to the central line of the tread[3]. The radial tire has advantages of small rolling resistance, good adhesion, good vibration absorption and heavy duty[4]. The higher speed the vehicle develops, the more fuel saved by the tire. The radial tire gains fuel economy of 7% reduction compared with the conventional bias-ply tire[5].

本节注释：[1]无内胎子午线轮胎；[2]帘布层帘线的方向；[3]胎面、胎冠；[4]承载能力大；[5]普通斜交轮胎。

REDUCING AIR RESISTANCE

Air resistance is in direct proportion to the square of the vehicle speed[1]. When the vehicle speed is more than 80 km/h, nearly half of the engine power would be consumed on air resistance. Improvement of the body shape has significance of fuel economy. If the drag coefficient[2] of a car reduces from 0.5 to 0.3, about 0.02 L/km of fuel can be saved. Air resistance of a truck equipped with fairings[3] would reduce by 20%. Driving at high speed, the truck can save 3 to 4% of fuel.

To reduce air resistance means that the styling of motor vehicles becomes smooth and round. Today's car styling is no longer the concept of 30 years ago, i. e. "a square base composed by stiff curved surfaces and sharp edges[4]", but is a subtle shape composed by round corners and fluent curved surfaces[5] (Fig. 6-22). Although the full-size luxury cars[6] are striving to keep their dignified[7] appearance, it is evident that their shape becomes round and flexible too. Fig. 6-23 shows a concept truck representing the future development tendency by British Leyland Company. It consists of a round head, smooth transition between the cab and the rear body, close connection of a big fairing with the top of the cab, skirt board attachments[8] on both sides of the underbody and air conductive curtains[9] on both sides of the rear body.

Fig. 6-22 Elegant Styling of GM's Concept Car Corvette Indy

本节注释: [1]与车速的平方成正比;[2]空气阻力系数;[3]整流罩、导流罩;[4]坚挺的曲面和凸棱构成的方基体;[5]圆滑的拐角和流畅的曲面构成的微妙形体;[6]

Fig. 6-23 English Concept Truck Leyland TX-450

高级轿车;[7]庄重的;[8]附加的裙板;[9]引道气流的布帘。

INCREASING GEARS IN TRANSMISSION[1]

Although the increase of the number of gears would make the gearbox more complicated, it provides possibility for the driver to select a proper transmission ratio to match the particular road condition better. A higher gear results in a smaller transmission ratio which means the smaller number of rotations of the engine crankshaft[2], i. e. less engine working cycles and less fuel consumption, within one kilometer. Therefore, it is a good way to improve traction performance and to save fuel.

In recent years, many new type motor vehicles tend to increase the number of gears. Even in small cars and small trucks, their four-gear gearbox is replaced by a five-gear gearbox. For example, the local made[3] medium truck Jiefang has been equipped with a new type gearbox of six gears to replace the old five-gear one.

本节注释: [1]增加变速器档位;[2]发动机曲轴的旋转次数;[3]国产的。

ALTERNATIVE FUEL[1]

Most of the energy sources of the motor vehicles come from gasoline and diesel. In fact, the world petroleum reserves are becoming less and less. The urgency to develop alternative fuel has been recognized worldwide. Some measures are suggested as follows.

Liquified Petroleum Gas (LPG) [2]

The main content of LPG is propane[3]. It is the by-product[4] of petroleum. Its advantages are high octane number[5], rich resources[6], low harmful emission, low price and easy reconstruction of the gasoline engine. Its disadvantages are low heat value[7] and big volume. A thick tank to keep it under pressure is much heavier than a gasoline tank.

Today, there are more than 4 million LPG vehicles throughout the world including Italy, Netherlands, U. S. A, Australia, Japan, etc.

本节注释: [1]代用燃料;[2]液化石油气;[3]丙烷;[4]副产品;[5]辛烷值;[6]资源丰富;[7]热值。

Compressed Natural Gas (CNG)[1]

The main content of CNG is methane[2]. Because of small density, it should be kept in a high pressure steel cylinder[3] of 20 MPa. Its advantages are high octane number, low harmful emission, low price, rich resources and easy reconstruction of gasoline engine.

Resources of natural gas in China are very rich, 38 000 billion cubic meters. We can expect to supply 500 thousand CNG vehicles which consume 7.5 billion cubic meters of CNG yearly. The disadvantages are difficulty for the high pressure cylinders to refill[4] and the requirement for construction of a lot of refilling stations[5] throughout the country.

本节注释: [1]压缩天然气;[2]甲烷;[3]高压钢瓶;[4]重新灌装;[5]加油站、加气站。

Ethanol and Methanol[1]

Their properties are nearly the same as gasoline. It is easy to mix gasoline with 20% ethanol or methanol without any reconstruction of the engine. Ethanol is easy to refine from plants[2]. For example, Brazil abounds in sugarcane[3] and uses sugarcane dregs to refine ethanol[4]. It is necessary to emphasize[5] that some people are keen on refining ethanol from corn[6], but it is not acceptable because it would make the prices of grain and forage rise up[7] and result in many economic problems.

本节注释：[1]乙醇和甲醇；[2]植物；[3]盛产甘蔗；[4]用甘蔗渣提炼乙醇；[5]须要强调；[6]玉米；[7]会使粮食和饲料涨价。

Hydrogen

Hydrogen may be a kind of inexhaustible[1] fuel. As it burns with oxygen, water molecules[2] are formed without any pollution to the environment. Its disadvantage is difficulty to prepare, transport and store. However, the research of hydrogen engine is just in the process of experiment and far from the level of large scale production[3].

本节注释：[1]耗之不尽的；[2]水分子；[3]远未达到大批生产的水平。

6.3.1.3 ENVIRONMENTAL PROTECTION

Pollution of motor vehicles and automotive industry to environment affects our life very much and is an important problem to be considered.

EMISSION CONTROL

In spite of the targets of average ownership and average density of motor vehicles[1] in China (40 units/1000 persons and 5 units/1 km^2 territory) are rather low compared to those in developed countries, we should clearly understand that there are more than 10 million motor vehicles squeezing[2] in some large cities with a total population of 50 million. Average ownership has been 1 unit/5 persons and pollution caused by motor vehicles in those cities has become a big social problem impossible to be neglected.

Some situations should be considered as follows. Firstly, on the city roads, motor vehicles, non-motor vehicles and pedestrians crowd together and make traffic conditions worse. Evidently, it is difficult for motor vehicles to develop their normal speed range in such traffic conditions. They have to slow down, stop and start again and again, which makes their engines work in unfavorable[3] conditions. Secondly, emission control equipments have not been seen in most of the local made[4] vehicles. Lastly, some of the vehicles have been overage[5] and have caused serious pollution problems. According to some primary investigations, harmful emissions of carbon monoxide and hydrocarbons[6] caused by motor vehicles have reached to 60 to 70% of their total amounts in China's large cities and nitro-oxides[7] has reached to 30%. Therefore, effective measures should be taken to limit the automotive emissions urgently.

Measures aiming at automotive harmful emissions should begin with improvement of the structure of the internal combustion engines. Firstly, the proportion of fuel and air should be correct. Secondly, ignition should be normal to make the mixture burn thoroughly. For example, the electronic controlled technique of multi-point injection[8] used in most of the engines can manage the fuel supply precisely to form a proper proportion of fuel and air and thus to provide perfect combustion. Lastly, a catalytic reactor[9] can be added into the exhaust pipe to oxidize[10] the carbon monoxide and the hydrocarbons and thus to reduce the content of harmful exhaust gas greatly.

本节注释: [1]汽车的平均拥有率和平均密度;[2]拥挤;[3]不良的、不利的;[4]国产的;[5]超龄;[6]一氧化碳和碳氢化合物;[7]氮氧化合物;[8]多点喷射的电控技术;[9]催化反应器;[10]氧化。

OTHER ISSUES

Noise[1] includes two kinds, interior and exterior. Interior noise affects the occupant's comfort whereas exterior noise is harmful to the environment. Noise of the motor vehicle comes from engine working processes (burning, intake and exhaust), mechanical vibrations and tire-road interactions mainly. Great research efforts are focused on the above aspects in recent years.

The evaluation target of noise is the "sound pressure level (SPL)[2]". SPL is 20 times the logarithm of the ratio of sound pressure divided by the lower limit of human audible sensation[3] (2×10^{-5}Pa). Its unit is decibel (dB)[4]. For example, noise caused by a passenger car measured at its side from a distance of 7.5 m should not exceed the limit of 82 dB by the National Standard.

The asbestos particles abraded from the clutch and brake friction liners[5] would lead to lung cancer[6]. Vapor[7] from fuel and odor[8] from chemical materials are harmful to human respiratory system[9]. Leakage of fluoric refrigerant[10] from the automotive air-conditioning system would spoil the ozone layer[11] of the atmosphere.

Every year more than 10 million motor vehicles through out the world are out of use because of collision damage or overage. Parts made of steel and other metals are easy to reuse and recycle[12], but parts made of plastics and composed materials[13] are not easy to reuse and decompose[14]. It is only possible to reuse them if the same kind of plastic parts are collected together. Therefore, in order to be sorted out[15], on the surface of an automotive plastic part words to express its material should be given clearly such as PU (polyurethane), PVC (polyvinyl chloride) and PP (polypropylene)[16].

本节注释:[1]噪声;[2]声压级;[3]声音压强与人的听觉下限(2×10-5Pa)的比率取对数的20倍;[4]分贝;[5]离合器和制动器摩擦衬片磨下的石棉微粒;[6]肺癌;[7]蒸汽;[8]气味;[9]呼吸系统;[10]含氟的制冷工质;[11]臭氧层。[12]再利用和再循环;[13]合成材料;[14]分解;[15]分类拣出;[16]聚氨酯、聚氯乙稀、聚丙烯。

POLLUTION FROM AUTOMOTIVE INDUSTRY

During the manufacturing processes of the motor vehicles, a great deal of waste gas, waste liquid, waste parts, powdered dust[1] and other chemicals (some of them may be poisonous) are exhausted, drained or thrown to the nature. For example, in a painting shop, various kinds of chemical liquids are used in the manufacturing processes such as pickling, phosphorizing and electrocoating[2]. Volatile matters[3] caused by paint spraying[4] would contaminate the air.

本节注释:[1]粉尘;[2]酸洗、磷化、电泳涂漆;[3]挥发性物质;[4]喷漆。

6.3.2 *LOOKING FORWARD TO THE FUTURE*

In such a versatile[1] world, it is not easy to predict the style and the structure of the future motor vehicle precisely because science and technology are keeping on changing rapidly. Perhaps, by reviewing the history and recent development of the motor vehicle, we can see the light of dawn[2].

本节注释:[1]多样的、千变万化的;[2]晨曦、黎明曙光。

6.3.2.1 ELECTRIC VEHICLE

Electric vehicle (EV)[1] is a category of road vehicle driven by electric motor and equipped with a power source itself, that is, not including those vehicles operating along rails[2] or supplied by overhead cable[3] such as tram, trolleybus or locomotive[4]. Electric vehicle and gasoline vehicle were born almost the same time in late 19th century. At that time, EVs were quite common because the gasoline engine was not good enough. For example, in the year of 1900 there were 8 000 vehicles in use in the U. S. Among them 4 000 were steam powered vehicles, 3 000 were EVs and only 1 000 were gasoline vehicles. After that, innovations of the internal combustion engine emerged in large numbers[5]. In the competition versus[6] gasoline vehicle electric vehicle was fading down[7].

Electric vehicle can be classified into three main kinds, i. e. zero-emission electric vehicle (ZEV), hybrid electric vehicle (HEV) and fuel cell electric vehicle (FCEV)[8].

本节注释:[1]电动车、电动汽车;[2]轨道;[3]电力架线;[4]有轨电车、无轨电车、铁路机车;[5]大量涌现、层出不穷;[6]对(可写成 vs);[7]衰败;[8]零排放电动汽车、复合动力电动汽车和燃料电池电动汽车。

ZERO-EMISSION ELECTRIC VEHICLE (ZEV)

The main feature of ZEV is to use a storage battery as its power source. Lead-acid storage battery[1] dominated[2] in ZEV for a long time. Its disadvantages are low capacity[3], heavy weight, low continuous mileage[4] and short life. Its specific energy[5] is only 40 W · h/kg, too small to compare with 10 000 W · h/kg of gasoline. For example, the electric car EV-1 developed by General Motors with 18 lead-acid storage batteries (28% of the total vehicle mass) can carry 4 persons only. Its cruising speed is 45 km/h, continuous mileage within one charge[6] is 120 km and rechargeable frequencies[7] are several hundred only. Evidently, it is too far to compare with a light weight and more powerful gasoline car which can carry 5 persons and operate at the cruising speed of 90 km/h and can go through the mileage of more than 500 km within one filling[8]. Therefore, it is almost impossible for an enterprise to earn money by putting ZEV into large scale production[9].

At the same time, the following advantages make ZEV very special.

ZEV would not require any kind of petroleum fuel. Recharged at midnight, it would consume the excess electricity developed by the electric power plant[10] without any influence on the daytime electric supply. An electric motor has a higher efficiency of 75% than an internal combustion engine of 15%.

A remarkable advantage of ZEV is no harmful emission on road. That is why it takes the name "zero emission". We would not say that ZEV is totally no harmful emission because its electricity comes from the electric power plant. Besides, during the charging process of the storage battery some pollutants[11] could be made because of the chemical reaction.

A special kind of ZEV supplied by solar cells[12] may be a real vehicle of no pollution.

Internal combustion engine can not work without oxygen but ZEV can be used in special environment such as the Moon, the space[13], underwater and vacuum.

The other advantages are easy operation (no clutch pedal, no requirement of shifting gears), easy to start, low noise, etc.

Figure 6-24 shows a ZEV named "Think". It is interesting that the designer uses an exclamation mark[14] "!" to replace the alphabet "i" in the spelling of the name. What does the designer want us to think?

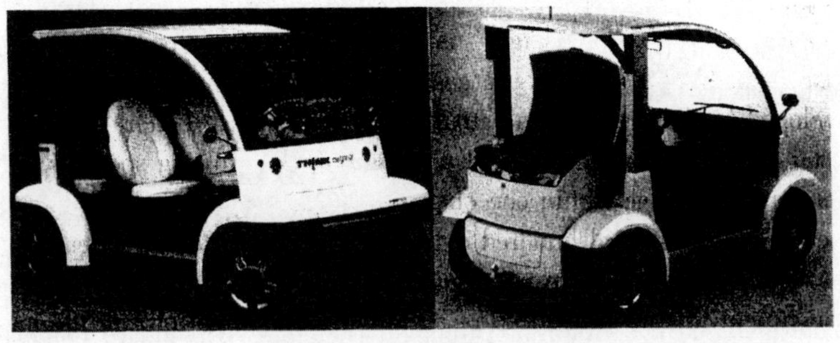

Fig. 6-24 A ZEV Named "Think"

本节注释: [1]铅酸蓄电池;[2]占优势;[3]容量低;[4]续驶里程低;[5]比能量;

[6]一次充电;[7]重复充电次数;[8]一次加油;[9]使 ZEV 大批投产;[10]发电厂;[11]污染物;[12]太阳能电池;[13]太空;[14]感叹号。

HYBRID ELECTRIC VEHICLE (HEV)

A hybrid electric vehicle has two power sources, normally a grouped IC engine-generator[1] and a storage battery (also called accumulator[2]). In the grouped IC engine-generator, the generator is driven by the internal combustion engine. When the vehicle is partially loaded[3], the generator supplies a part of the electricity to the electric motor and the excess part can be kept in the storage battery. When the vehicle is full loaded, both the generator and the storage battery supply the electric motor.

A remarkable advantage of HEV is its engine size smaller than half the size of the engine of a conventional vehicle[4]. At a constant speed of high efficiency, working condition of the engine of HEV is quite different from that of the engine of a conventional vehicle. Therefore, more fuel economy and less harmful emission can be obtained by HEV compared with the conventional vehicle. It is rather easy for HEV to meet the crucial targets of fuel consumption and emission control given by new regulations. The main disadvantage of HEV may be its complicated structure and expensive cost[5]. If it can be put into large scale production, high manufacturing cost may reduce.

Figure 6-25 shows a hybrid concept car named "Synergy 2010" developed by Ford Motor Company. It is equipped with two sets of power sources, i. e. a diesel engine-generator and a high speed flywheel-accumulator. Its drag coefficient[6] is only 0.20 and volume of its diesel engine is only 1 liter. Therefore, fuel consumption and harmful emissions are

Fig. 6-25 Ford's Concept Car "Synergy 2010"

only 1/3 of those of a conventional car.

本节注释：[1]内燃机－发电机组；[2]储能器；[3]部分负载；[4]其发动机尺寸比普通汽车发动机尺寸的一半还小；[5]结构复杂和成本高；[6]空气阻力系数。

FUEL CELL ELECTRIC VEHICLE (FCEV)

The operation principle of FCEV may be described briefly as follows. Firstly, the fuel (for example methanol) decomposes in the converter[1]. Secondly, hydrogen obtained in the converter can be conducted to the fuel cell[2]. Lastly, electricity is generated by the fuel cell through chemical reaction of hydrogen and oxygen.

Advantages of FCEV are the possibility of fuel changing into electricity directly and also no pollution. In recent years fruitful progresses have been made in the research of FCEV but its cost is too high.

Figure 6-26 shows a concept car developed by GM. It is an advanced FCEV named "Autonomy", so-called "a new episode of the 21st century[3]". It is very special that all the engine and chassis components are packed in a flat piece with a thickness of only 1/2 ft (152.4 mm).

Fig. 6-26 GM's Concept Car "Autonomy"

本节注释：[1]转化器；[2]燃料电池；[3]21 世纪的新篇章。

6.3.2.2 INCREASE RATE OF UTILIZING SPACE[1]

Prediction shows that the number of motor vehicles would continue to increase, the environment would be more and more crowded and traffic jams and shortage of parking lots would be long term problems in the near future.

A car has the length about 4 meters and occupies the area about 7.5 square meters. If space between vehicles is included, road area occupied by each car would not be a small figure. Almost all the cars have two rows of seats for 5 occupants. According to a report made by German traffic department, the average occupied rate[2] of car interior in this country is 1.4 persons per car. In most of the cars there is only one person and the other seats are free. A large number of free seats mean great waste of interior room and result in great needs of fuel and road area. Maybe, most of the German cars should cut down the number of seats, reasonably from 5 to 2. Experts have discussed that with the increase of car ownership, small cars of two seats (Fig. 6-27) should play an important role in road transportation.

Fig. 6-27 Concept Car of Two Seats Developed by Chrysler

In order to save the lateral space between two cars in a parking lot, it may be reasonable to replace the front hinged door[3] with swiveled wing door[4] (Fig. 6-28), sliding door (Fig. 6-29) and tilted roof[5] (Fig. 6-27).

With the improvement of light weight and high efficiency of the automotive components, skillful design may lead to tight package of the components and more room for the passengers and goods. Figure 6-30 shows a car equipped with an engine of high efficiency. From the figure we can see that the car has a small exterior and a roomy interior and its four wheels are pushed to the corners. Thus, high rate of utilizing space can be obtained.

本节注释: [1]提高空间利用率;[2]占用率;[3]顺开式(前部装铰链的)车门;[4]旋翼式车门;[5]翻转式(掀开式)车顶。

Fig. 6-28 Toyota Concept Car AXV-Ⅱ

Fig. 6-29 Japanese Daihatsu Concept Car TA-X80

Fig. 6-30 An Example of High Rate of Utilizing Space

6.3.2.3 WHAT WILL THE FUTURE VEHICLE BE?

It may be an attractive and interesting topic for everybody.

With the development of computer technology, we can expect that the control system of the future vehicle would be more electronic and automatic (Fig. 6-31 and Fig. 6-32) and the performances would be improved greatly, i. e. faster, safer, more comfortable and more economical.

Fig. 6-31 Central Computer System of English Concept Truck Leyland TX-450

Fig. 6-32 Voice Control System of Ford's Concept Car Synergy 2010

Application of new kinds of energy would lead to innovations of automotive engines. Application of new materials and cutting-edge manufacturing methods would lead to light weight, reliability and durability[1]. Wonderful study of aerodynamics[2] combined with fresh inspiration of aesthetics[3] would lead to a perfect style of smoothness, fluency and elegance (Fig. 6-33).

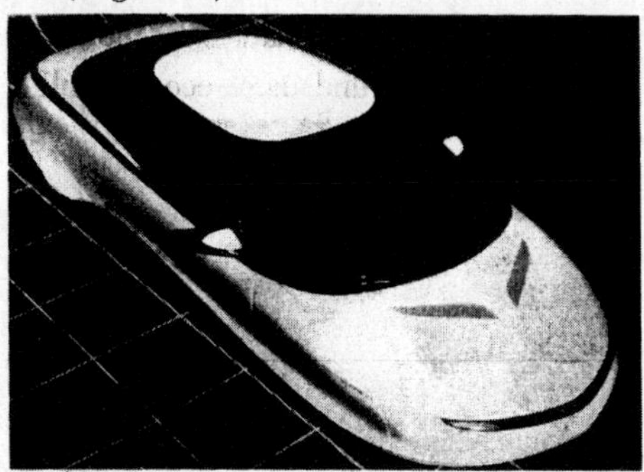

Fig. 6-33 Concept Car Developed by Pontiac Division of GM

At the end of this book the author would like to emphasize that transportation situations are different from place to place, requirements are also different from people to people and there would not be a single draft to describe what future vehicle will be like.

The author does not want to dream, to guess or to build a castle in the air[4]. In fact, many concept cars are good innovations aiming at current problems and courageous steps towards the future.

The society is making more and more progresses. Science and technology are changing day by day. Motor vehicle, a great companion of our society, will bring us to a glorious tomorrow.

本节注释: [1]可靠性和耐久性;[2]空气动力学;[3]新颖的美学灵感;[4]空想、建空中楼阁。

本章参考文献

6.1 肖国普. 现代汽车营销. 上海:同济大学出版社,2002

6.2 陈永革. 汽车服务贸易概论. 北京:机械工业出版社,2006

6.3 马芳武,门永新. 赛车世界. 北京:人民交通出版社,1995
6.4 乌尔里希 · 赛费特,彼得 · 瓦尔泽 著. 严机 等译. 汽车技术未来展望. 北京:中国展望出版社, 1989
6.5 日本汽车研究所. 刘秀娟 译. 二十一世纪汽车社会. 长春:吉林科学技术出版社, 1991
6.6 张纪康 编著. 奔驰世纪. 成都:四川人民出版社,2000
6.7 John Fenton. Advances in Vehicle Design. Bury St Edmunds Professional Engineering Publishing, 1999.
6.8 Paul Nieuwenhuis and P. E. Wells. The Automotive Industry and the Environment: A Technical, Business and Social Future. Cambridge, U. K. Woodhead Publishing, 2003.

INDEX
CELEBRITIES IN AUTOMOBILE CIRCLE
(车坛名人索引)

Agnelli, Giovanni	2.2.7
Alonso, Fernando	6.2.2
Austin, Herbert	2.2.6
Barzini, Liugi	2.2.10
Beau de Rochas, Alphonso	2.1
Benz, Karl	2.1
Bertha	2.1
Bertone, Nuccio	2.3.10, 5.1.2
Bouton, Georges	2.2.1
Borghese, Scipio	2.2..10
Braham, John	6.2.2
Breedlove, Craig	6.2.1
Briscoe, Benjamin	2.3.5
Buick, David Dunbar	2.3.4
Burman, R.	6.2.1
Cadillac, Antoine	2.3.2
Campbell, Malcolm	6.2.1
Donald	6.2.1
Chasselop-Laubat, Comte Gaston	2.2.1, 6.2.1
Chevrolet, Louis	2.3.4
Chrysler, Walter Percy	2.3.5
Citroen, Andre	2.3.6
Cobb, John Rhodes	6.2.1
Cugnot, Nikolas Joseph	2.1
Daimler, Gottlieb	2.1

Debottaville, Eldouard Delamarre	2.1
De Dion, Albert Marqius	2.2.1
Diesel, Rudoph	2.1
Dodge, John	2.2.3
Horace	2.2.3
Dunlop, John Boyd	2.2.5
Durant, William Crapo	2.3.4, 2.3.5
Duryea, Charles	2.3.1
Earl, Harley Jefferson	2.3.10
Eldridge, Ernest	6.2.1
Evans, Oliver	2.3.1
Eyston, George	6.2.1
Fangio, Juan Manucl	6.2.2
Farmer, Moses	2.2.2
Firestone, Harvey	2.2.5
Fisher, Carl	6.2.2
Ford, Henry	1.2.2, 2.3.1, 2.3.3, 2.3.7
Edsel	2.3.3
Gabelich, Gary	6.2.1
Gandini, Marcello	5.1.2
Giugiaro, Giorgetto	5.1.2
Goodyear, Charles	2.2.5
Green, Andy	6.2.2
Guiness, Kenelm Lee	6.2.1
Haynes, Elwood	2.3.1
Hemery, Victor	6.2.1
Homstead, L. G.	6.2.1
Horch, August	2.2.9
Irving, Jack	6.2.1
Issigonis, Alec	2.3.10
Janazy, Camille	2.2.1, 6.2.1
Jano, Vittorio	2.3.10
Jellinek, Emil	2.2.3
Mercedes	2.2.3
Johnson, Claude	2.2.6
Keech, Ray	6.2.1
King, Charles	2.3.1

Knight, John Henry 2.2.6
Lancia, Vincenzo 2.2.7
Lauda, Niki 6.2.2
Lenoir, Etienne 2.1
Levassor, Emile 2.2.1
Leland, Henry Martin 2.3.4
Loewy, Raymond 2.3.10, 5.1.2
Macdonald, Arthur 6.2.1
Mansell, Nigel 6.2.2
Marcus, Siegfried 2.1
Maxwell, Johnathan 2.3.5
Maybach, Wilhelm 2.1
McLaren, Bruce 6.2.2
Meyer, Louis 6.2.2
Michelin, Andre 2.2.5
Edouard 2.2.5
Morris, William Edouard 2.2.5
Moulton, Alex 2.3.10
Newcomen, Thomas 2.1
Nobel, Richard 6.2.1
Olds, Ransome 2.2.3, 2.3.1, 2.3.4
Opel, Adam 2.3.4
Fritz 2.2.11
Otto, Nikolas 2.1, 3.2.2
Palma, Ralph 6.2.1
Panhard, Louis 2.2.1
Peugeot, Armand 2.2.1
Pininfarina, Battista 2.3.10, 5.1.2
Piquet, Nelson 6.2.2
Porsche, Fedinand 2.3.7
Prost, Alain 6.2.2
Renault, Fernand 2.2.4
Marcel 2.2.4
Louis 2.2.4
Rolls, Charles Stewart 2.2.6
Royce, Henry 2.2.6
Schumacher, Michael 6.2.2

Segrave, Henry 6.2.1
Seiberling, Frank 2.2.5
Senna, Ayrton 6.2.2
Serpollet, Leon 2.2.2
Sloan, Alfred Prichard Jr. 2.3.4
Stanley, E. E 2.2.2
E. O 2.2.2
Stewart, John 6.2.2
Szisz, Ferenc 2.2.8
Thomas, John Godfrey Parry 6.2.1
Toyota, Sakichi 2.3.12
Kiichirou 2.3.12
Eiji 2.3.12
Wankel, Felix 3.2.13
Watt, James 2.1
White, Rollin 2.2.2
Womack, James P. 1.2.4